IMAGES
of America

Maine's Hunting Past

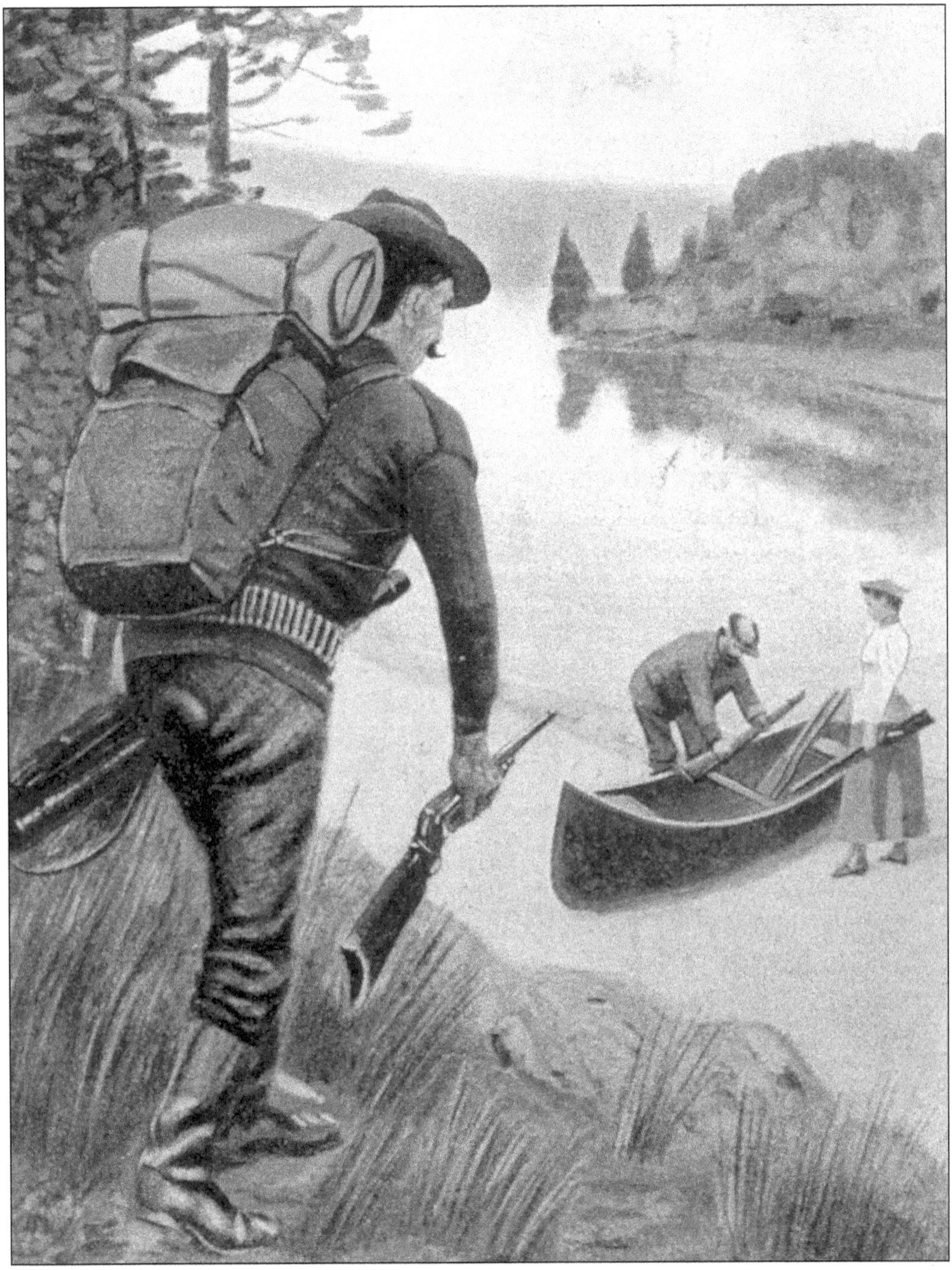

Filled with anticipation, a hunter totes his gear to the canoe where his companions are waiting. They will either hunt the stream from the canoe or land at another location to hunt inland from the waterway.

On the cover: Two deer at East Outlet Camps (now Wilsons Camps) are attended to by a future hunter and his father *c.* 1920.

IMAGES
of America

MAINE'S HUNTING PAST

Donald A. Wilson

ARCADIA
PUBLISHING

ISBN 978-0-7385-0500-8

Published by Arcadia Publishing
Charleston, South Carolina

Library of Congress Catalog Card Number: 2001086552

For all general information contact Arcadia Publishing at:
Telephone 843-853-2070
Fax 843-853-0044
E-mail sales@arcadiapublishing.com
For customer service and orders:
Toll-Free 1-888-313-2665

Visit us on the Internet at www.arcadiapublishing.com

Dedicated to the Maine Department of Inland Fisheries and Wildlife and its law enforcement, who have endeavored through the years to maintain wild game populations for us all to enjoy, whatever our pleasures or intentions.

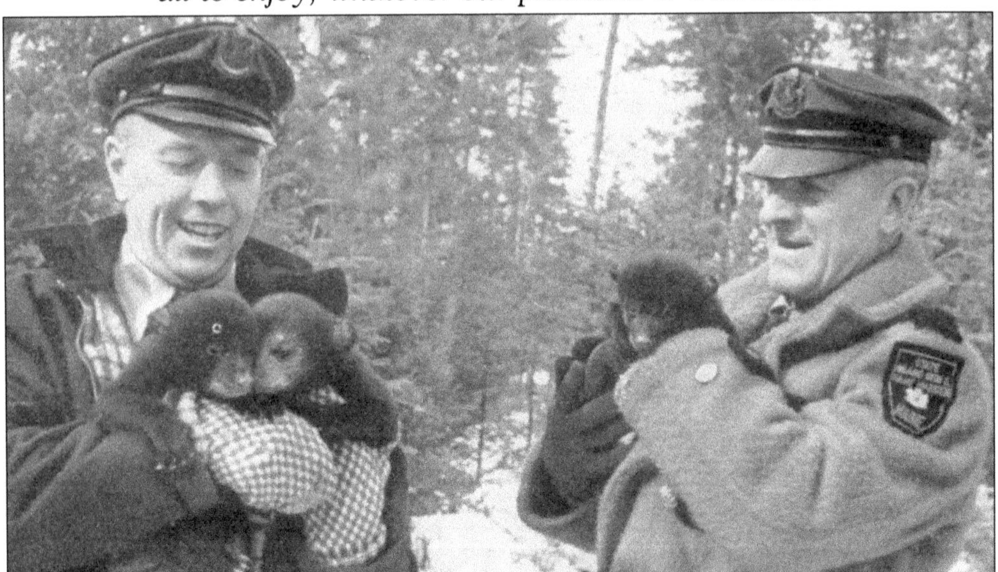

Game Wardens Peasley and Brown check on the welfare of three bear cubs near Passadumkeag c. 1940. (From *In the Maine Woods*, 1940.)

CONTENTS

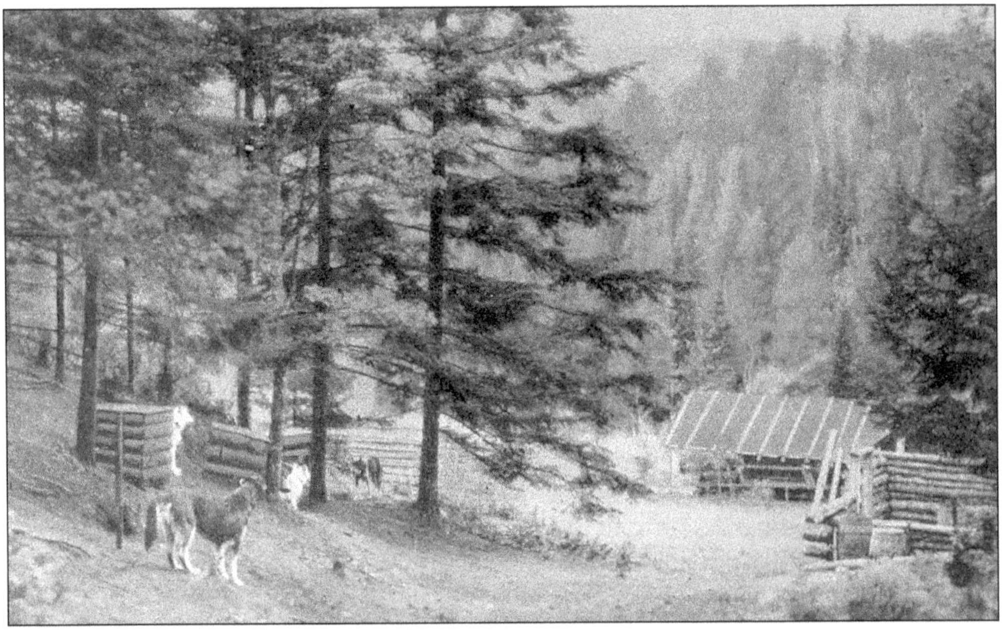

Greetings from Maine—hunter's paradise.

ACKNOWLEDGMENTS

Once again, much appreciation goes to the Bangor & Aroostook Railroad Company, who granted permission to use selections of text as well as advertisements from *In the Maine Woods*, their yearly promotional publication produced for six decades. While I relied on limited sections of text for historical and statistical information, I borrowed freely from their advertisements as a supplement to my personal collection of photographs. Their impressive photograph collection of early game animals is equaled in few places. Credit is due to them for sharing with us material that rounds out this treatment in a way that could not have been accomplished otherwise.

I also want to thank Steve Rainsford, who graciously offered and unselfishly shared part of his extensive collection of Maine woods memorabilia. His photographs helped to fill in some obvious gaps.

Other publications by Donald A. Wilson:
New Hampshire Fishing Maps (with Charlton J. Swasey), DeLorme, 1982.
Smelt Fly Patterns, Frank Amato, 1996.
Maine Aquatic Insects: Mayflies, Caddisflies & Stoneflies, Adventures in Angling, 1997.
Glimpses of Maine's Angling Past, Arcadia Publishing, 2000.

One

Hunting in Maine

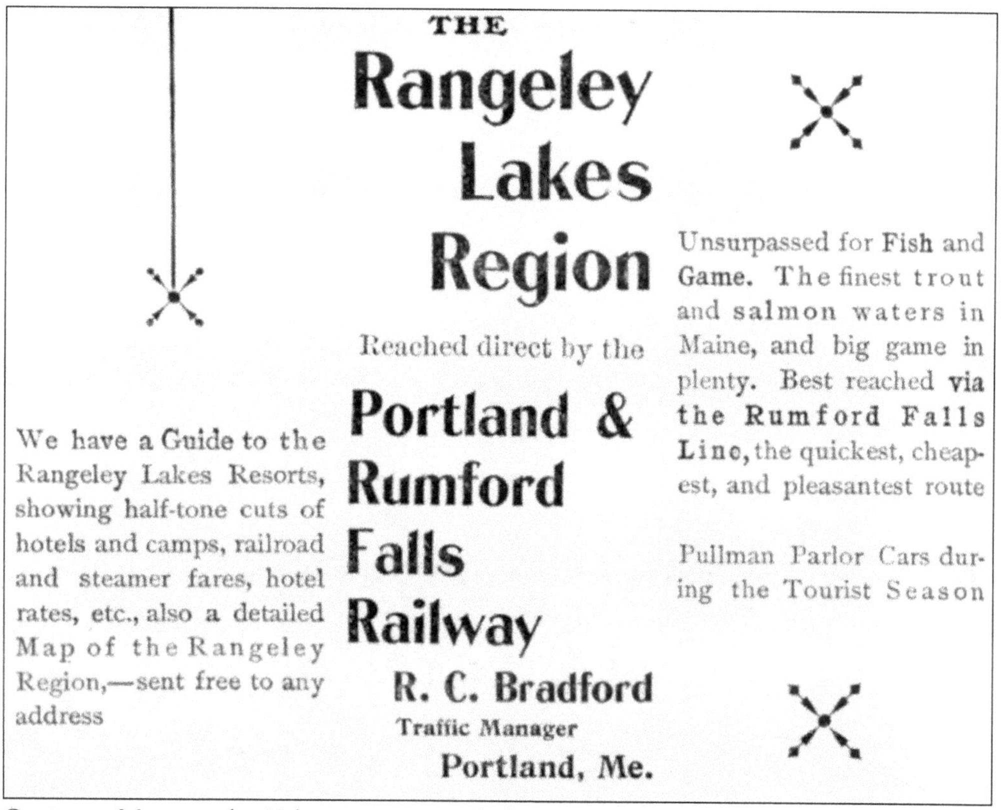

Getting to Maine in the 19th century was a challenge until the railroads were established about mid-century. It used to mean a long, hard journey from Bangor by stage, bateau, and canoe in order to penetrate to the runways of the forest denizens. After the railroads came in, the sportsman could board an evening train out of Boston and not leave his Pullman until its arrival at a Maine destination by the next forenoon. From that point, other smaller railroads and stage lines, local buckboards, or canoes would get them to their chosen sporting camp or hunting location.

This is an advertisement for one of the smaller railroads in the southern part of the state. Even the smaller lines promoted the magnificent hunting and fishing in the areas they served. (From *In the Maine Woods*, 1904.)

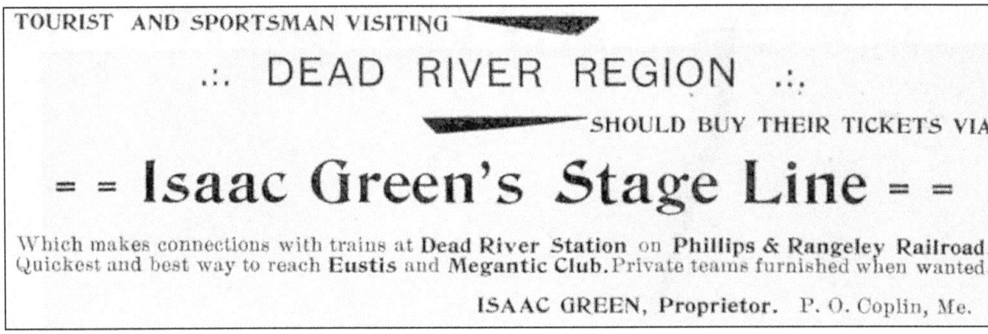
TOURIST AND SPORTSMAN VISITING

.:. DEAD RIVER REGION .:.

SHOULD BUY THEIR TICKETS VIA

= = Isaac Green's Stage Line = =

Which makes connections with trains at **Dead River Station** on **Phillips & Rangeley Railroad.** Quickest and best way to reach **Eustis** and **Megantic Club.** Private teams furnished when wanted.

ISAAC GREEN, Proprietor. P. O. Coplin, Me.

Stage lines were established at prime locations and at popular railroad stations. At less populous locations, camp owners in buckboards or other types of conveyances would meet parties at railroad stops. Horses used for transportation were commonplace. (From *The Maine Central*, May 1894.)

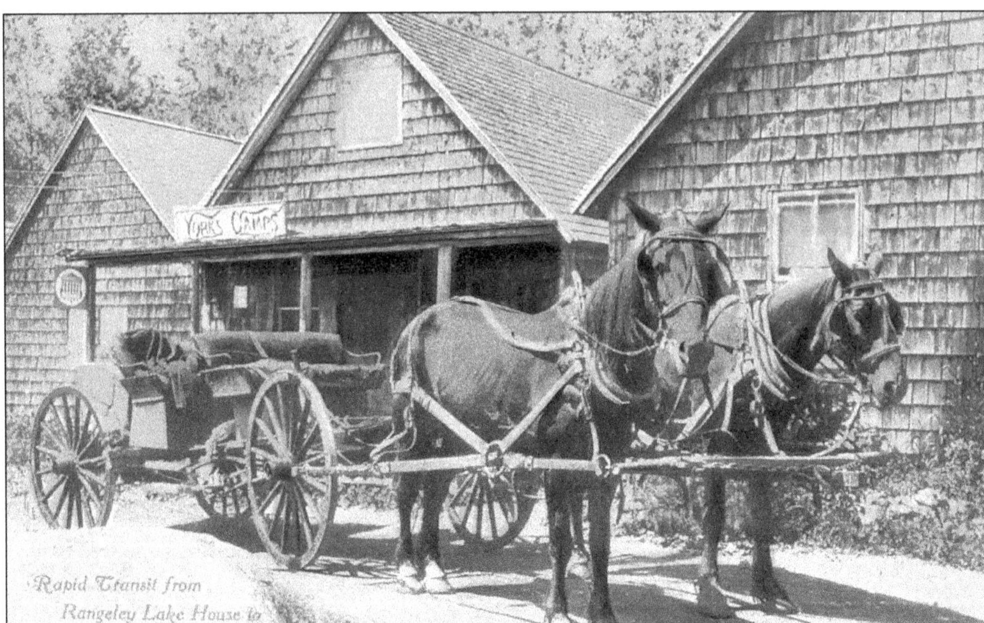

Shown here is one of the modes of transportation. This particular one, parked in front of Yorks Camps in the Kennebago area, took people around the Rangeley Region from the Rangeley Lake House.

The Phillips and Rangeley Railroad. The only ALL-RAIL ROUTE to **RANGELEY.**

The central point and natural headquarters for all sportsmen visiting the great RANGELEY REGION, including **KENNEBAGO, SEVEN PONDS, Etc.** This road also furnishes the quickest and by far the easiest route to **EUSTIS,** the central point for sportsmen visiting the great hunting grounds of the **DEAD RIVER REGION.**

For map and guide to hotels, camps, etc., address

H. H. FIELD, G. P. & T. A., - Phillips, Maine.

...THE...

Patten and Sherman Railroad

REACHES THE BEST

Hunting and Fishing Regions

in the State.

Shipped in Open Season of 1899, - - 406 Deer and 36 Moose.

All express business on this road done by the American Express.

P. C. NEWBEGIN, Supt., - Patten, Maine.

Two of the smaller railroad lines catering to sportsmen are advertised here. By this time, even the most remote areas of the state could be reached. (From *In the Maine Woods*, 1900.)

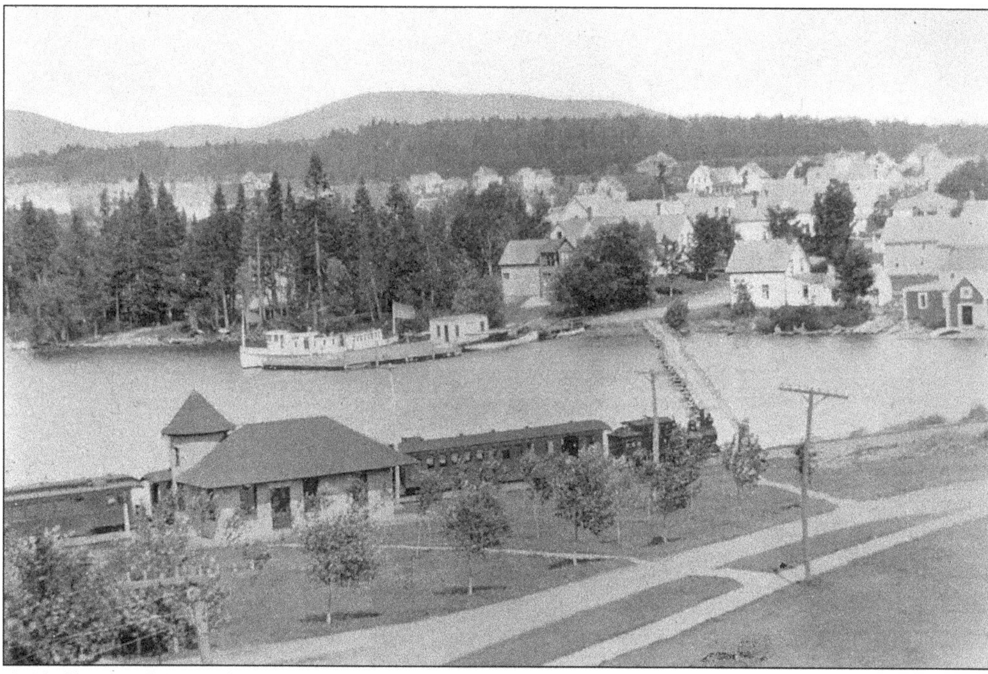

A Phillips and Rangeley train is parked beside the marble station at Rangeley Village. This was a narrow-gauge railway that advertised plush Pullman cars, shown here.

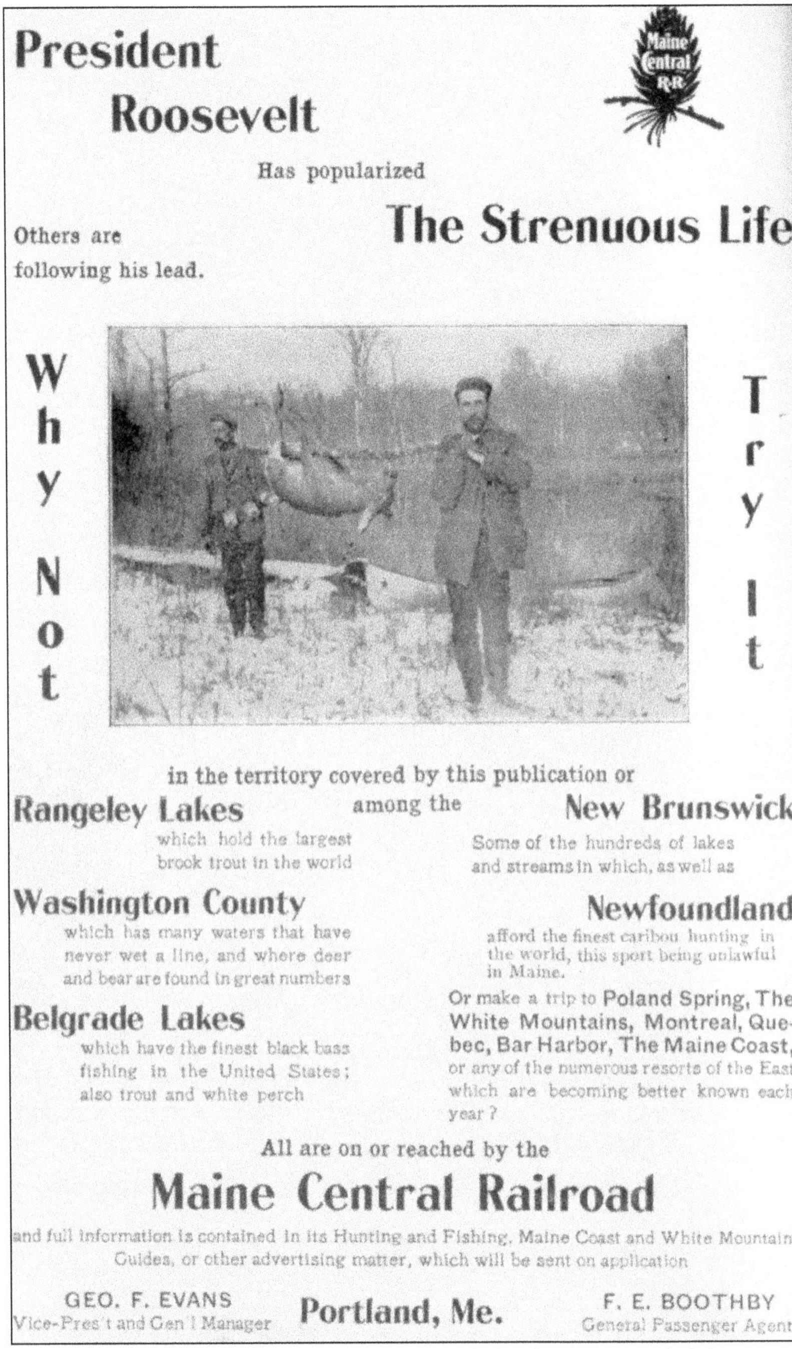

Railroads immediately recognized Maine's potential for hunting and fishing and heavily promoted the idea that the state was a hunter's paradise abundant with big game. They undertook advertising campaigns of their own to entice travelers and sportsmen to utilize their transportation services. Lines from Boston and New York took sportsmen to key Maine locations, such as Portland to Sebago and the Rangeley Region, Bangor to the Moosehead and Jackman Regions, Down East to the Machias Region, and to the great north wilderness of Aroostook County and the Allagash Region. (From *In the Maine Woods*, 1903.)

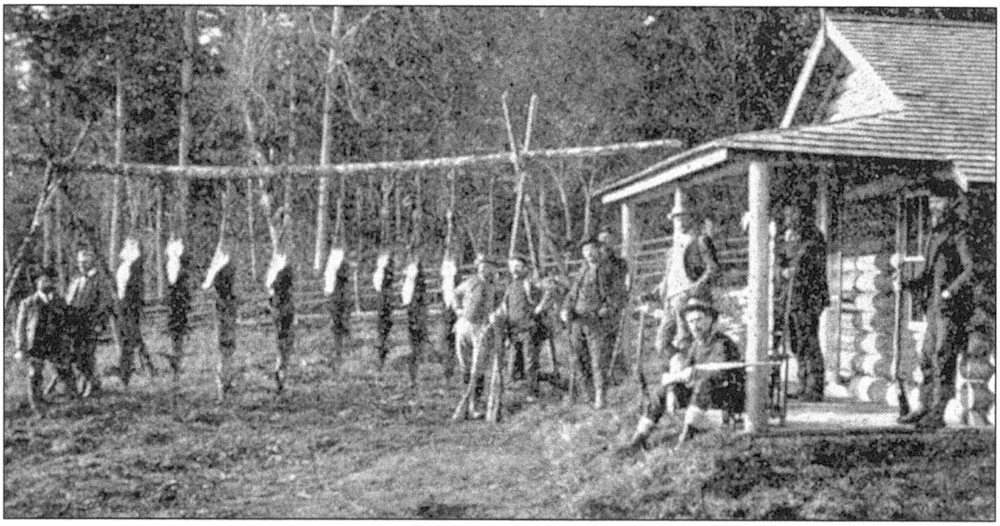

This is one of the postcards frequently sent by the Maine Central Railroad to promote trophy hunting. It reads, "It is easy to get a good Deer Head in Maine. Ask for booklet which tells all about it. Address, F.E. Boothby, Gen'l Passenger Agent, Portland, Me."

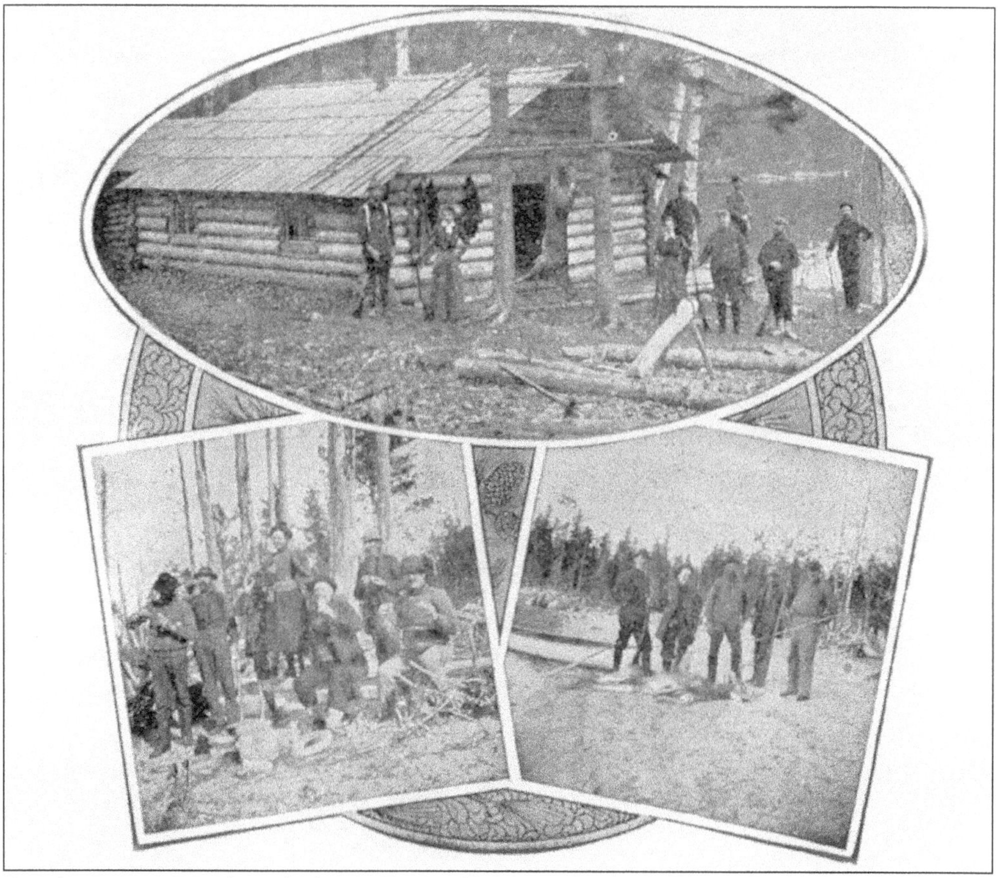

Another promotional card, this one aimed at women, reads, "The ladies are taking to the Maine Woods to hunt and fish and grow strong. Outdoor life is now the proper thing."

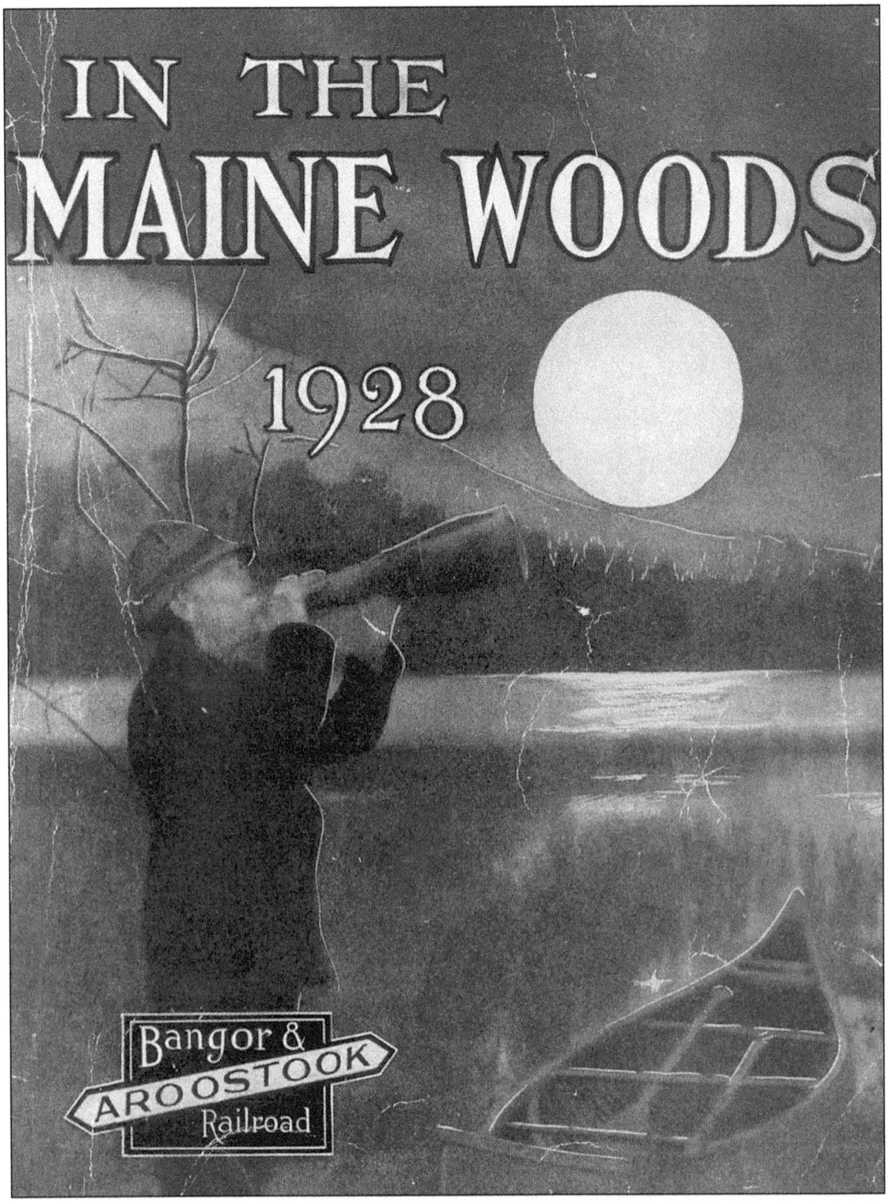

The three major railroad companies used extensive advertising to entice sportsmen and vacationers alike to come to Maine's wilderness. From the late 1800s to the 1950s, books and pamphlets were distributed containing hundreds of photographs, maps, and articles regarding the woods of Maine. One of the most extensive and long lasting was an annual publication entitled *In the Maine Woods*, produced by the Bangor & Aroostook Railroad.

The cover on this issue features Alfred Saulnier, well known for his moose-calling ability, demonstrating the use of a birch-bark horn. Saulnier was born in New Brunswick in 1886 and began his guiding career in the Greenville area in 1919. He guided on more than 75 trips on the Allagash, Miramichi, Restigouche, the East and West Branches of the Penobscot, and the Rangeley area. He trapped during the winter, setting out some 100 traps. According to him, his best profits were from mink and "blackcat," or fisher. (From *The Moosehead Gazette*, September 2, 1977.)

This Bangor & Aroostook Railroad promotion pretty much tells it all. The records of game shipment and the comfort of travel would have had to be very enticing at this time. (From *The Maine Central*, May 1896.)

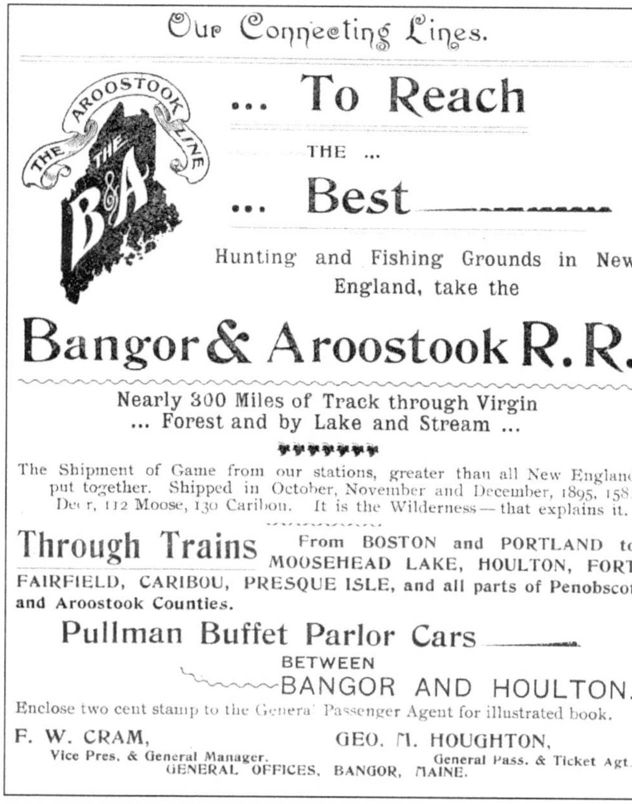

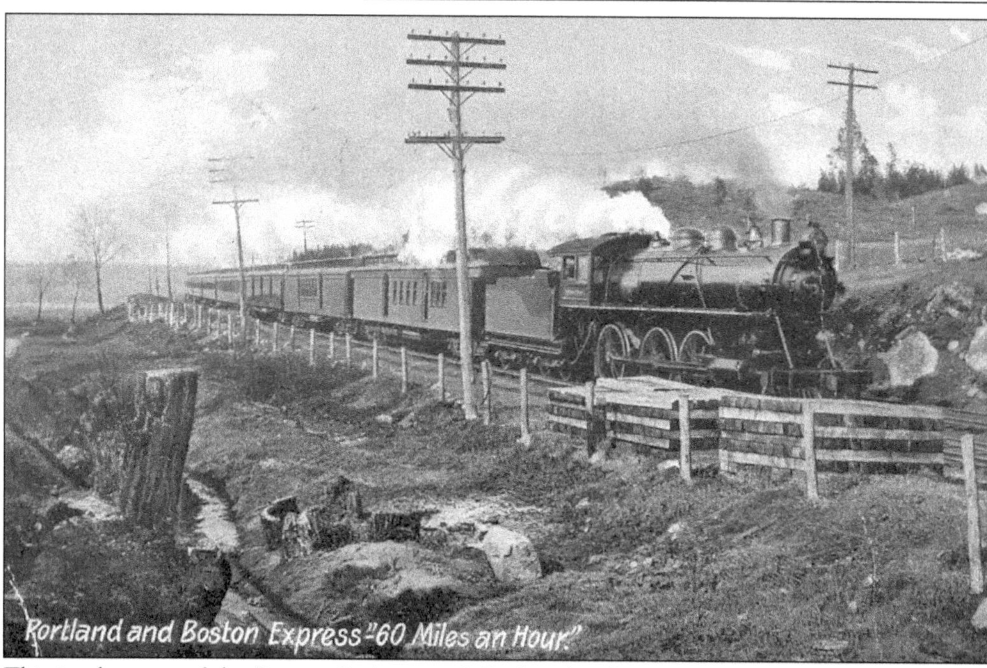

This is what one of the Bangor & Aroostook Railroad Pullman trains would have been like. It could obviously travel at a fast speed to get sportsmen to their destinations in a short amount of time.

The Most Famous

FISHING AND HUNTING REGIONS

Of the Country
are reached by the

BOSTON & MAINE R. R.

Direct route to the Aroostook and Dead River regions, Millinocket, Norcross, Twin Dam, Rangeley and Moosehead, Connecticut and Winnepesaukee, Memphremagog, Sunapee, and Willoughby Lakes, Lakes St. John and Champlain, and New Brunswick and Nova Scotia resorts.

Through Express Trains,

modernly fitted with Pullman Parlor and Sleeping Cars, to all leading sporting grounds. Descriptive and illustrated literature of Northern New England catalogued on opposite page.

BOSTON TICKET OFFICES:

322 Washington Street and at Union Station.

D. J. FLANDERS, Gen. Pass. and Tkt. Agt., Boston.

The Boston & Maine Railroad had similar advertisements and had its own publications. Although these publications differed from *In the Maine Woods* by being mostly pictures, they still emphasized the areas they served and the types of things that would interest travelers—lakes, mountains, and so on. (From *In the Maine Woods*, 1900.)

STATIONS SHIPPED FROM	October			November			December			Total		
	Deer	Moose	Bear	Deer	Moose	Bear	Deer†	Moose‡	Bear	Deer	Moose	Bear
Blanchard	....	....	....	32	....	....	....	....	....	32	....	....
Shirley	....	....	....	41	1	....	....	....	....	41	1	....
Greenville	157	....	....	596	....	2	....	....	....	753	....	2
Iron Works	....	....	....	46	....	....	....	....	....	46	....	....
Norcross	11	....	1	60	2	3	....	....	....	71	2	4
Grindstone	2	....	....	27	1	....	....	....	....	29	1	....
Stacyville	2	....	....	57	....	3	....	....	....	59	....	3
Patten	31	....	1	332	8	3	....	....	....	363	8	4
Oakfield	3	....	....	51	2	....	....	....	....	54	2	....
Howe Brook	13	....	....	60	....	....	....	....	....	78	....	....
Griswold	4	....	....	33	1	....	....	....	....	37	1	....
Masardis	66	....	3	225	1	....	....	....	....	291	1	3
Ashland	42	....	....	165	....	....	....	....	....	207	....	....
Portage	14	....	1	52	....	....	....	....	....	66	....	1
Stockholm	9	....	....	15	....	....	....	....	....	24	....	....
Sidings	....	....	....	44	1	....	....	....	....	44	1	....
Other Stations	31	....	....	292	2	3	....	....	....	323	2	3
Total	390	....	6	2128	19	14	....	....	....	2518	19	20
Total Shipped 1895	669	53	....	501	21	....	411	38	....	1581	112	....
" " 1896	1029	79	....	718	19	....	498	35	....	2245	133	....
" " 1897	1246	55	....	1023	37	....	671	47	....	2940	139	....
" " 1898	1348	71	....	1347	77	....	682	54	....	3377	202	....
" " 1899	1433	80	....	1960	63	....	363	23	....	3756	166	....
" " 1900	1298	83	....	1516	63	....	565	64	....	3379	210	....
" " 1901	1331	99	....	1905	97	....	646	64	....	3882	259	....
" " 1902	1469	68	....	2192	110	....	834	66	....	4495	224	....
" " 1903	1350	79	....	1758	106	....	678	47	....	3786	232	....
" " 1904	1088	62	....	1813	101	....	657	59	....	3558	222	....
" " 1905	1538	81	15	2187	87	15	909	39	8	4634	207	38
" " 1906	838	65	9	1678	90	3	861	43	5	3377	198	17
" " 1907	678	56	14	1559	92	17	916	107	28	3153	255	59
" " 1908	1111	44	6	1992	48	5	412	17	....	3515	119	11
" " 1909	683	43	13	1652	62	17	931	70	14	3266	175	44
" " 1910	1225	56	2	2216	68	2	1165	89	9	4606	193	13
" " 1911	622	38	12	1572	35	10	831	115	20	3025	188	42
" " 1912	543	15	18	1689	25	13	861	57	35	3093	97	66
" " 1913	376	....	5	1452	26	4	805	32	1	2633	58	10
" " 1914	364	....	10	1614	25	27	569	29	8	2547	54	45
" " 1915	530	*	23	1358	*	13	708	*	5	2596	*	41
" " 1916	380	*	3	1614	*	1	702	*	1	2696	*	5
" " 1917	449	*	2	1325	*	4	778	*	2	2552	*	22
" " 1918	246	*	3	797	*	2	472	*	1	1515	*	6
" " 1919	344	‡	7	1609	‡23	5	†	‡	....	1953	23	12

In 1908, it was reported that "big-game totals in northern Maine are not to be figured by the hundreds, but in thousands; for between three and four thousand moose, deer and bears are killed in this section and shipped out of the state every season, while additional thousands are killed by residents of the state or consumed in camps. One would naturally suppose that such tremendous totals would soon deplete the forest of its hulky denizens, yet the wardens, guides and other best informed woodsmen say that game is really more plenty now in Maine than it has been for some years past. It would seem, therefore, that seekers for moose, deer or bears can count on splendid results in northern Maine for many years to come, even though industrialism should push further and further into the forest, and civilization tame a wide border of what is now a wilderness unfettered and untouched." (From *In the Maine Woods*, 1908.)

This report of game shipped by the Bangor & Aroostook Railroad covers the period of 1895 to 1920. By that time, caribou hunting was over and moose hunting had been closed for five years. (From *In the Maine Woods*, 1921.)

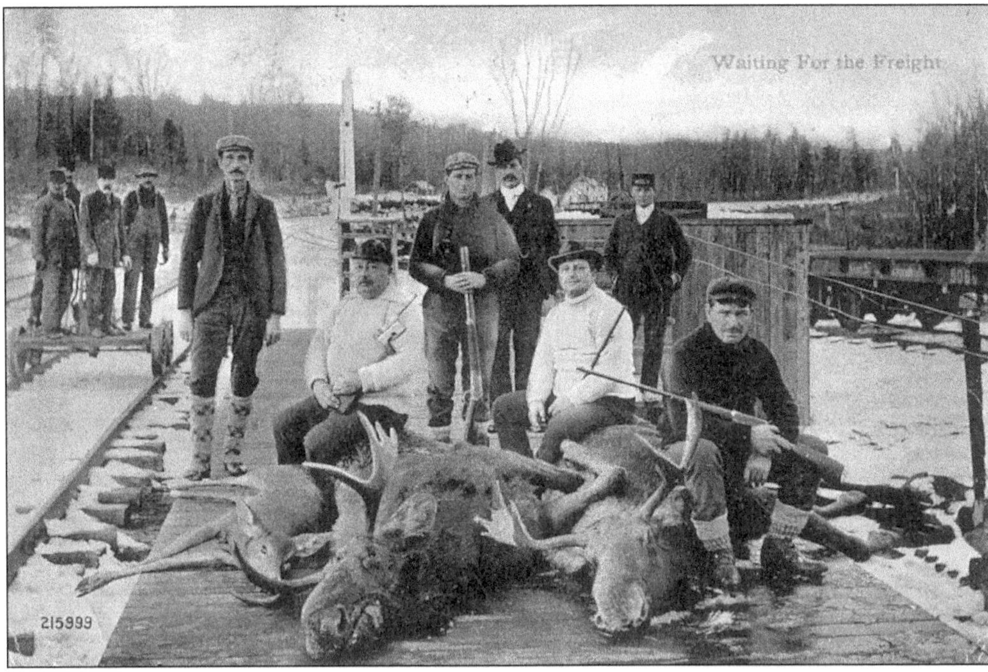

Railroads got double duty from sportsmen. Not only did they transport people to and from locations, but they also transported their bounty of meat, trophies, and furs back home or to market. This was big business for them, something that no longer exists. Today, most of what is shipped by rail from Maine is pulpwood and potatoes, and much of that is shipped almost exclusively within the state.

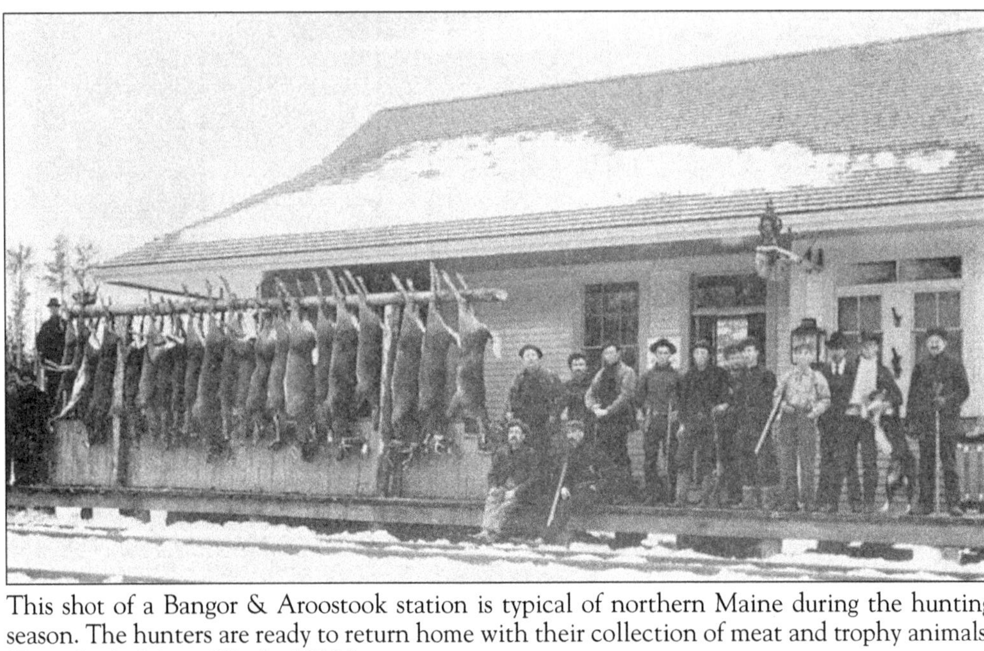

This shot of a Bangor & Aroostook station is typical of northern Maine during the hunting season. The hunters are ready to return home with their collection of meat and trophy animals. (From *In the Maine Woods*, 1900.)

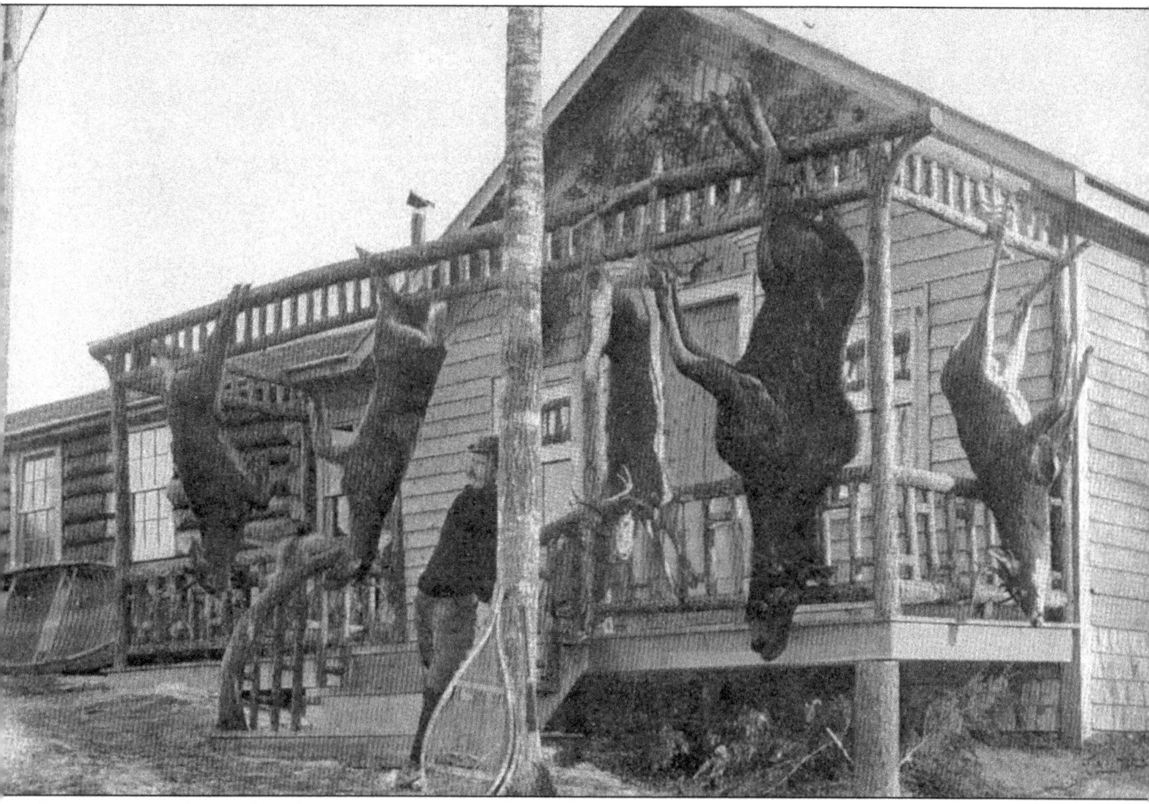

Beginning in the mid-to-late 1800s, sporting camps sprang up throughout the state, mostly in the northern sections. Many of them catered to both hunting and fishing and a few to just one or the other popular sports. Sportsmen were of both types, so many establishments became known as "sporting camps" and "hunting camps" and seldom "fishing camps" or "fishing lodges."

This is Gerrish's Camp at North Twin Dam, identified from a picture in Cornelia "Fly Rod" Crosby's personal photograph album, which is now in the collection at the Maine State Museum in Augusta. This camp was one of several either visited or frequented by Crosby as she hunted and fished the popular areas, while promoting the sporting qualities of the state of Maine.

MAINE'S GAME LAWS.

Regulations Concerning employment of Guides, Camping, and the Taking and Shipment of Game by Sportsmen.

THE GUIDE LAW — Non-resident sportsmen going into the woods to hunt or fish, and to camp on the wild lands of the state, must be accompanied by a registered guide during the months of June, July, August, September and October. This does not apply to hunters stopping at registered hunting camps, who have no intention of camping out or building fires. Residents of the state are not required to hire guides. Non-resident owners of wild lands may hunt on their own land without employing a guide, and may invite friends to do the same. Persons who keep places of resort for inland hunting or fishing parties are obliged to take out a license. No person shall engage in the business of guiding unless registered by the commissioners of inland fisheries and game.

Sunday is close time on all game in Maine.

Caribou are protected for six years from October 15th, 1899.

MOOSE — Between October 15th and December 1st., any sportsman may legally kill one bull moose, having at least two prongs on his horns. Cows and calves are protected at all times. Penalty for killing more than one moose is a fine of not less than $500 nor more than $1,000, or imprisonment for not more than four months. One bull moose, or portions, may be shipped out of the state without being accompanied by the hunter when marked with a special official shipping tag, supplied by express agents or station agents, the cost of a tag for moose being $5. No tag is required for moose or other game, and there is no shipping fee, when the owner accompanies the game. Penalty for falsely representing the ownership of a moose in transportation, or for failing to plainly mark the game with owner's name, is $40. Moose meat cannot be sold or given away for transportation out of the state ; penalty, $100.

DEER — One deer may be killed in September, for food purposes, to be eaten in the general neighborhood where killed, and the head and hide may be kept, by each holder of a special license, which can be obtained at all towns and railroad stations, at a cost of $6 for a non-resident, and $4 for a resident of the state. Between October 1st and December 15th, any sportsman may legally kill two deer, in addition to the one previously killed for food in September. Deer taken in October may be shipped out of the state, when officially tagged, the cost of a tag for a whole deer or portions being $2. No tag is required when owner accompanies game. Penalty for illegally killing a deer, $40 ; for misrepresenting ownership in transportation, $40. The only legal method of killing deer is shooting. Deer meat cannot be given away or sold for transportation out of the state ; penalty, $100.

GAME BIRDS — Partridge (ruffed grouse) and woodcock may be gunned from September 15th to December 1st ; quail, October 1st to December 1st ; wood duck, black duck, teal and gray duck, September 1st to May 1st ; plover and snipe, August 1st to May 1st. Only 15 birds of any one variety may be legally killed in a day by one person, except plover and snipe. Penalty for illegal killing, $5 a bird. Use of traps and snares is forbidden. Partridge cannot be offered for sale, nor can any person have partridge in his possession except for his own consumption. Hunters from outside the state may ship home one pair of game birds, except partridge, on buying a special shipping tag at 50 cents. No resident of the state is allowed to give away any game birds, nor any one to accept them, for the purpose of transportation out of the state, under penalty of $1 for each bird.

BEARS, WOLVES AND WILDCATS — These animals can be legally killed whenever found. There is a bounty of $5 on wolves and $2 on wildcats.

MINK, SABLE, MUSKRAT AND FISHER — Open time is from October 1st to May 1st. Beaver can be legally killed only by written permission of the commissioners.

Here is an outline of the game laws in effect for 1900. Note that caribou hunting was closed in 1899, but a hunter could take one bull moose and two deer. Another provision existed whereby one deer could be taken for food purposes prior to the regular season by special permit. At this time, there was no closed season or bag limit on bear, wolves, or wildcats and there was a bounty on the latter two. Later, the state instituted a bounty on bear and porcupine and increased the bounty for wildcat because the animals became a nuisance. They removed the bounty on wolves because they were either extremely scarce or absent. (From *In the Maine Woods*, 1900.)

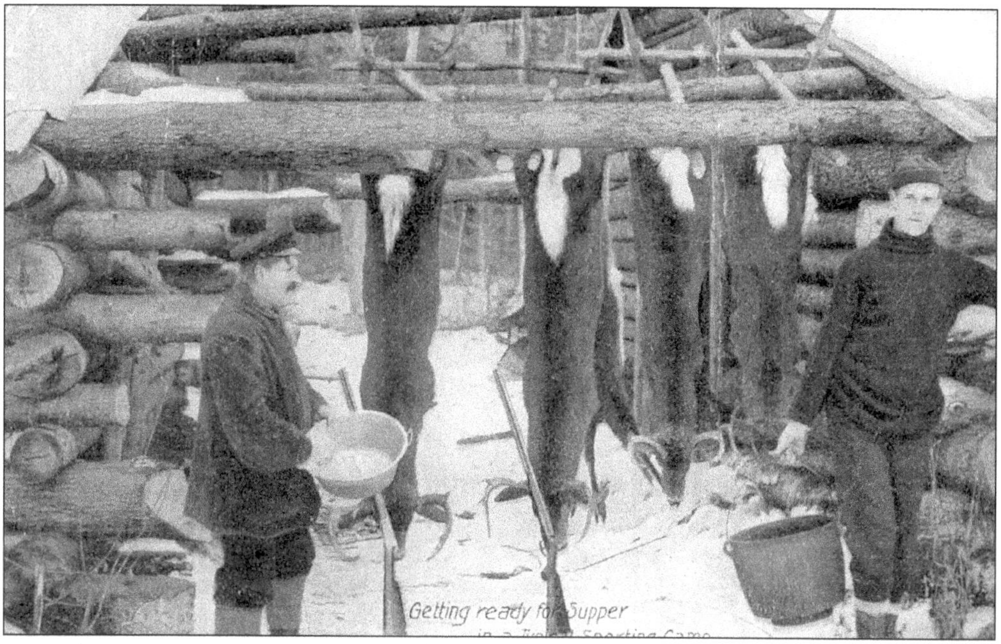

Two other types of camps became popular, and both were probably abundant long before the more formal lodges and commercial establishments became known. Small single camps owned by individual hunters, guides, or small groups are found throughout prime hunting areas. Some of these are used on a regular basis. Others are used each year, but only during the hunting season. These are truly known as "hunting camps."

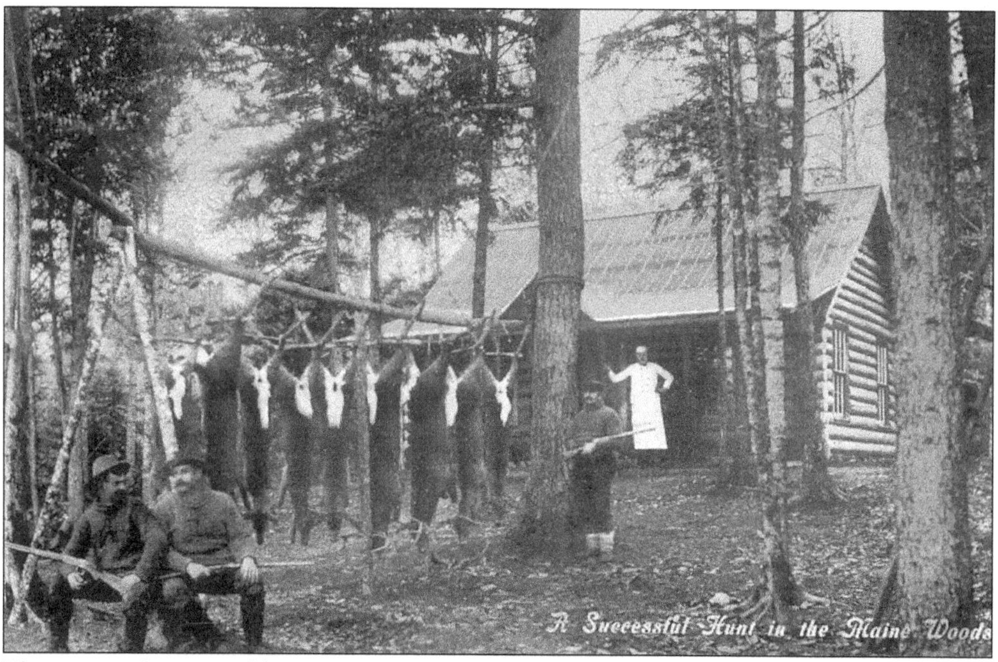

This camp is being used by a group of hunters who have hired a cook to take care of the camp and get the meals while they concentrate on hunting. This practice was common, and the guide for the party was often the cook.

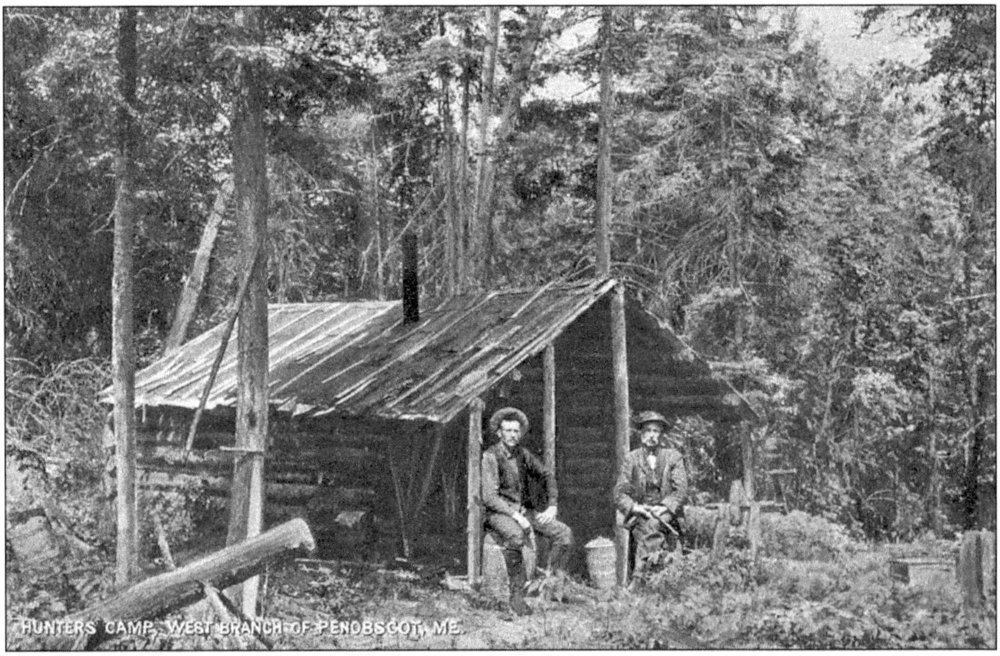

Some shelters were temporary lean-tos or tents that were intended for a one-time or one-season use. Some were placed on regular campsites, and others were set down at some convenient place in the wilderness. Today, many of these temporary shelters have been replaced with the more functional and luxurious trailers and campers.

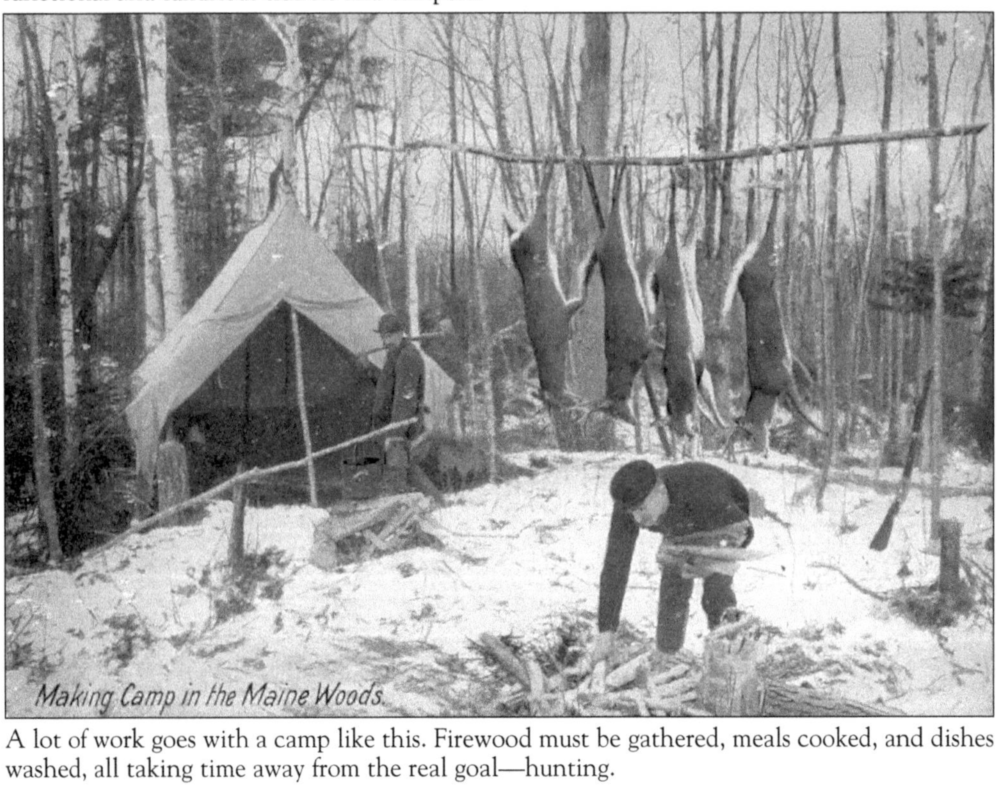

A lot of work goes with a camp like this. Firewood must be gathered, meals cooked, and dishes washed, all taking time away from the real goal—hunting.

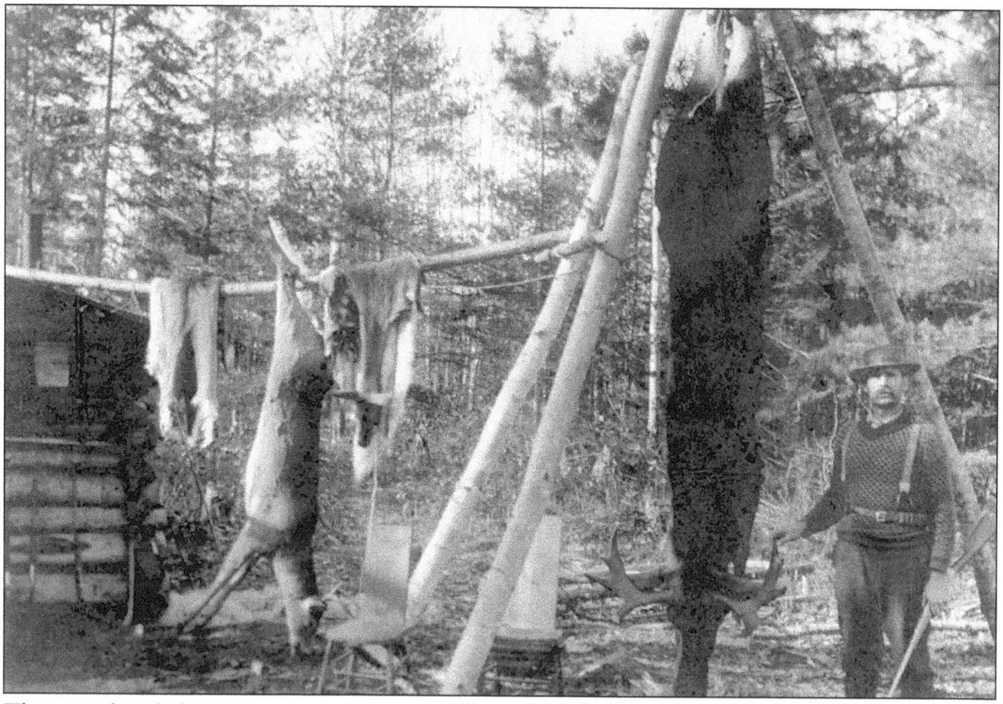

This was the plight of many outdoorsmen: relying on fishing in the spring and summer, hunting in the fall, and trapping in the winter in order to supply a regular income throughout the year. Those who did not trap often worked at other pursuits during the winter. Logging, carpentry, and similar jobs often occupied them while seasons were closed for the taking of fish and game.

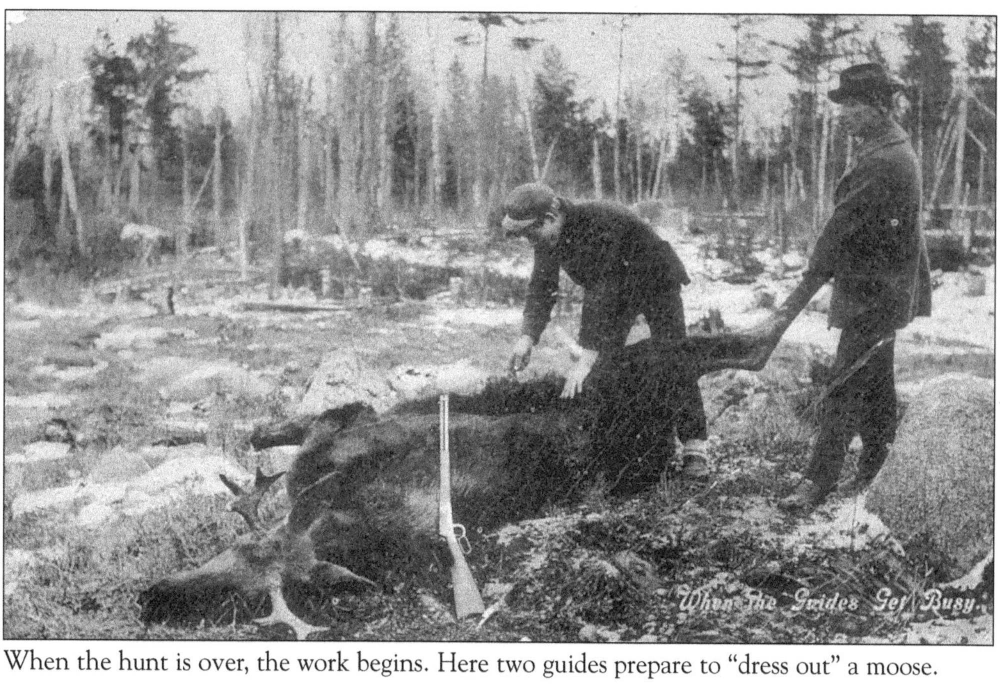

When the hunt is over, the work begins. Here two guides prepare to "dress out" a moose.

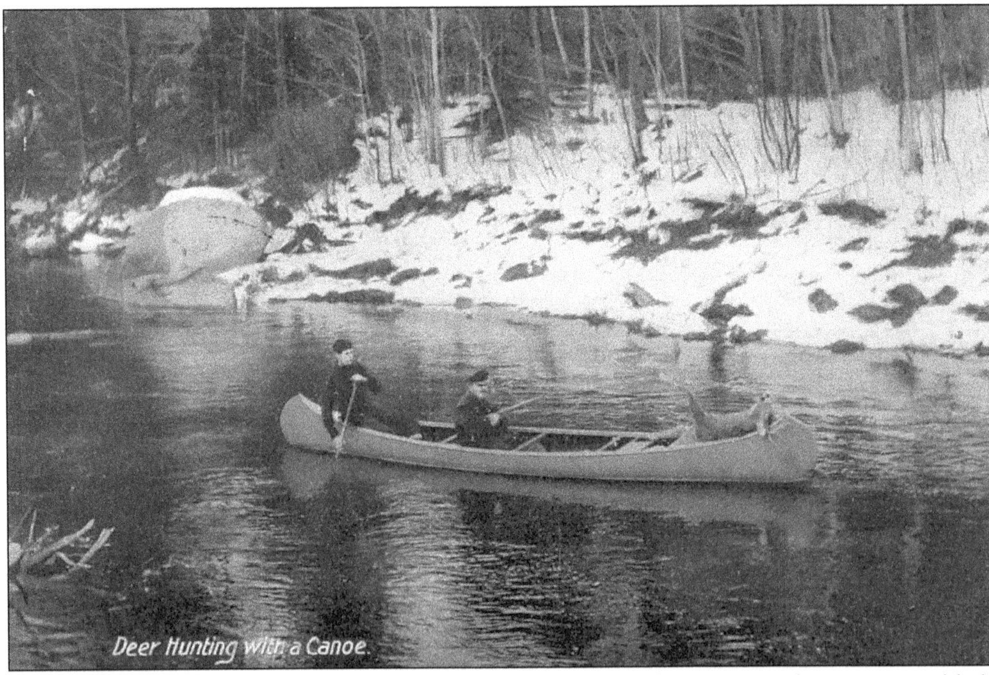

Besides hunting on foot, canoe travel is a way of working the streams where game is likely to frequent.

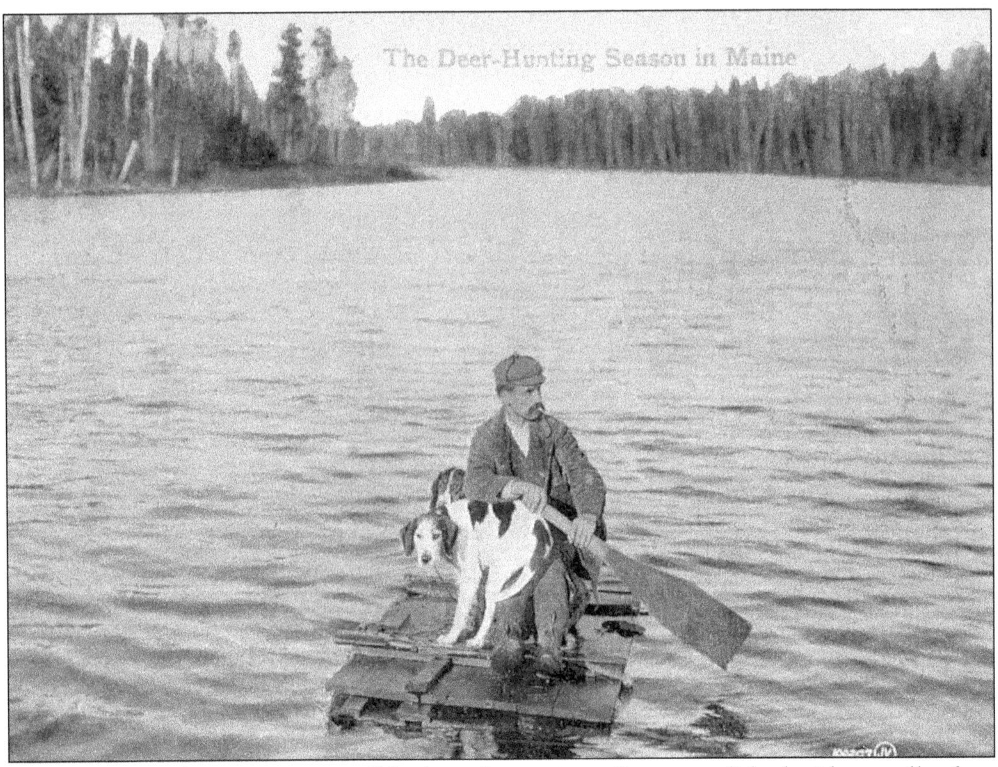

When hunting alone, crossing small bodies of water is easily accomplished with a small raft.

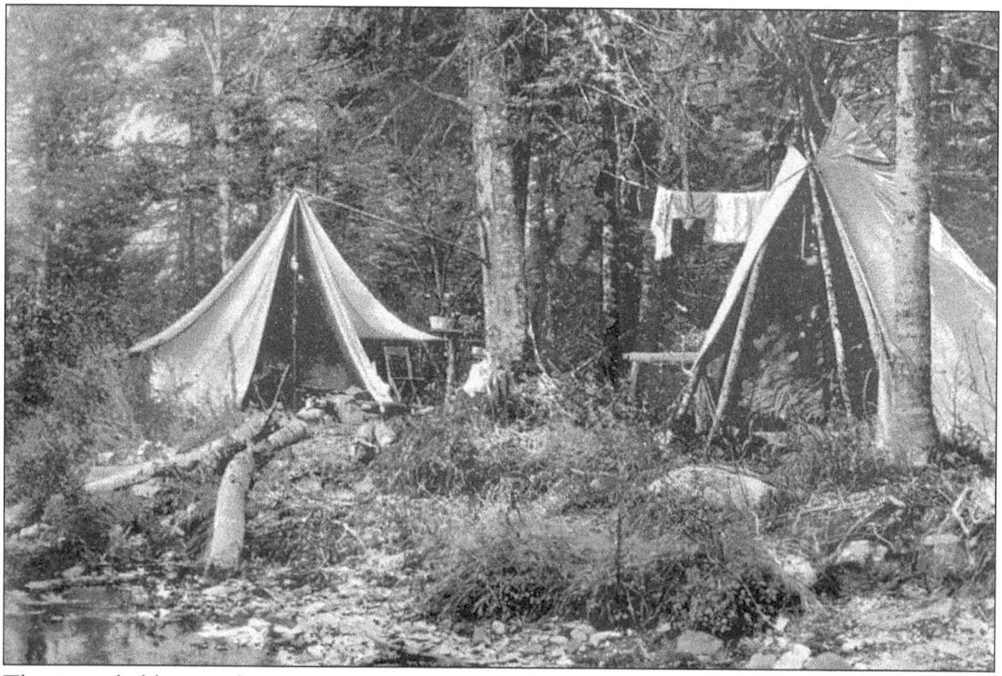

This is probably a guide's setup, with one tent for him and one for the sport.

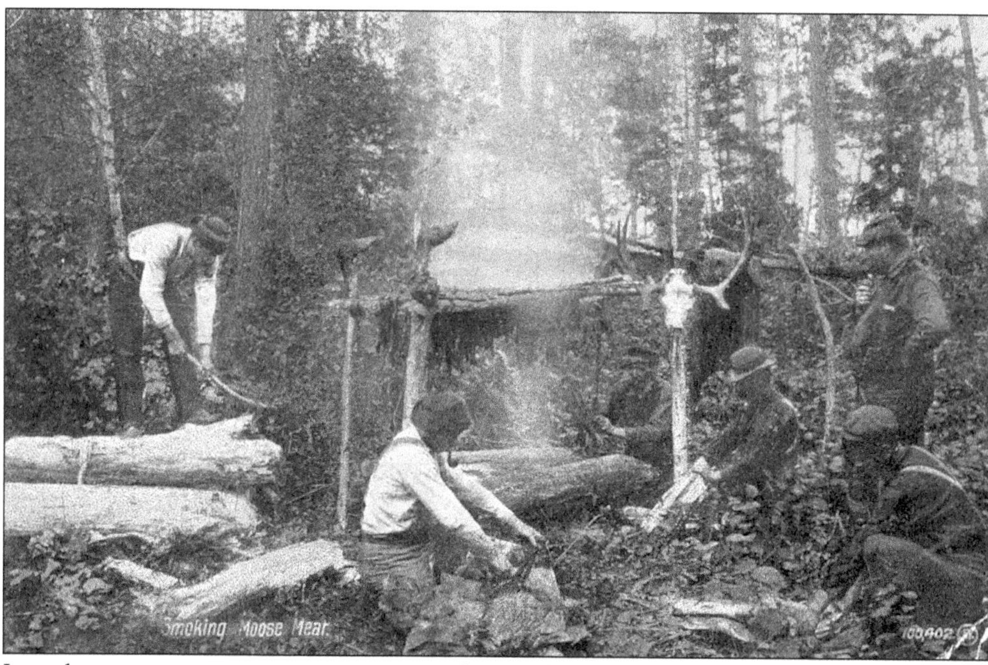

In order to preserve moose meat, it was frequently smoked on the spot. Here is a typical operation for that purpose.

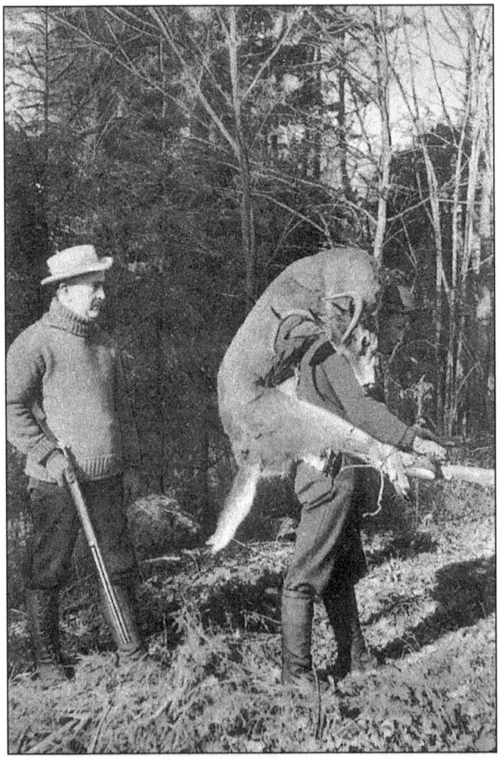

Most discussions center around dragging a deer out of the woods, but older photographs show that many of them were carried. This method seemed to be rather common and, looking at the dense underbrush and blowdowns so frequent in the Maine woods, one can easily understand why dragging an animal would not work in many locations.

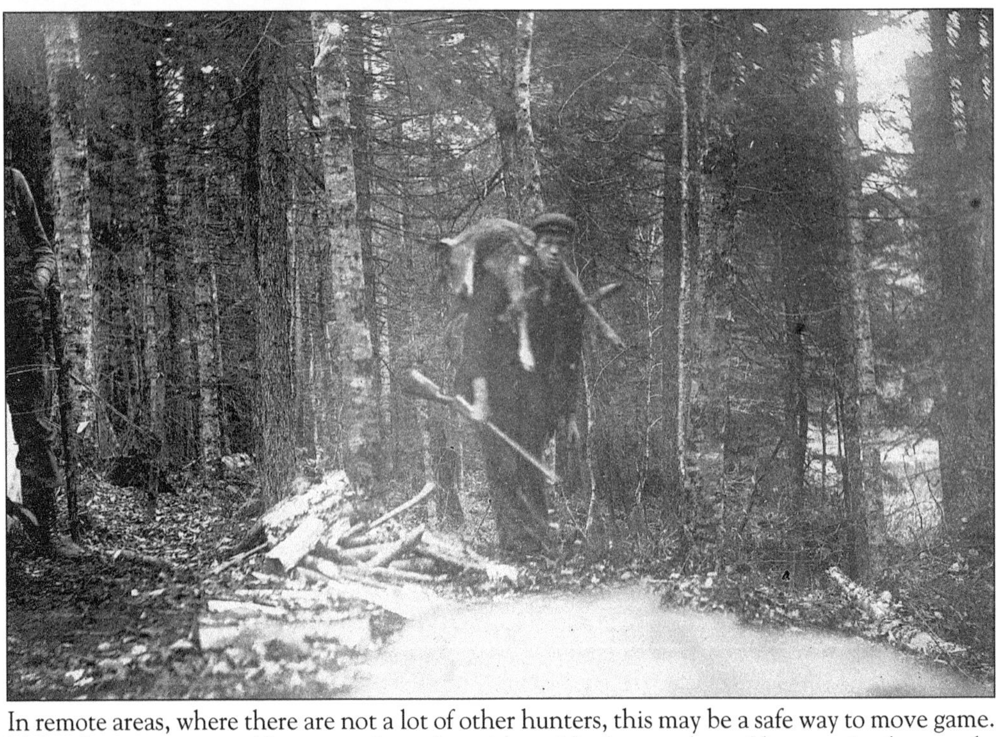

In remote areas, where there are not a lot of other hunters, this may be a safe way to move game. Today, however, it would seem to be rather risky with the number of hunters in the woods. Under the right lighting conditions, a person could easily be mistaken for an animal.

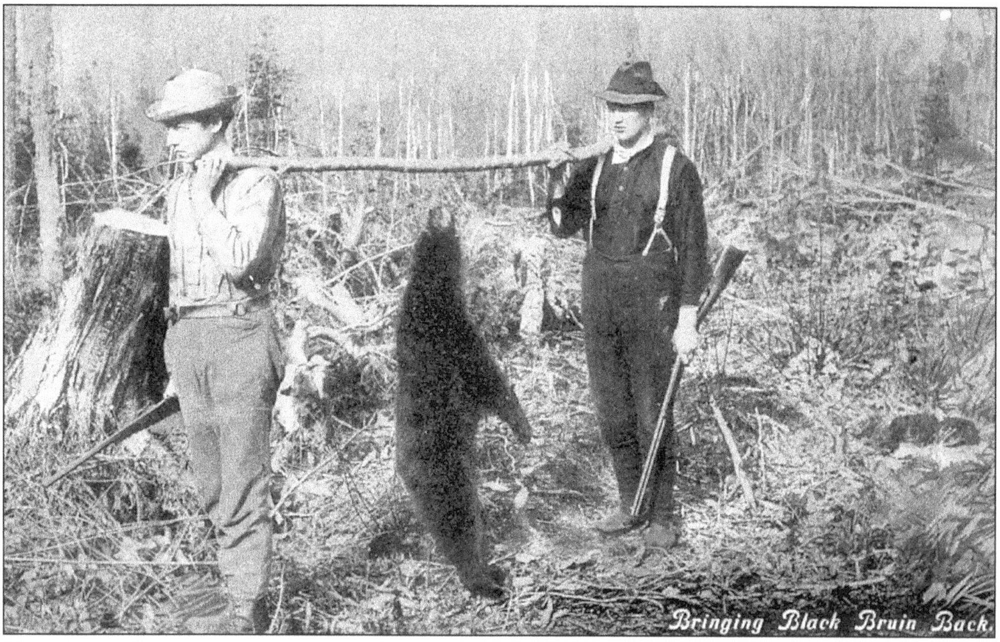

Here is another common way to take game out of the woods, especially a trophy animal that should not be dragged over rough terrain, thus ruining its coat. Many bear have been shot for their hides to be made into rugs, so protecting the soft fur is important.

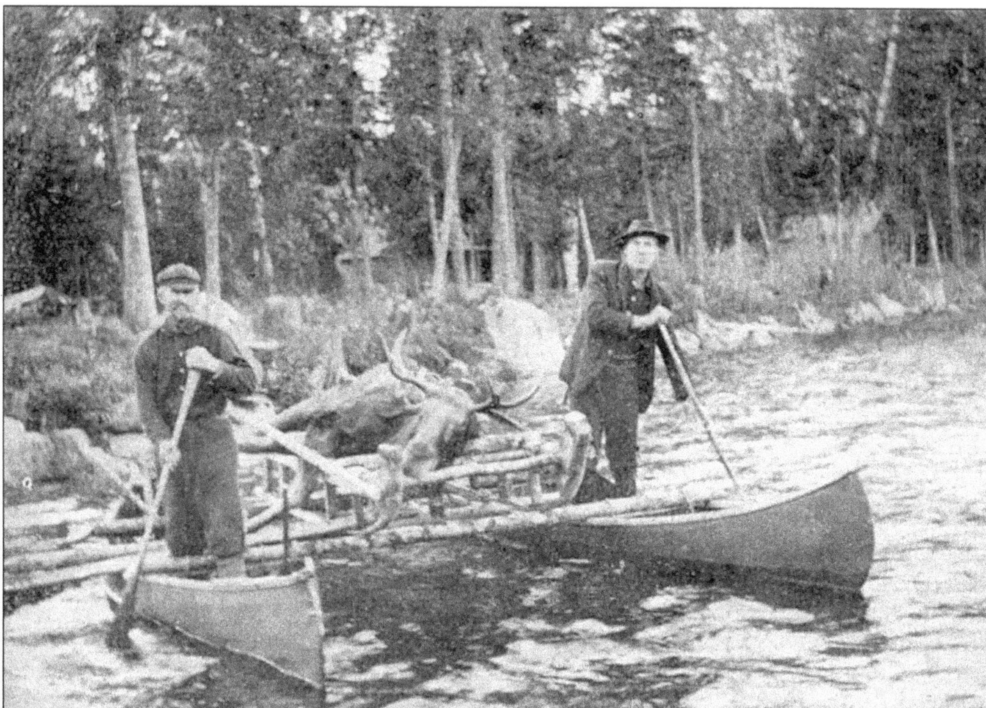

Since moose are too large for the average canoe and too heavy to carry, they are sometimes moved this way or with wagons and sleds. Here two hunters take their large animal across Northwest Pond, near Schoodic-Seboeis. (From *In the Maine Woods*, 1912.)

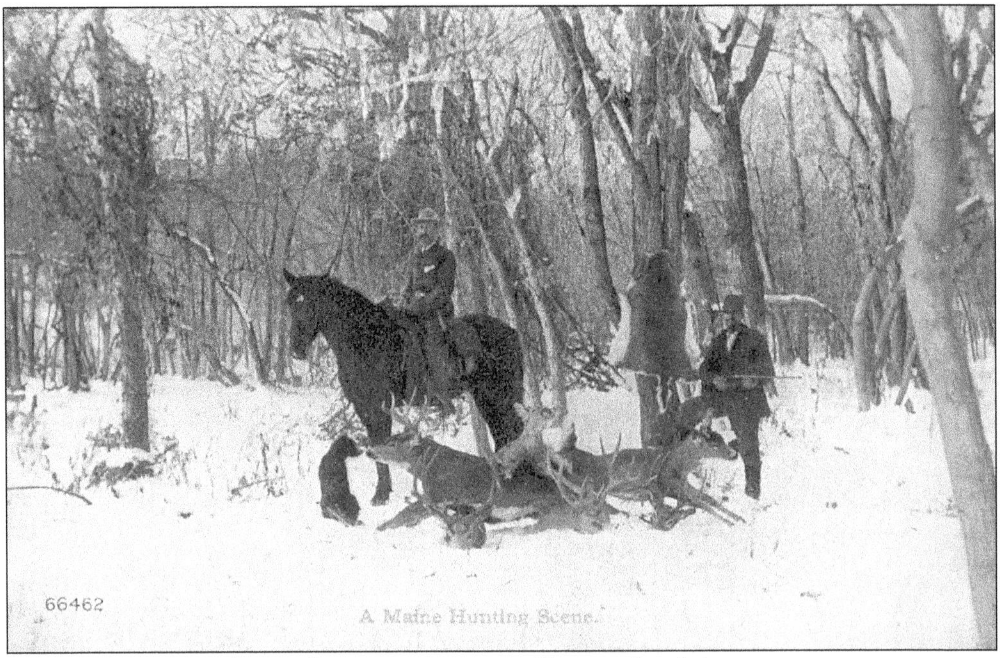

Larger game or several animals at a time were usually moved with horses.

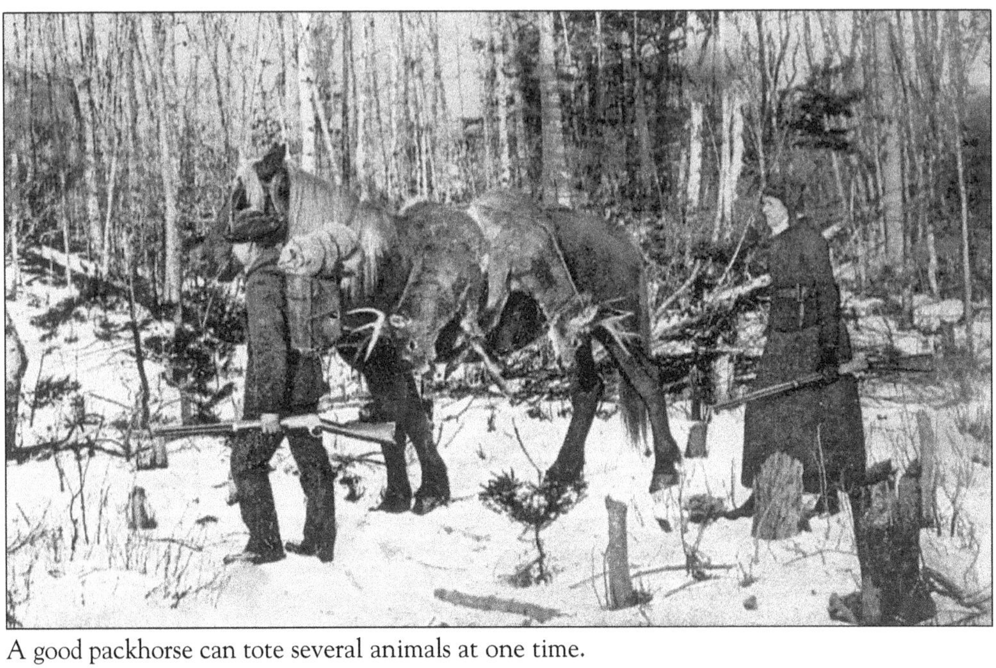

A good packhorse can tote several animals at one time.

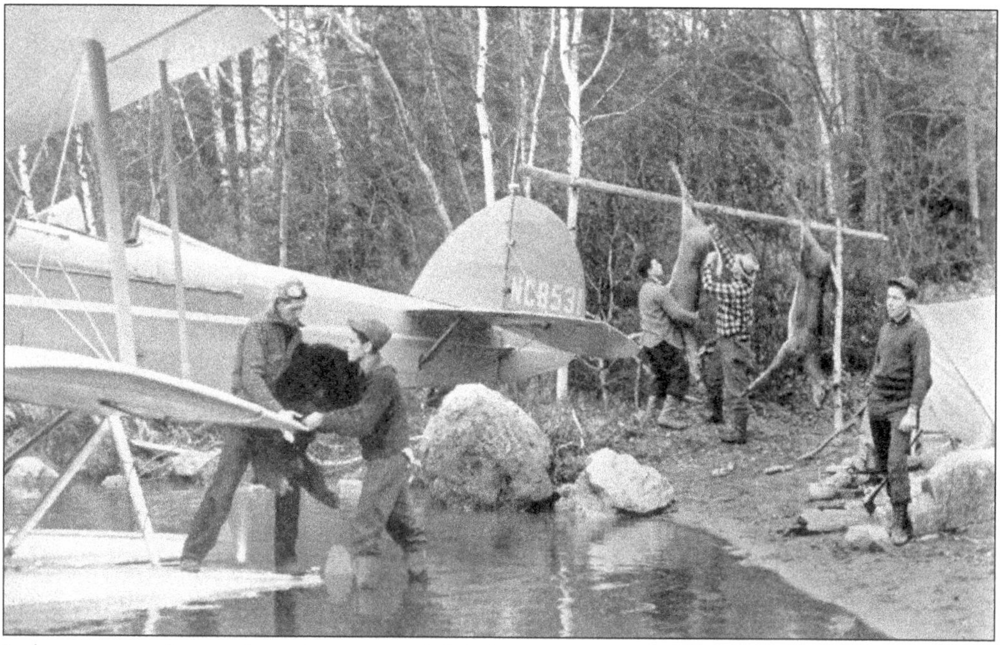

In later years, after airplanes became useful for hunting, game was taken out by lashing it to the pontoon. Here Buck Sherman, known as "Maine's Flying Guide," loads on game for the trip out. (From *In the Maine Woods*, 1940.)

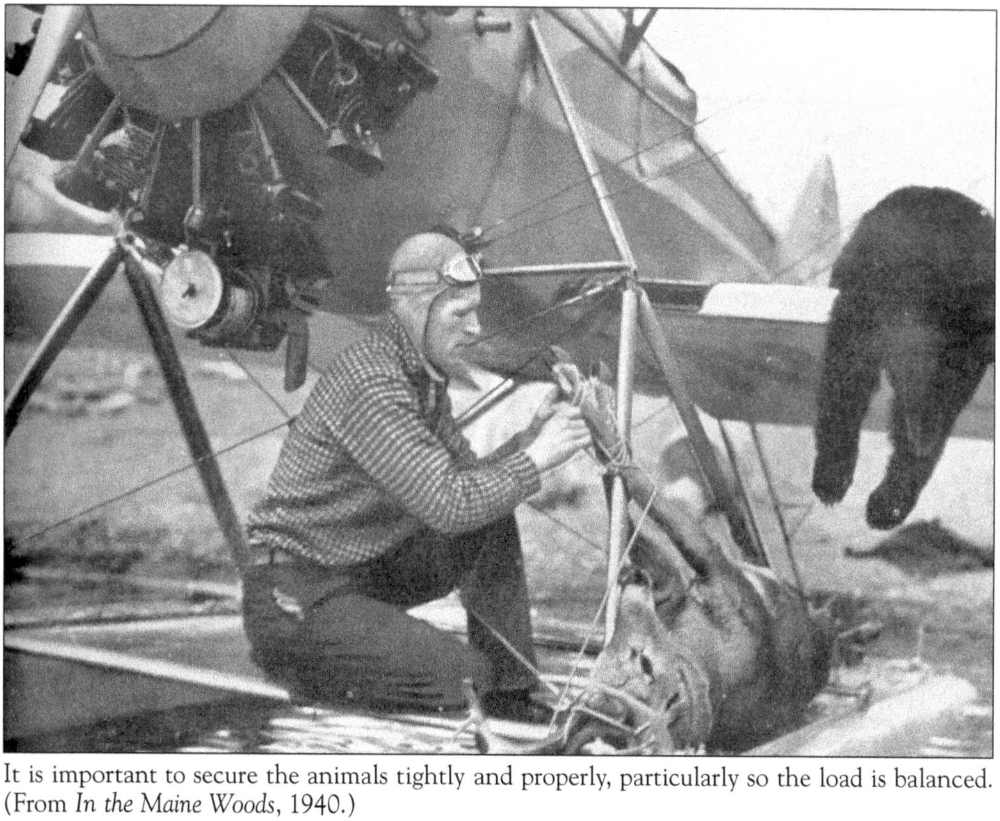

It is important to secure the animals tightly and properly, particularly so the load is balanced. (From *In the Maine Woods*, 1940.)

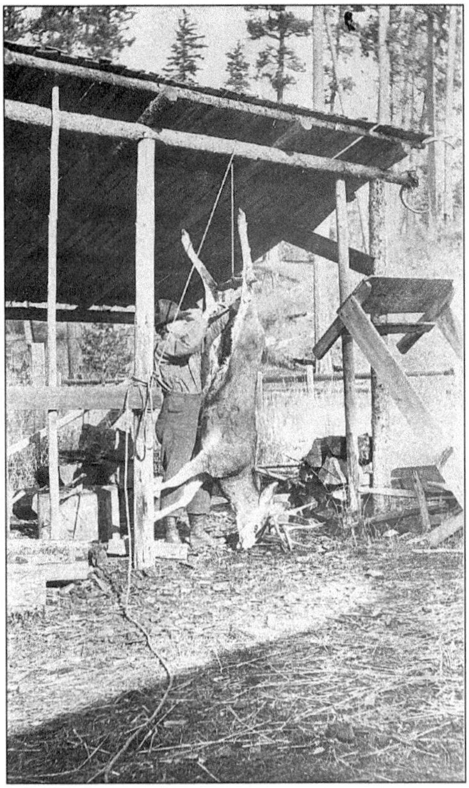

This successful hunter is hanging his deer in his shed for a few days to cure the meat.

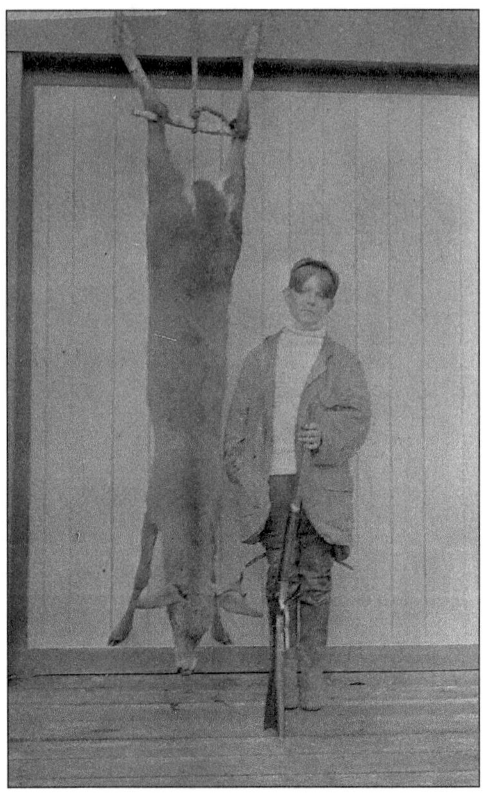

A young man poses at home with what is probably his first deer. The image appears on a postcard made from a personal home photograph, and the sender writes on the back that they wish they "had not put such an old coat" on the boy.

Two

Big Game in the Maine Woods

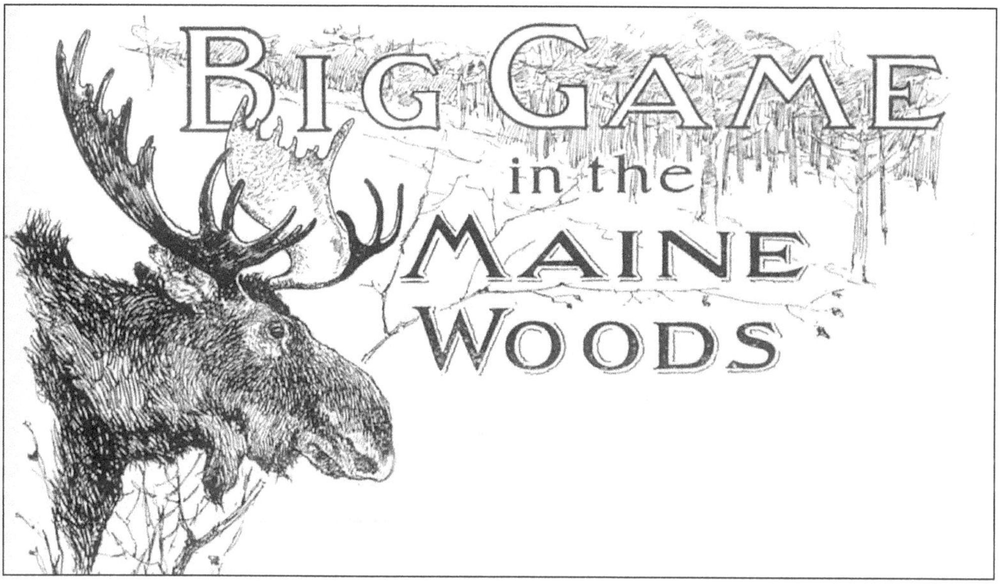

Owing to certain ownership conditions of the wild lands in northern Maine, nearly the whole north half of the state, which is about 15,000 square miles in area, is practically one great game preserve. The wild lands, once the property of the state, are now owned by men who wish to keep them in their wild state as long as possible, due to the returns to be had from the timber on them. The state assumes the right of eminent domain over these lands in the matter of hunting and makes laws governing hunting on them, thus conserving the supply of game and making better sport as the years go by. Game is so abundant in this great forest preserve of the north that anyone who can handle a gun and walk the forest is almost certain of getting a shot at a deer. Hunters who go for moose seldom come out of the woods without having come up with their game. Whether they secure their trophy of a pair of antlers or not depends on their skill. The game is there. The success that hunters have had in this great game region is shown in the number of moose, deer, bear, and caribou heads and rugs adorning dens, club rooms, hotel corridors, and offices all over the country. (From *In the Maine Woods*, 1900.)

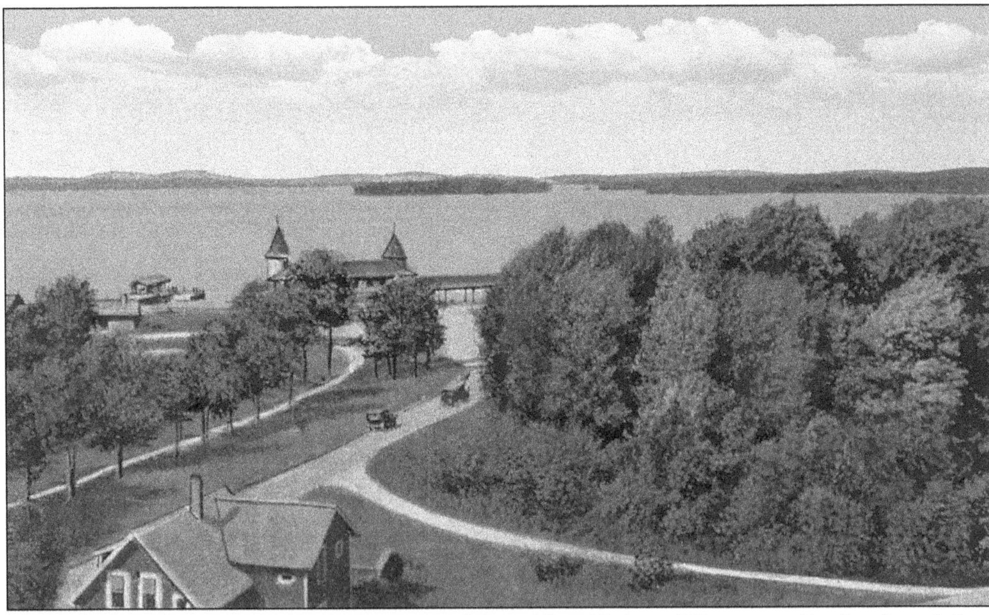

The Sebago Lake Region was easily accessed from New York and Boston to Portland, and then to the Sebago Lake Station, shown here. This view includes the Maine Central Railroad station and, to its left, the ferry landing from which boats transported travelers to other parts of the lake and beyond.

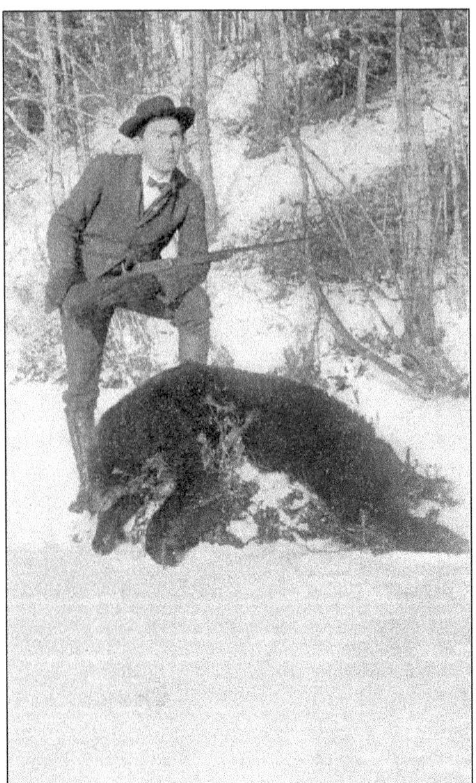

While not widely known, since it was not considered part of the wilderness, the Sebago Lake Region provided ample sport for game enthusiasts, as shown in this photograph. Carlton D. Martin shot this 257-pound bear at East Sebago on January 13, 1908.

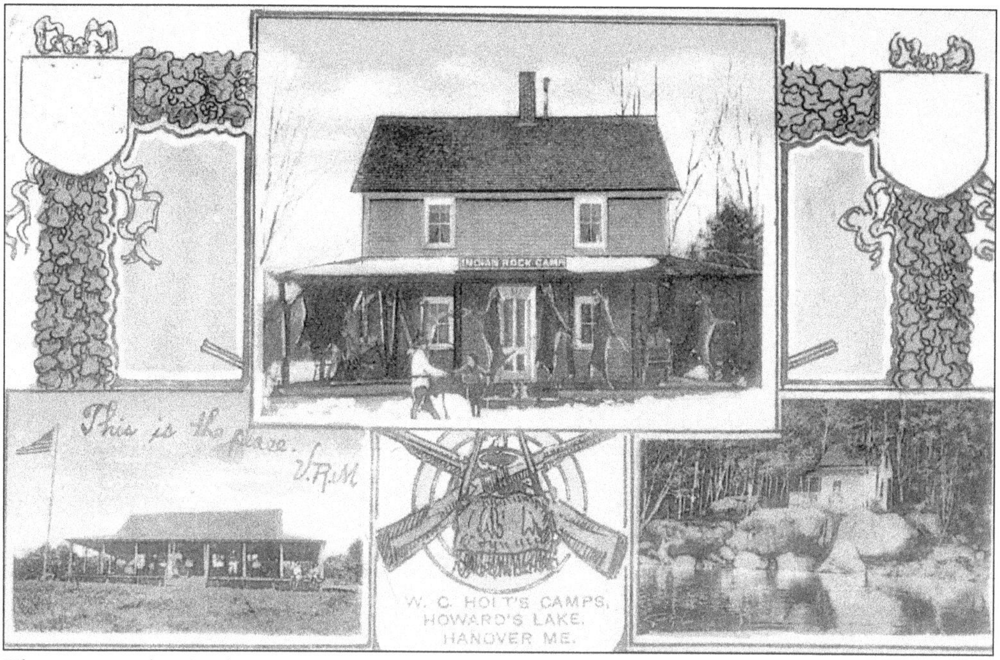

The area north of Sebago was also popular for big game. This camp has displayed several deer and a bear.

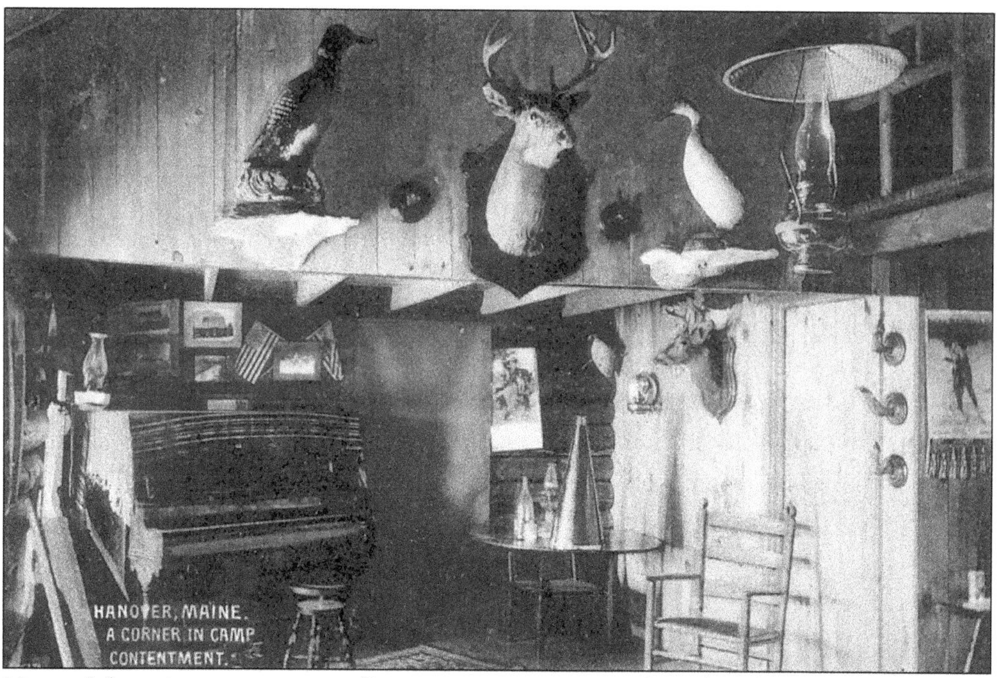

Many of the private camps, as well as sporting camps, are adorned with trophies of all kinds. Here we see birds, deer, and coat hangers made from deer feet.

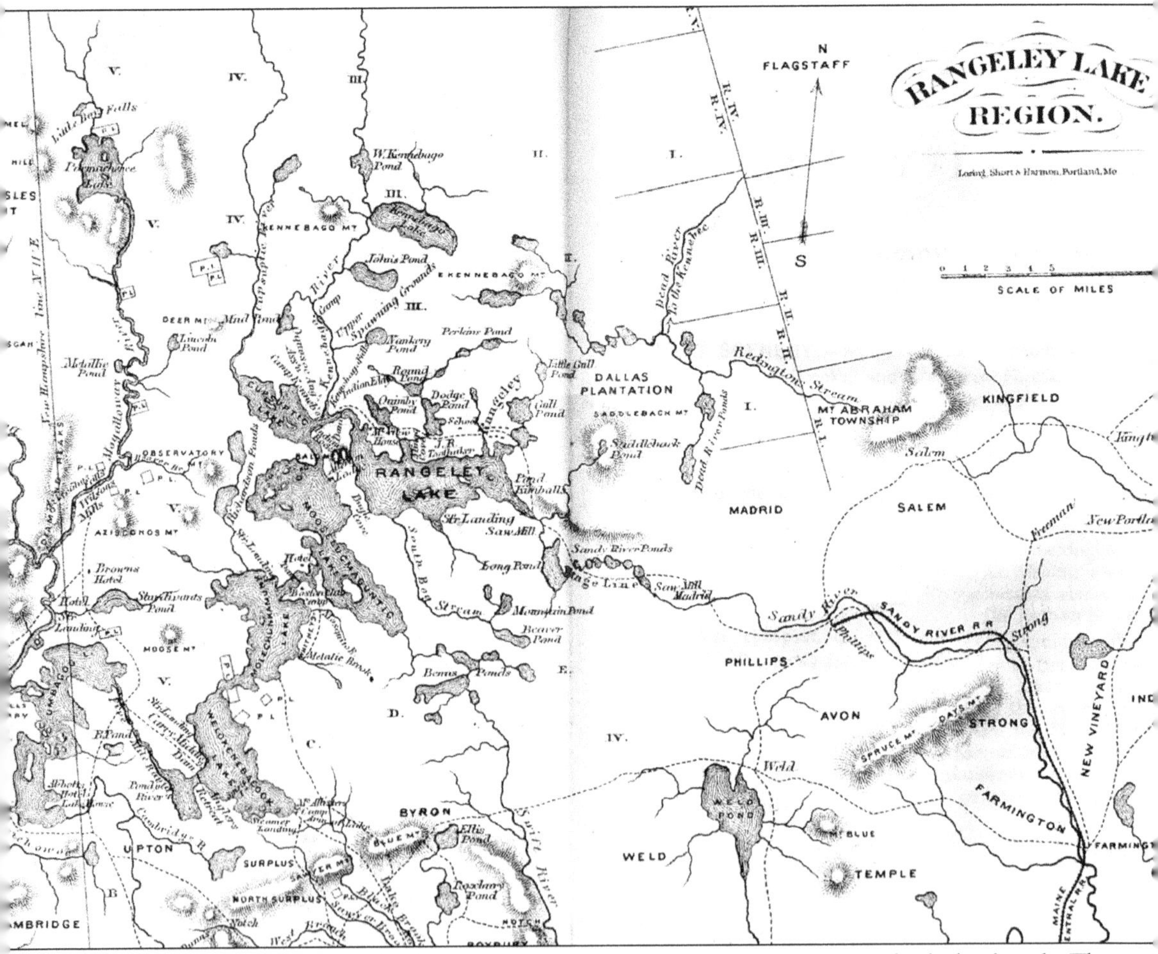

This *c.* 1880 map shows the Rangeley Region and surrounding area. Note the lack of roads. The Maine Central Railroad went as far north as Farmington, the Sandy River to Phillips, and then a passenger took the stage on to Rangeley and Kennebago. (From *Guide to the Rangeley Lakes*, 1880.)

THE RANGELEY LAKES.

THE MAINE CENTRAL RAILROAD

In connection with the Stage Lines from Farmington and Phillips, forms the

ONLY DIRECT ROUTE

To this remote and romantic series of Lakes, of which it has been said no other waters in the world produce such large trout as these pure cold streams in the

Wilderness of Maine.

There is no equally accessible portion of our whole country which offers such attractions to sportsmen.

Trains leave Portland daily for Farmington on arrival of trains from Boston, making close connection with stage for Phillips same evening. The stage leaves Phillips for Rangeley every morning at 7.30, arriving at Greenvale at 11.30 A. M., and Rangeley at 12 M. From each of these points the

Steamer "Molly Chunkamunk," (Capt. C. W. Howard,)

May be taken for

Mountain View House, Indian Rock, Camp Kennebago, Soule's Camp, and the Lower Lakes.

Time for Indian Rock and Camp Kennebago, the headquarters of the Oquossoc Angling Association

Three Hours Ahead of any other Route.

At Indian Rock and Haines' Landing (Soule's Camp) connection is made with the steamer Oquossoc, running on Lake Mooselucmaguntic, to and from Upper Dam and the Lower Lakes.

Returning, stage leaves—after arrival of Steamer from Indian Rock and Mountain View House—from Rangeley at 1.30 P. M. and Greenvale at 2.00 P. M., arriving at Phillips for supper, and leaving in the morning in season to connect with morning train from Farmington to Portland and Boston.

Excursion Tickets

From Philadelphia by Pennsylvania R. R. from New York, by all of the Sound Lines and from Providence, Worcester and Nashua by the W. & N. R. R.; from Boston, tickets will be for sale at the depots of the Eastern and Boston & Maine R. R.'s, and also at No 3 Old State House and No. 214 Washington St.

Fares to Rangeley and return:—Boston, $14.00; Portland, $11.00; Bath, $10.00; Brunswick, $9.75; Lewiston, $9.50; Indian Rock and Return, $1.25 additional.

Remember this is the cheapest and most popular route to this great sporting region, the favorite haunt of the deer and trout; and also to Kennebago and Parmachenee Lakes. The Parmachenee Lakes are reached by this route with only a five-mile carry from Cupsuptic Lake.

Ask for Tickets via the Maine Central R. R.

The Maine Central Railroad heavily promoted its ability to get the hunter to two prime hunting areas: Rangeley and, by 1906, Moosehead. The early transportation included stage travel, while additional railroads and extensions came later. (From *Guide to the Rangeley Lakes*, 1880.)

FARMINGTON, PHILLIPS AND RANGELEY LAKES.

D. CLARK & SON,

PROPRIETORS OF THE

FIRST CLASS STAGE LINE

BETWEEN

Farmington and Phillips.

FARE $1.50.

This is an old established route, and the line is thoroughly equipped with fine and comfortable coaches, a large stud of steady and well-trained horses, and careful and experienced drivers.

MESSRS. CLARK & SON look personally after the comfort of their passengers, and all who patronize this line are sure to be landed speedily and safely at the hotels in Phillips.

Express Matter promptly Forwarded.

Parties wishing for conveyance from Farmington to Rangeley Lake other than the regular stage will find it for their interest to procure the same of D. CLARK & SON, of Farmington, up, and Samuel Farmer, of Phillips, back, on account of their extra facilities at both ends, and cheapnesss of keeping on the route.

For further information address,

D. CLARK & SON,

3 **Farmington, Maine.**

While the Wells Fargo Company became nationally famous, smaller local lines offered some of the same services on a more limited basis. This advertisement explains how accommodating some stage lines were in taking care of travelers' needs. (From *Guide to the Rangeley Lakes*, 1880.)

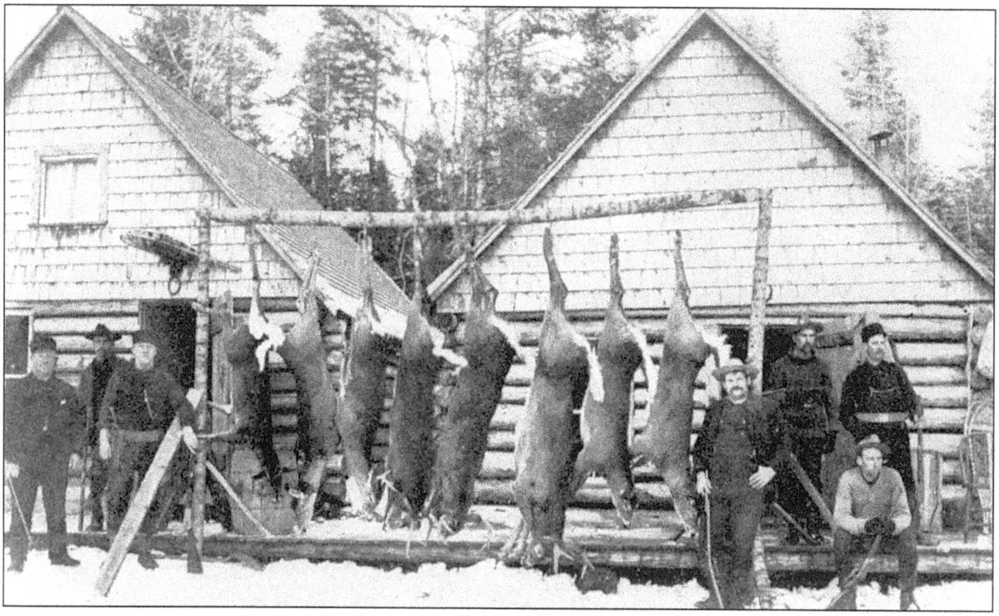

Many camps were founded in the Rangeley Region. In this picture, Porter and Kimball's Camp, near Quimby Pond, displays a particularly successful hunt.

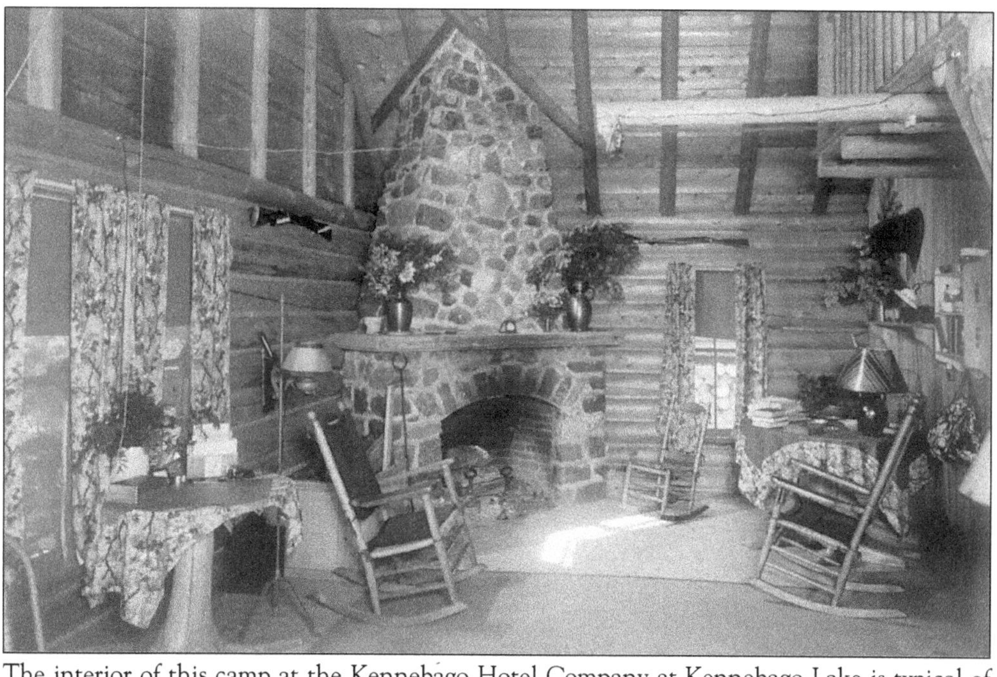

The interior of this camp at the Kennebago Hotel Company at Kennebago Lake is typical of hunting camps of this era. There are rifles hanging on the walls, which were also adorned with trophies. This camp even displays a boar's head.

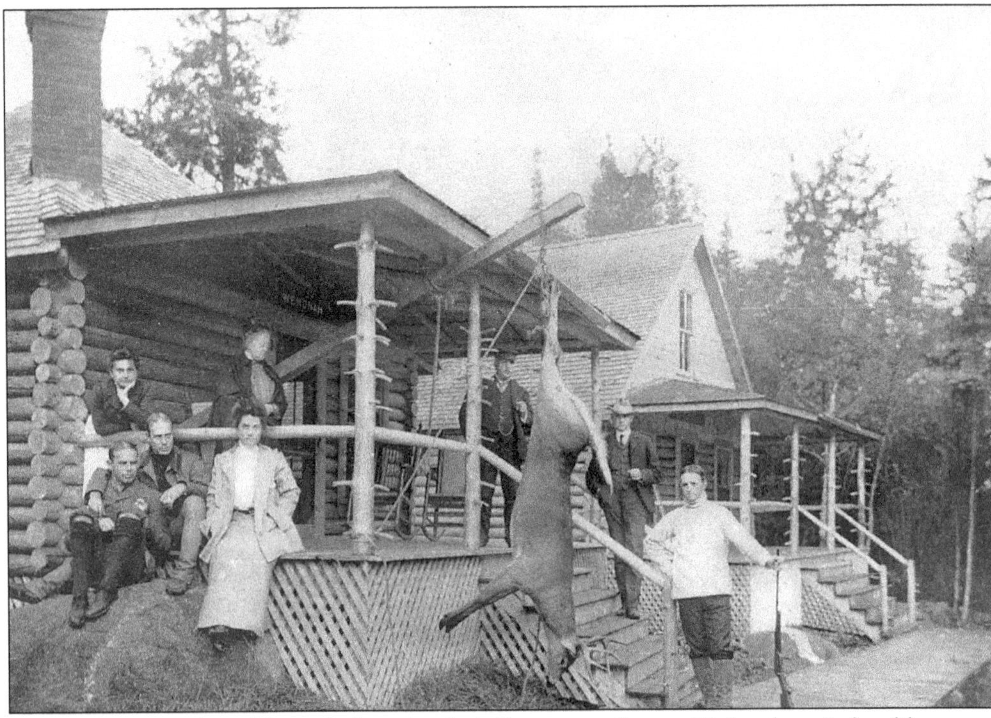

Although primarily a fishing lodge, Angler's Retreat at Lower Richardson Lake, like many lodges, remained open during the hunting season. (From *Scenic Gems of Rangeley Lakes*.)

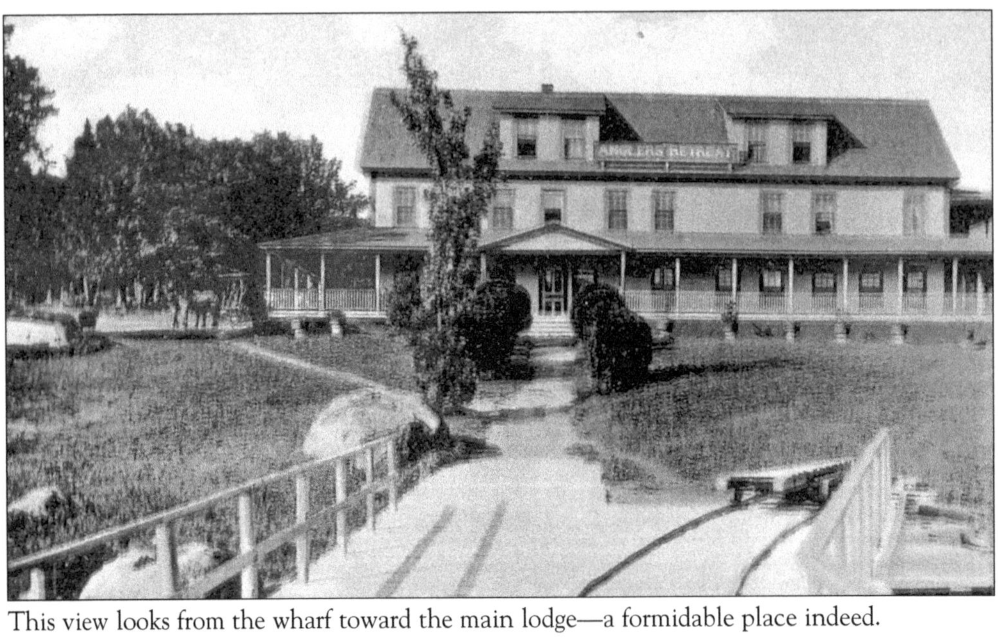

This view looks from the wharf toward the main lodge—a formidable place indeed.

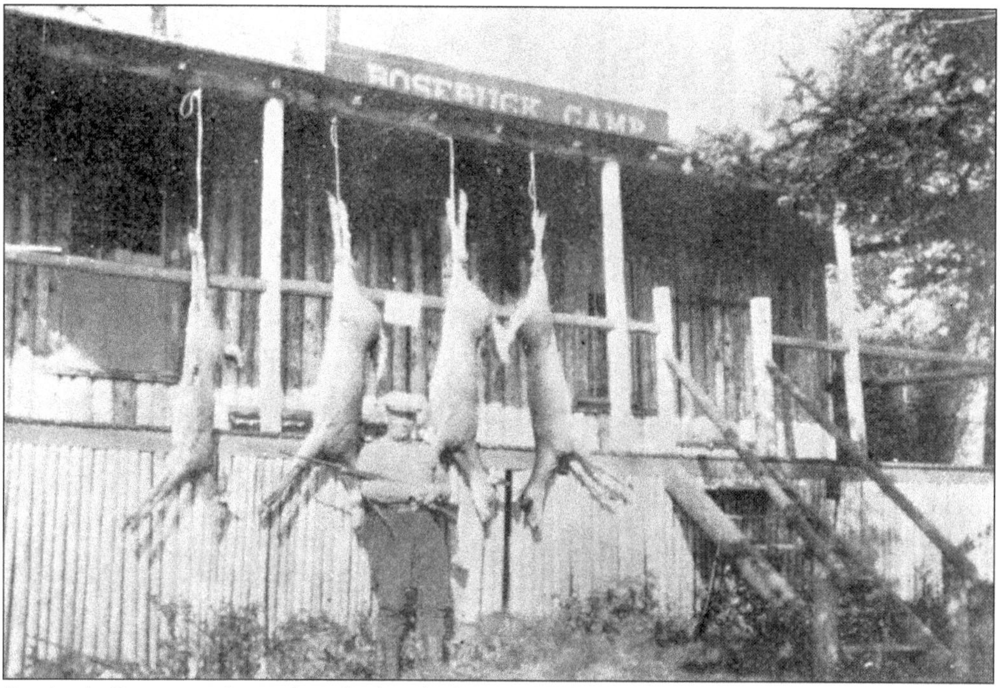

Bosebuck Camps are located at the head of Sawyer Lake, where the Big and Little Magalloway Rivers meet, 12 miles from Wilsons Mills. They were obviously situated in a prime hunting area.

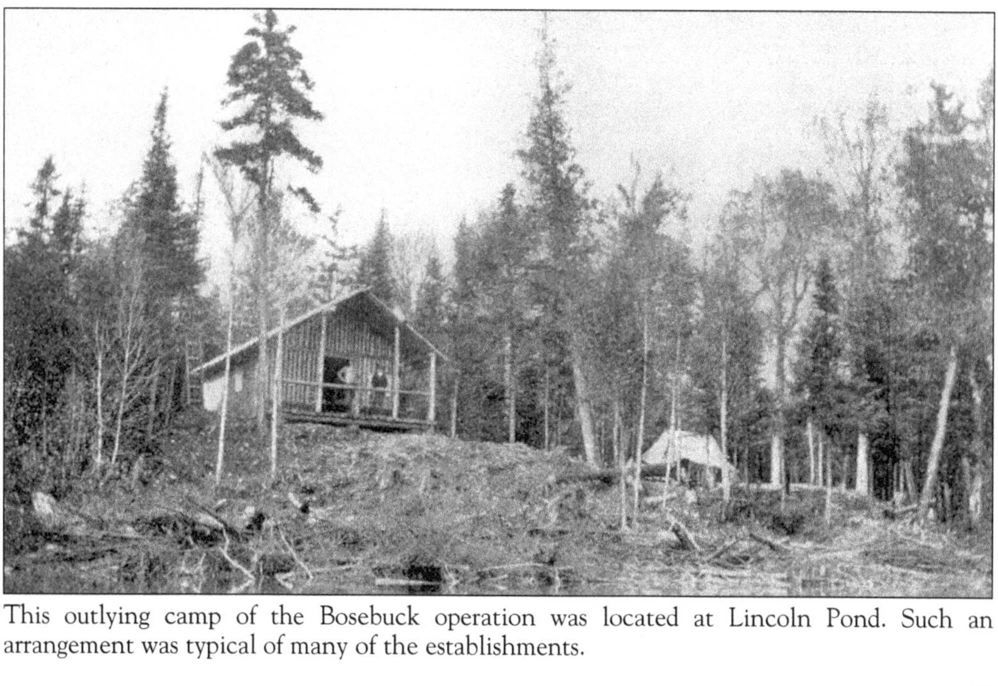

This outlying camp of the Bosebuck operation was located at Lincoln Pond. Such an arrangement was typical of many of the establishments.

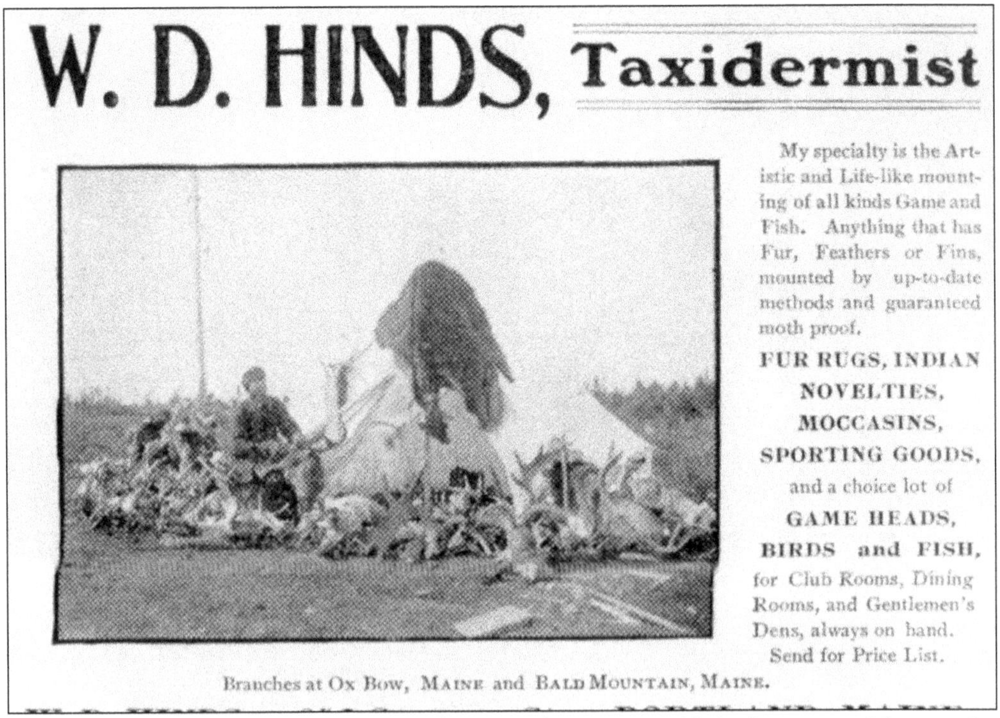

To accommodate the trophy hunter, taxidermy studios were established at most of the popular hunting locations or hubs. Hinds had several shops around the state. In 1904, three were advertised. (From *In the Maine Woods*, 1904.)

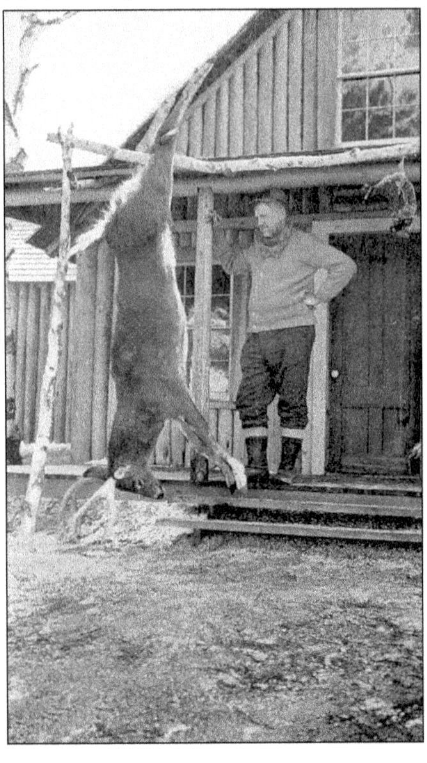

The deer shown in this photograph is unquestionably a trophy animal. The proud and satisfied hunter admires his trophy, no doubt contemplating getting the head mounted. (From *In the Maine Woods*, 1916.)

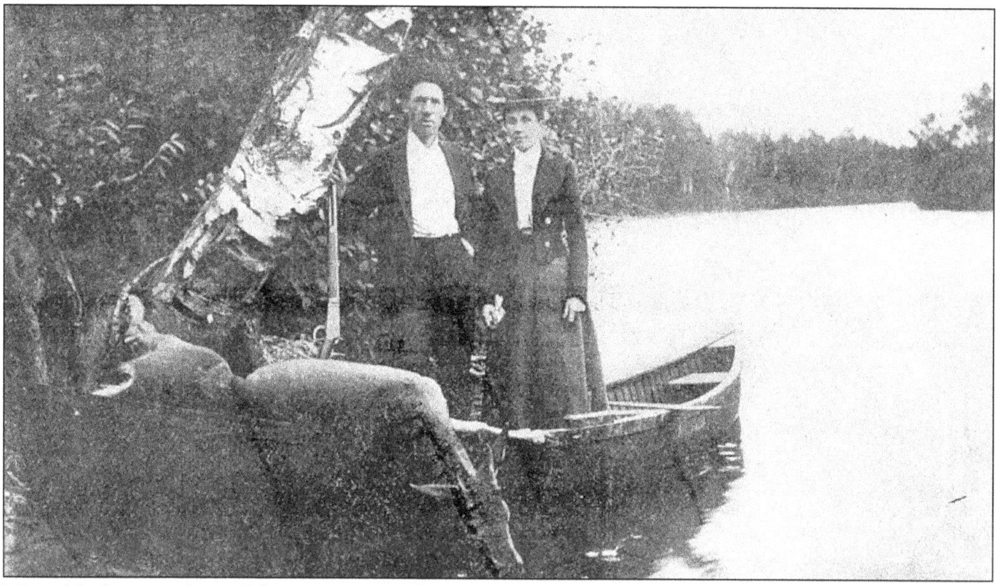

Most likely a guide and his sport pose here with their game transported by canoe. The lever-action rifle was a popular model for deer hunting and, around the turn of the century, many women took up the sport. In 1903, it was written that "the hunts*woman* is of comparatively recent origin. It has only been in late years that petticoated vacationers have shouldered their rifles at the advent of the big-game season and gone into the Maine wilderness in quest of handsome trophies."

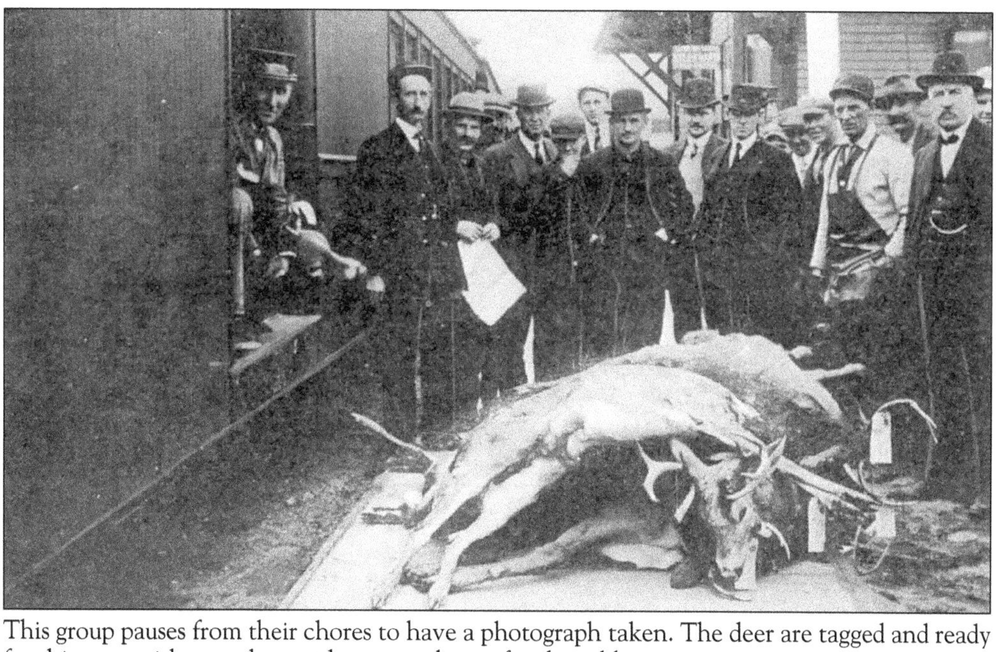

This group pauses from their chores to have a photograph taken. The deer are tagged and ready for shipment either to the taxidermist or home for the table.

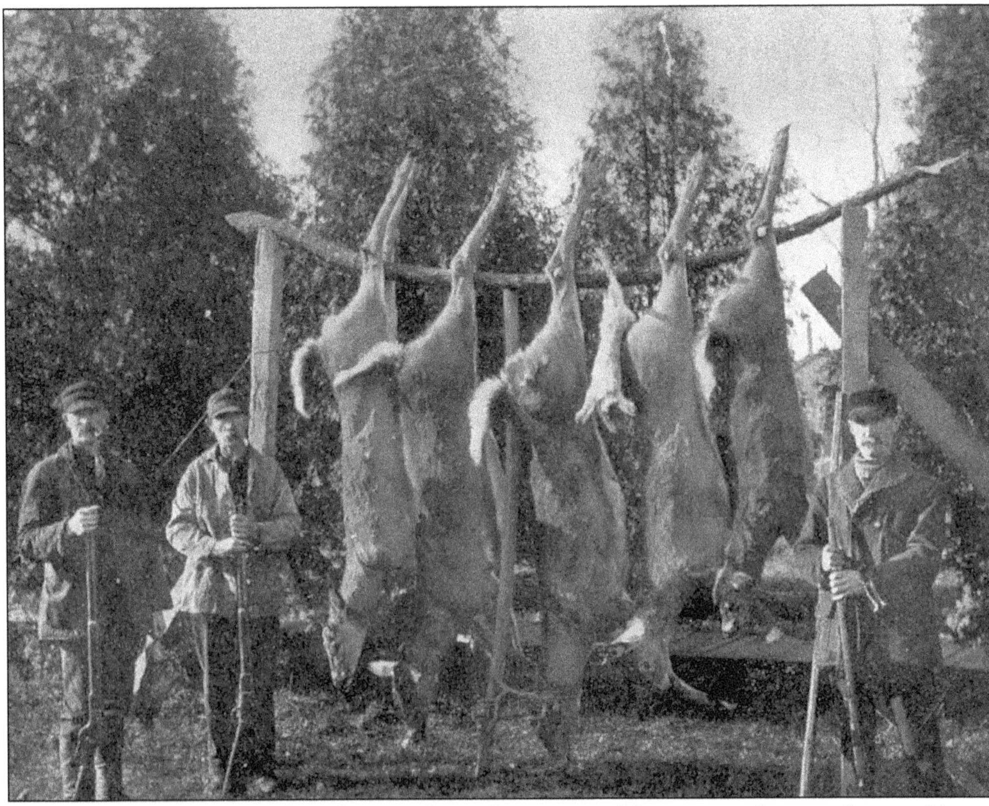

Three hunters pose with their limits of two deer apiece. Note again the popularity of lever-action rifles. This postcard is marked "Clifton, Maine."

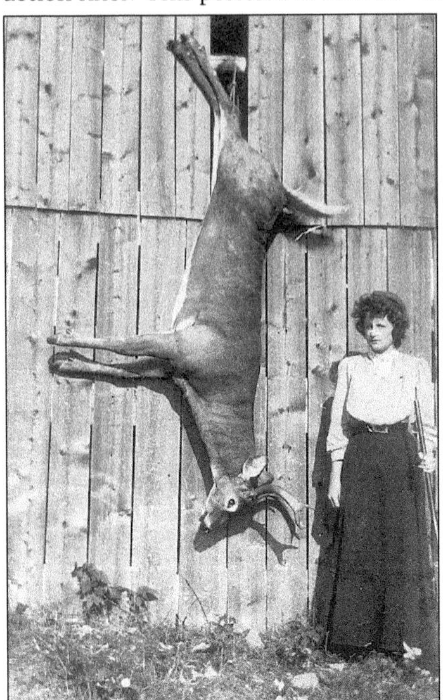

The chances are this woman bagged this nice buck. The card is postmarked "Flagstaff, 1910." (Steve Rainsford collection.)

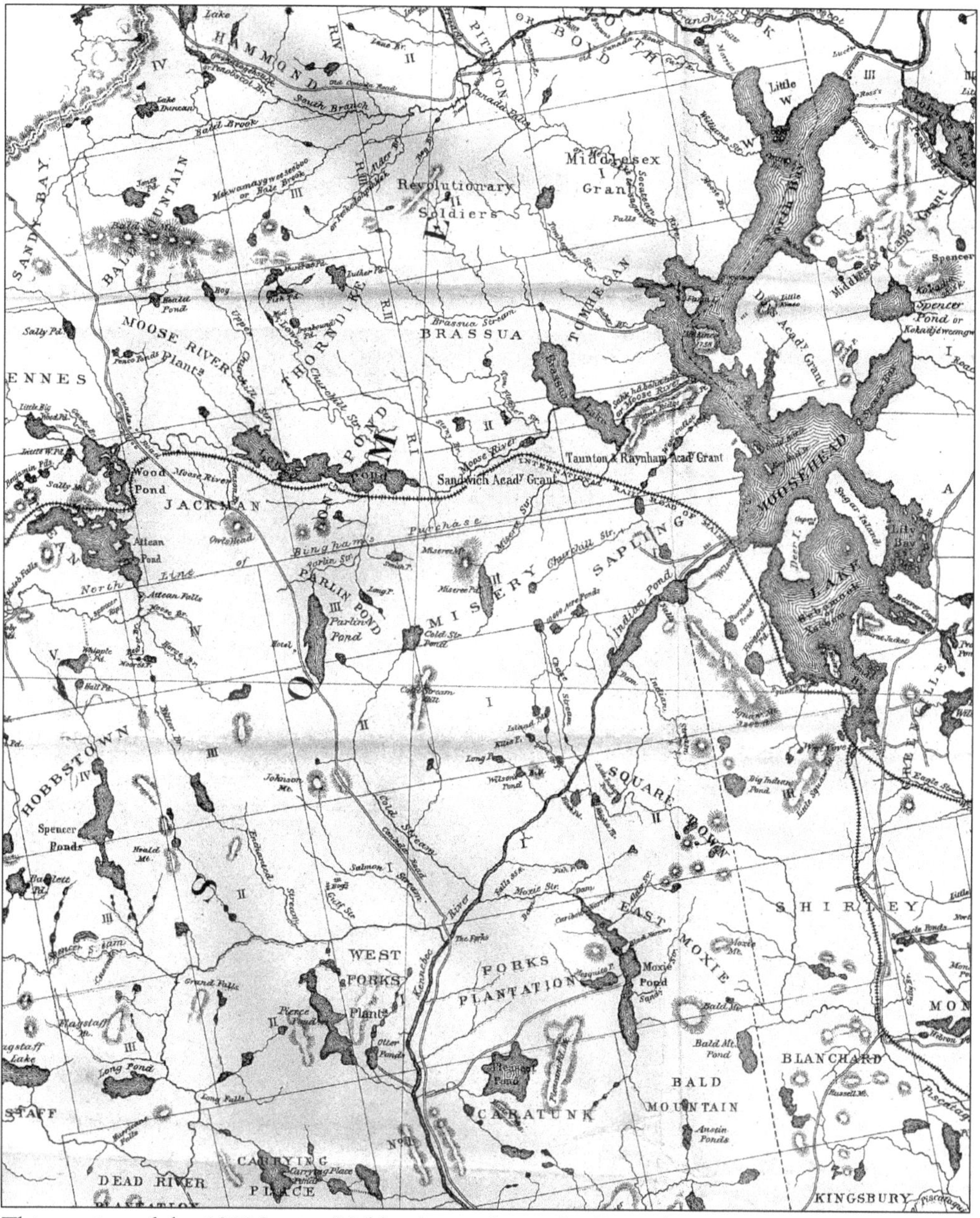

This section of the 1900 Lucius Hubbard map shows the Kennebec River Valley, just north of Rangeley-Farmington, and northward, including Moosehead, the Moose River Valley, and the West Branch of the Penobscot River.

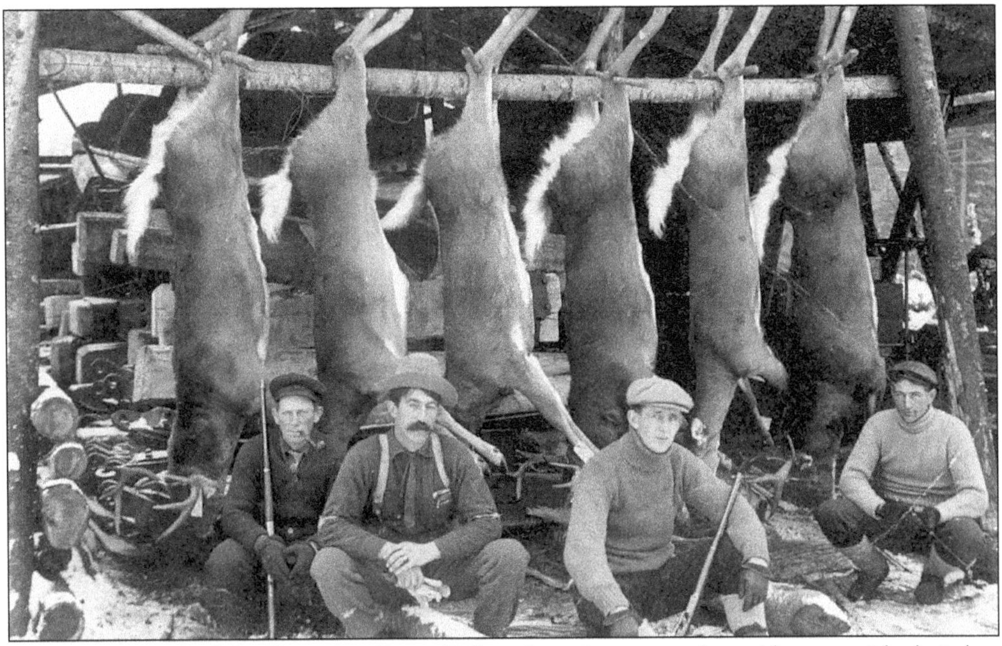

At the lower end of the Kennebec River Valley, these hunters and a guide pose with their bag limits—two deer each. This postcard is stamped "Madison, 1909." (Steve Rainsford collection.)

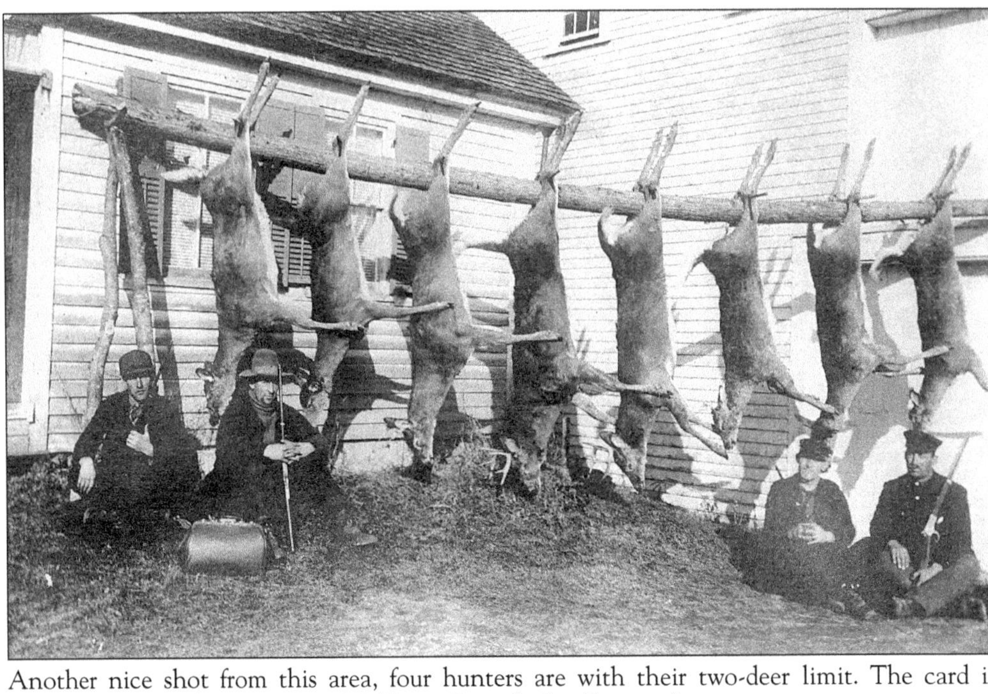

Another nice shot from this area, four hunters are with their two-deer limit. The card is postmarked "North Anson, 1909." (Steve Rainsford collection.)

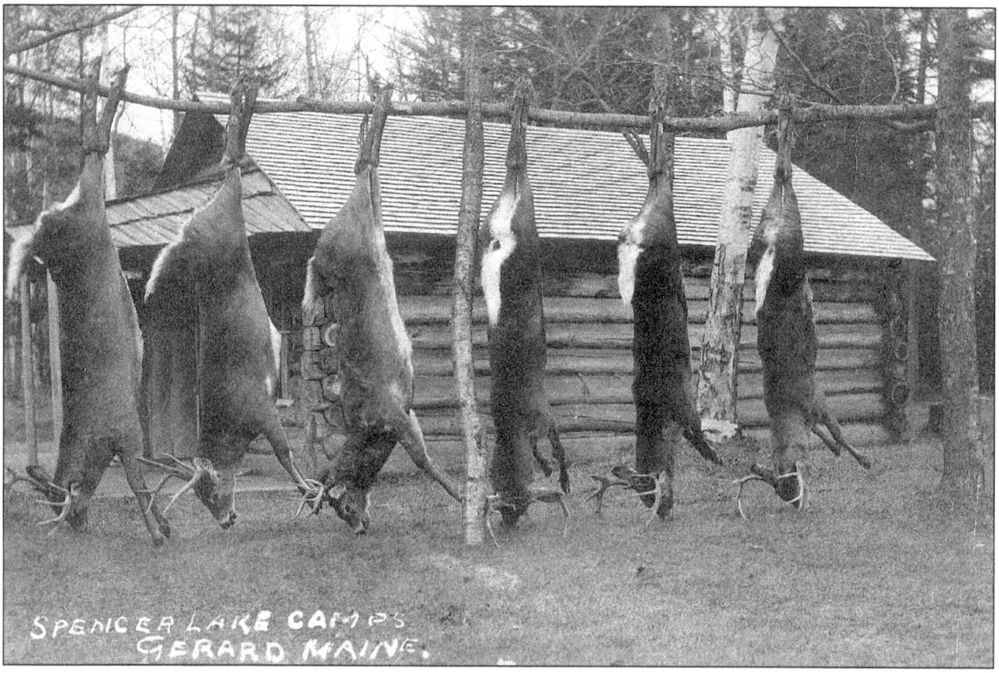

Spencer Lake Camps in Gerard were slightly off the beaten path, located well off the main road. The camps advertised, "Deer and bear are very plentiful, and moose are seen each season near the camps. Partridge shooting is excellent and ducks in their fall flight frequent these waters in large numbers. These camps have been advertised in a very limited way, thus preserving the hunting and fishing until the present time." Owing to the nature of the location and its lack of accessibility, chances are little that it has changed.

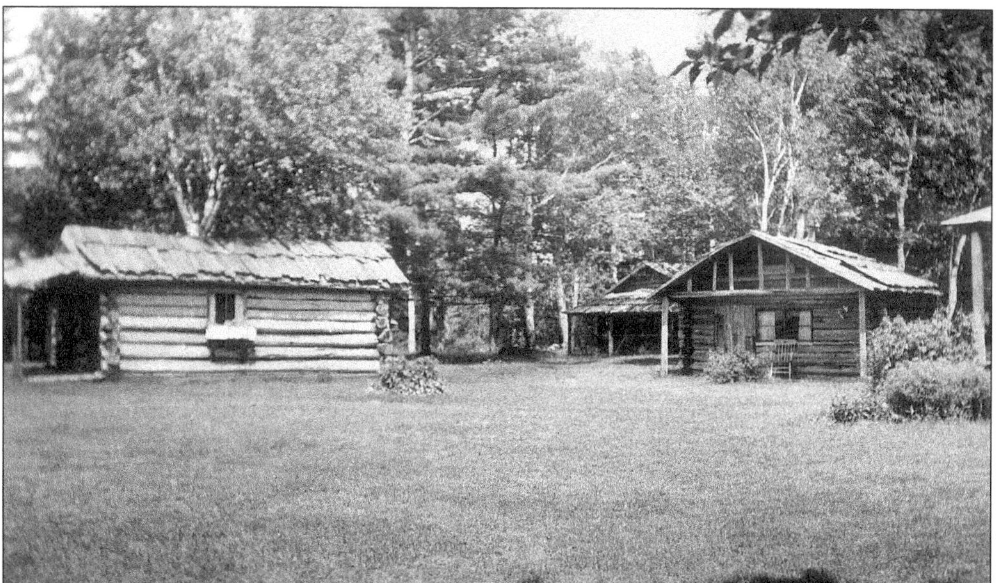

Another view of the Spencer Lake Camps shows the character of the dwellings.

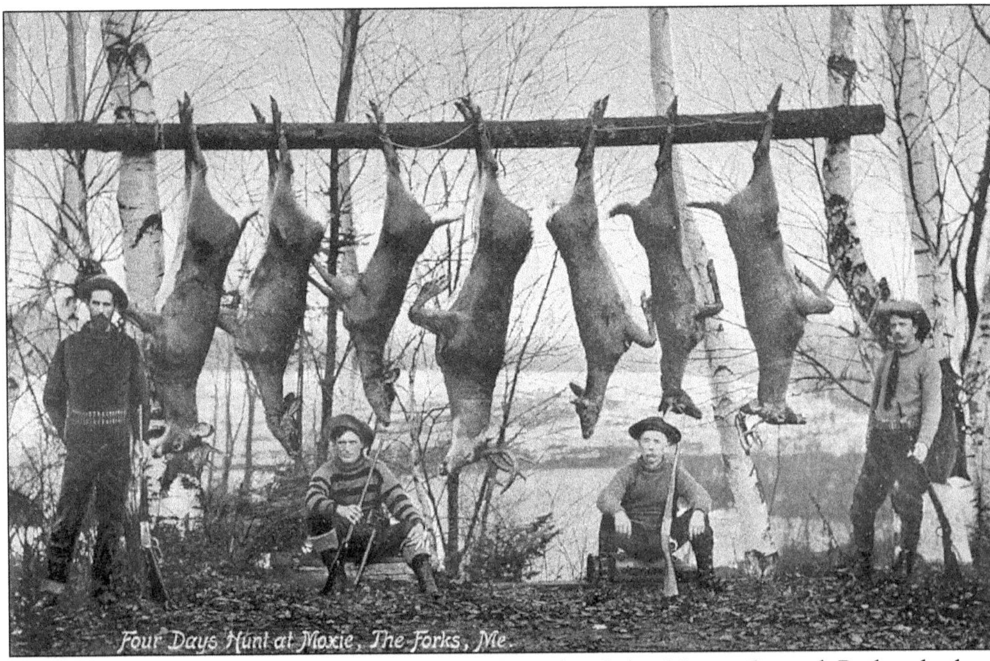

At Moxie, accessible only by the Somerset Branch of the Maine Central Railroad, there were several remote establishments. This area has always been known for large expanses of timberland with an abundance of large game.

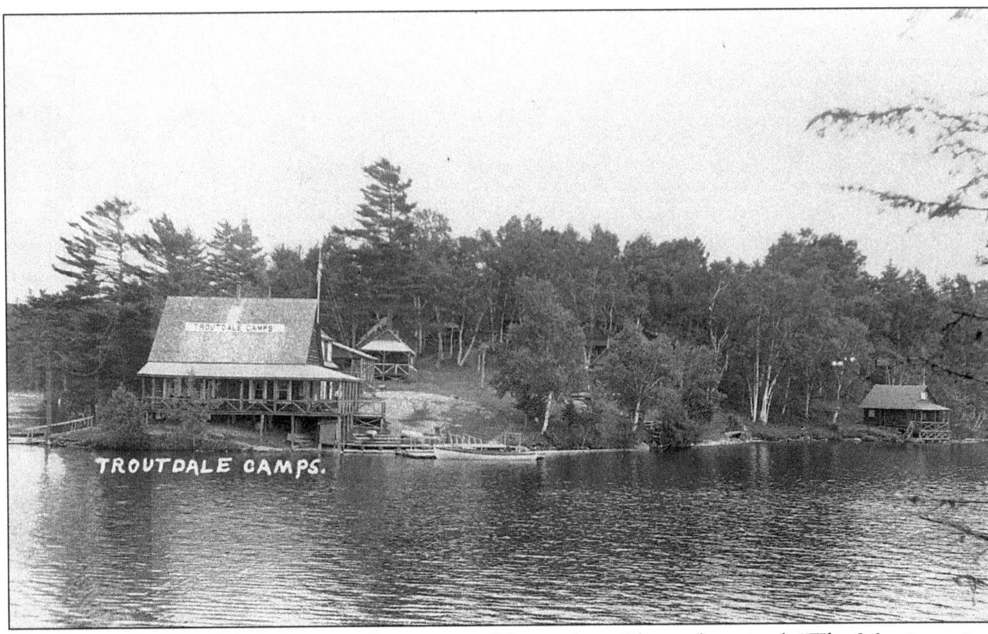

Troutdale was one of the most popular camps of the region. They advertised, "The Moxie region is out of reach of the roadside hunter, and its old road and cut-over lands support an abundance of deer, birds, and other game."

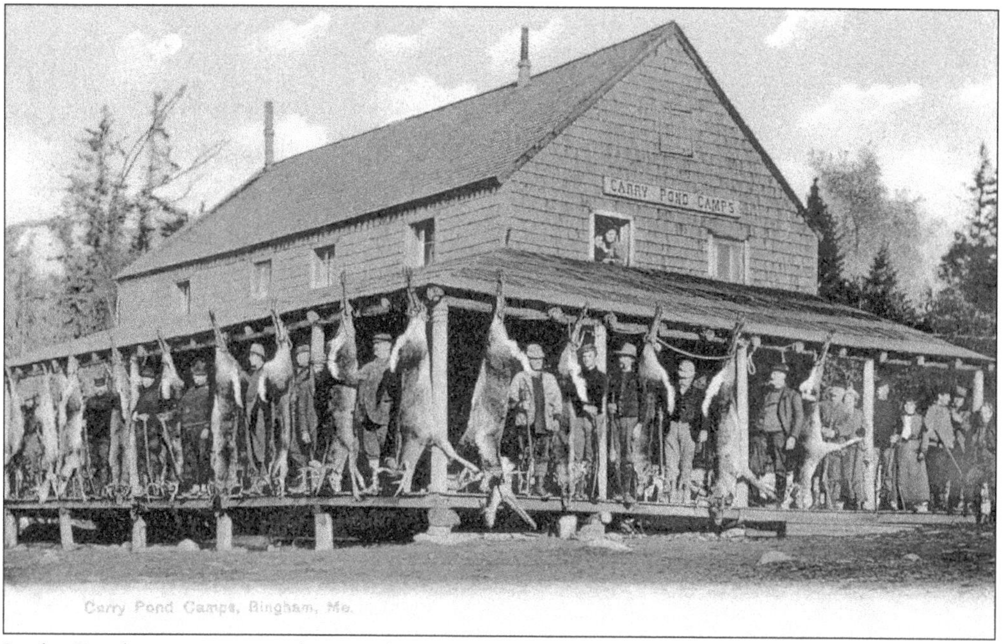

In the Bingham area, a popular set of sporting camps was at Carry Pond. Here a gang of hunters shows off an impressive number of big bucks.

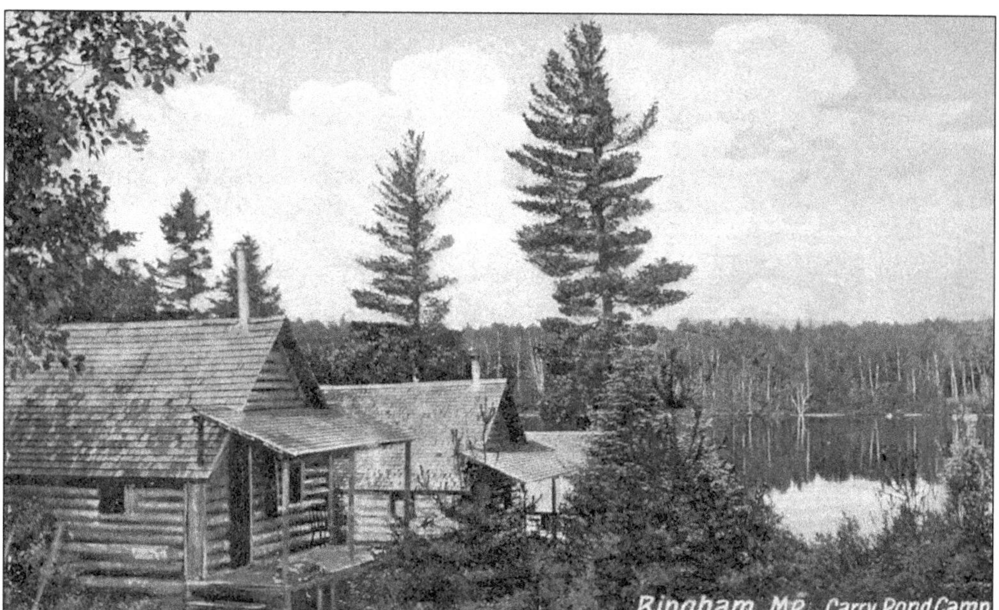

This shot of the camps takes in the pond itself and provides a look at a truly wilderness setting.

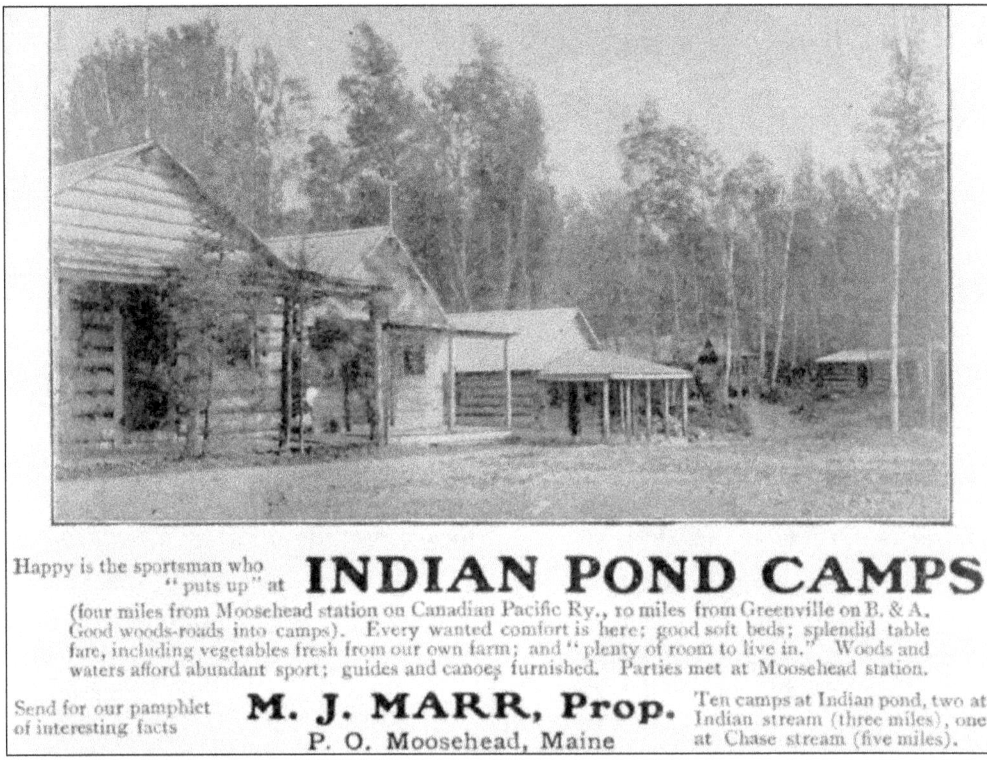

Located just off the Somerset Branch Railroad, Marr's was a popular establishment until the mid-1950s, when the completion of Harris Station resulted in the enlargement of Indian Pond, completely flooding this site. Note that Marr's had three outlying camps in addition to the 10 at the main location. (From *In the Maine Woods*, 1903.)

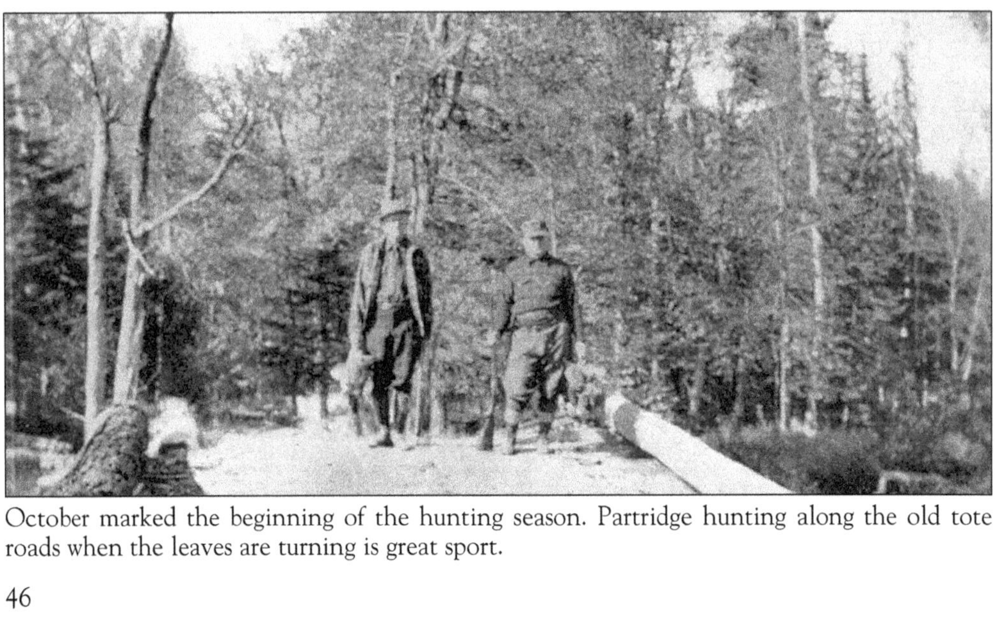

October marked the beginning of the hunting season. Partridge hunting along the old tote roads when the leaves are turning is great sport.

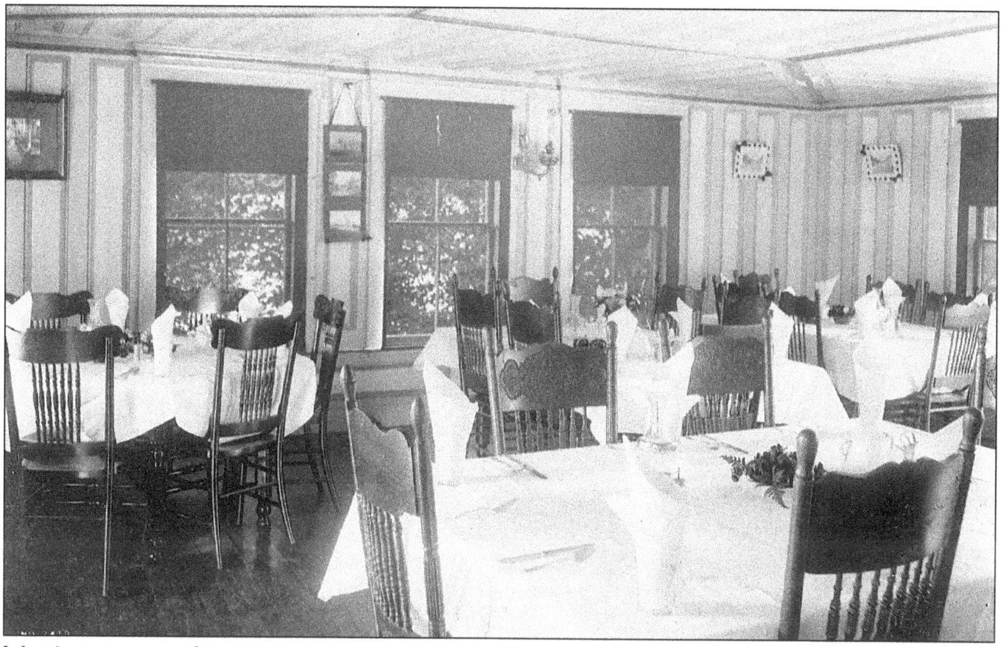

Marr's was one of many camps with a fancy dining room. Most establishments offered the American plan of accommodations, whereby one price included lodging and three meals.

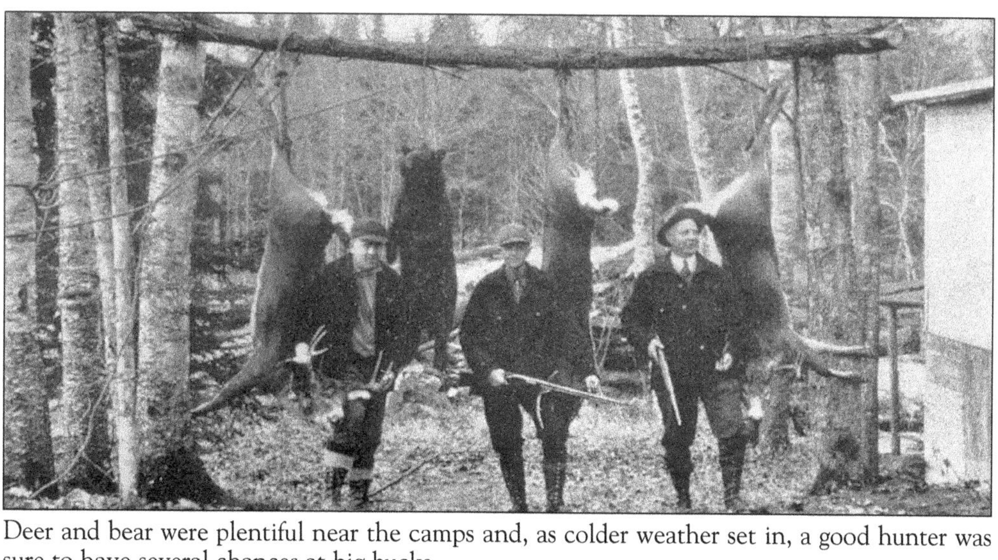

Deer and bear were plentiful near the camps and, as colder weather set in, a good hunter was sure to have several chances at big bucks.

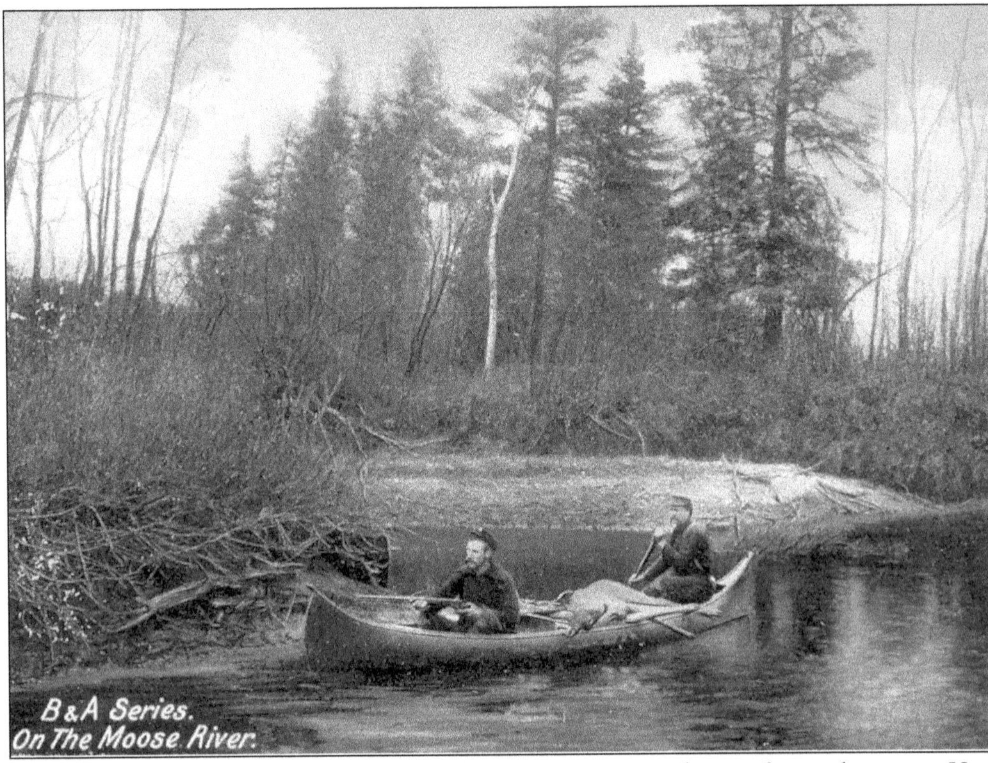

With few roads, a lot of hunting in the Jackman Region was either on foot or by canoe. Here the hunter watches carefully as the guide slowly maneuvers the canoe along the margin of the river. The party has bagged one deer and is looking for a second one to "fill out his tag."

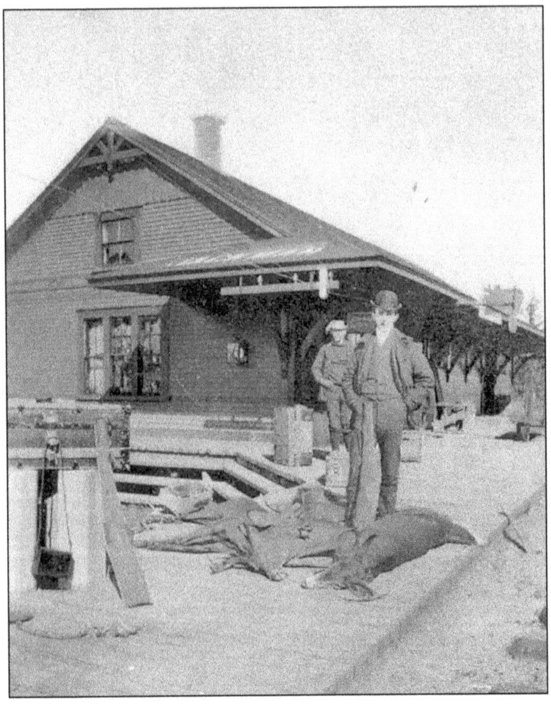

Hunters in the Jackman Region area usually shipped their game out on the Canadian Pacific line, which ran from Quebec across Maine to New Brunswick. Here hunters await their transportation back home after a successful hunt.

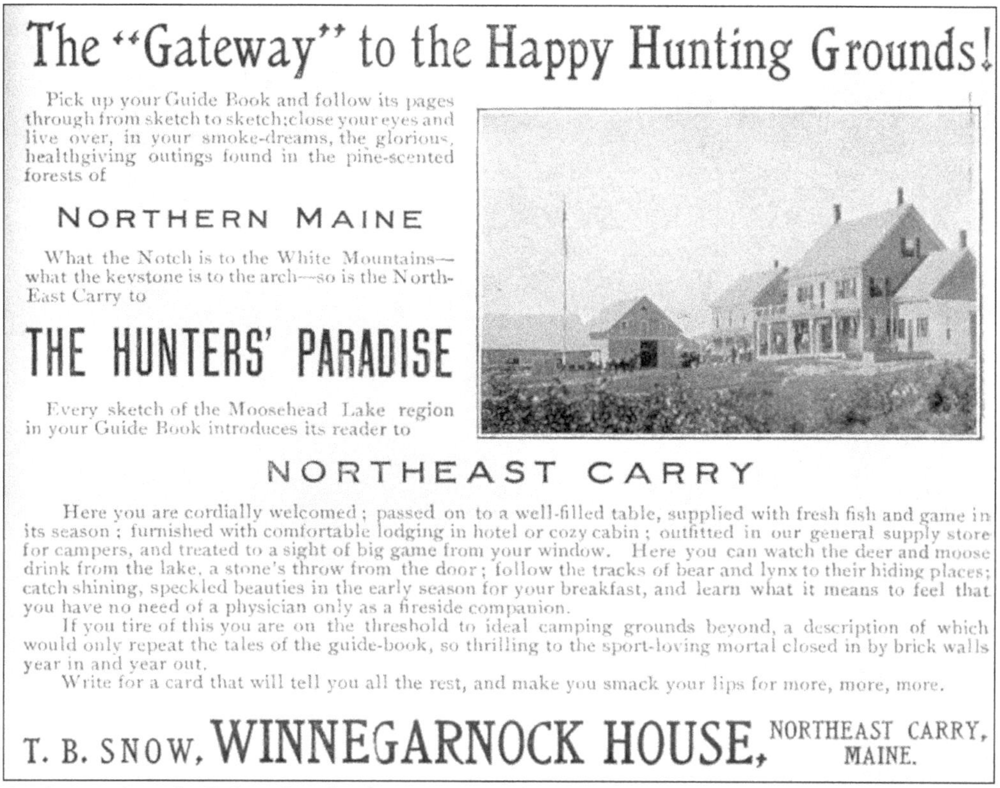

The "Gateway" to the Happy Hunting Grounds!

Pick up your Guide Book and follow its pages through from sketch to sketch; close your eyes and live over, in your smoke-dreams, the glorious, healthgiving outings found in the pine-scented forests of

NORTHERN MAINE

What the Notch is to the White Mountains—what the keystone is to the arch—so is the North-East Carry to

THE HUNTERS' PARADISE

Every sketch of the Moosehead Lake region in your Guide Book introduces its reader to

NORTHEAST CARRY

Here you are cordially welcomed; passed on to a well-filled table, supplied with fresh fish and game in its season; furnished with comfortable lodging in hotel or cozy cabin; outfitted in our general supply store for campers, and treated to a sight of big game from your window. Here you can watch the deer and moose drink from the lake, a stone's throw from the door; follow the tracks of bear and lynx to their hiding places; catch shining, speckled beauties in the early season for your breakfast, and learn what it means to feel that you have no need of a physician only as a fireside companion.

If you tire of this you are on the threshold to ideal camping grounds beyond, a description of which would only repeat the tales of the guide-book, so thrilling to the sport-loving mortal closed in by brick walls year in and year out.

Write for a card that will tell you all the rest, and make you smack your lips for more, more, more.

T. B. SNOW, WINNEGARNOCK HOUSE, NORTHEAST CARRY, MAINE.

At the north end of Moosehead Lake were several establishments, accessible only by steamboat for a long time. This one, located at Northeast Carry, was one of the most popular. (From *In the Maine Woods*, 1908.)

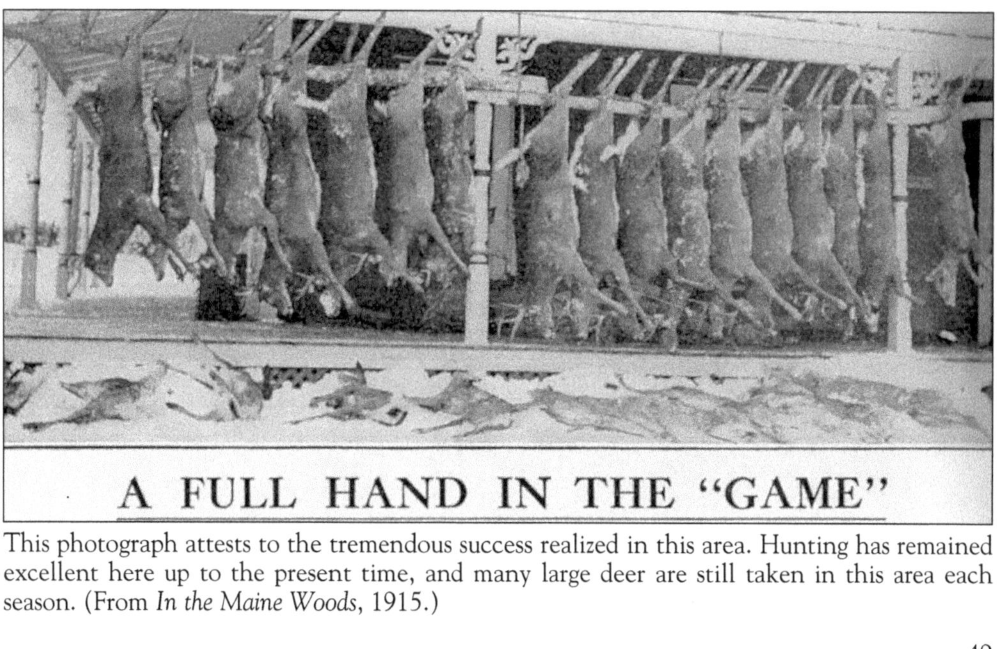

This photograph attests to the tremendous success realized in this area. Hunting has remained excellent here up to the present time, and many large deer are still taken in this area each season. (From *In the Maine Woods*, 1915.)

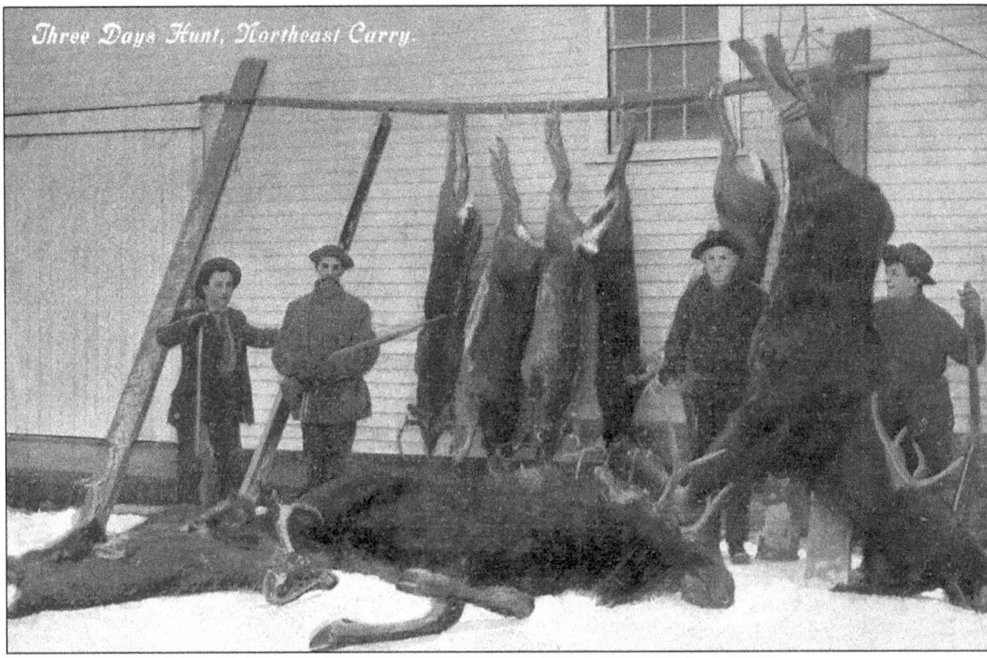

Two large moose are included in this 1910 photograph.

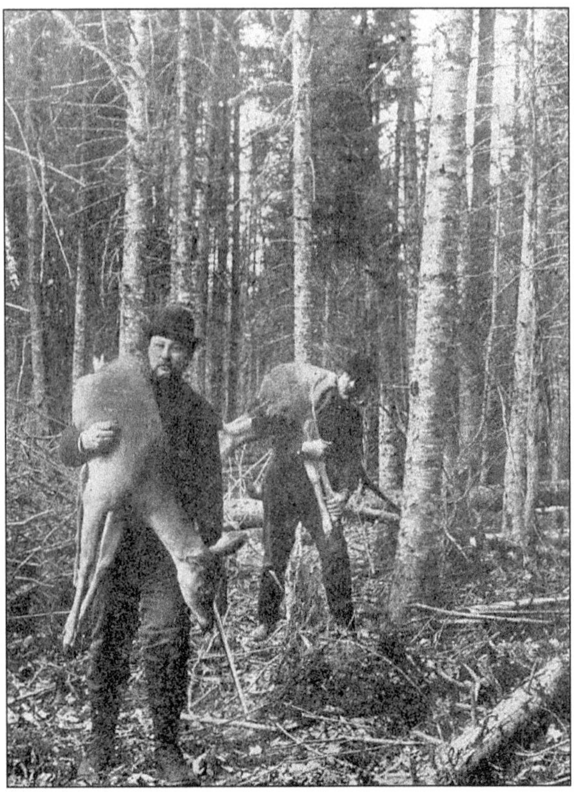

Two hunters carry their recently bagged game back to camp. It is easy to see in this photograph why carrying an animal out of the woods is much easier than trying to drag it. The back of this card is stamped "Northeast Carry, 1909."

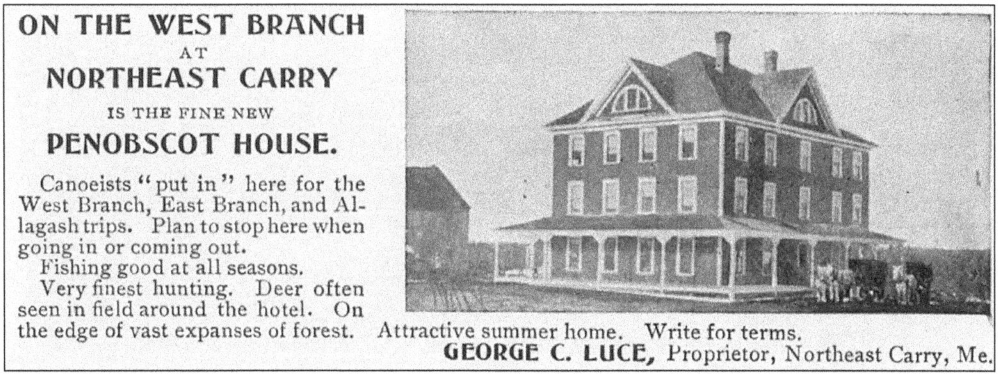

This facility was a key location for travelers and hunters. It was located on the West Branch of the Penobscot River, three miles from Northeast Carry on Moosehead Lake. The establishment burned in 1903. (From *In the Maine Woods*, 1900.)

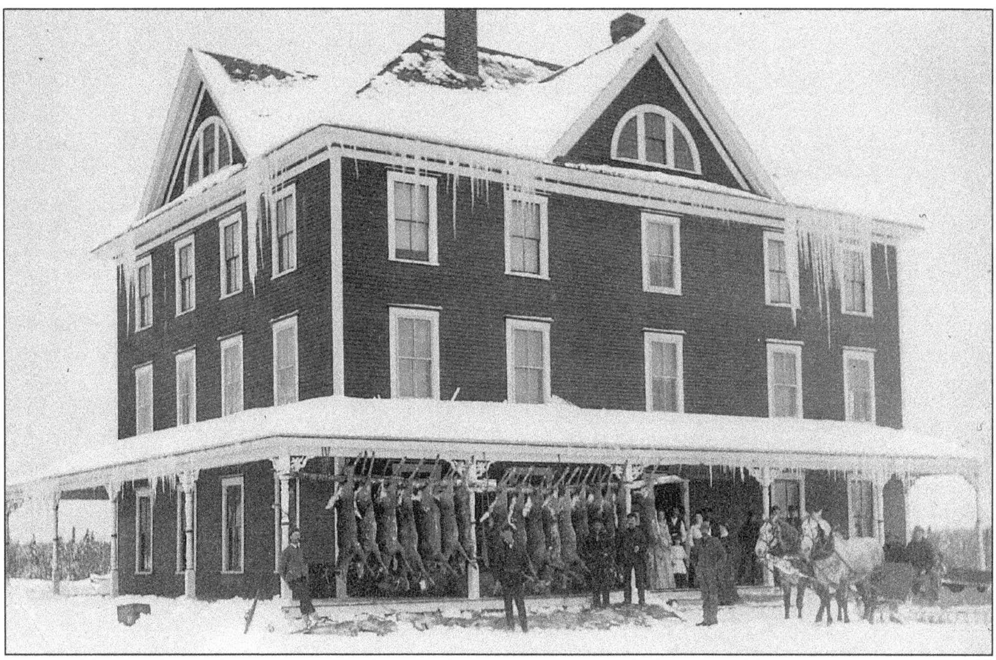

This close-up of the hotel shows 17 deer hanging, plus at least 12 more lying on the snow in front. The photograph was taken well into the snow season judging from the icicles on the building.

Kineo

Stands for all that a vacationist can want—big game in abundance; the best trout and togue fishing in America; ideal canoeing waters; magnificent scenery; and health and rejuvenation in fullest measure.

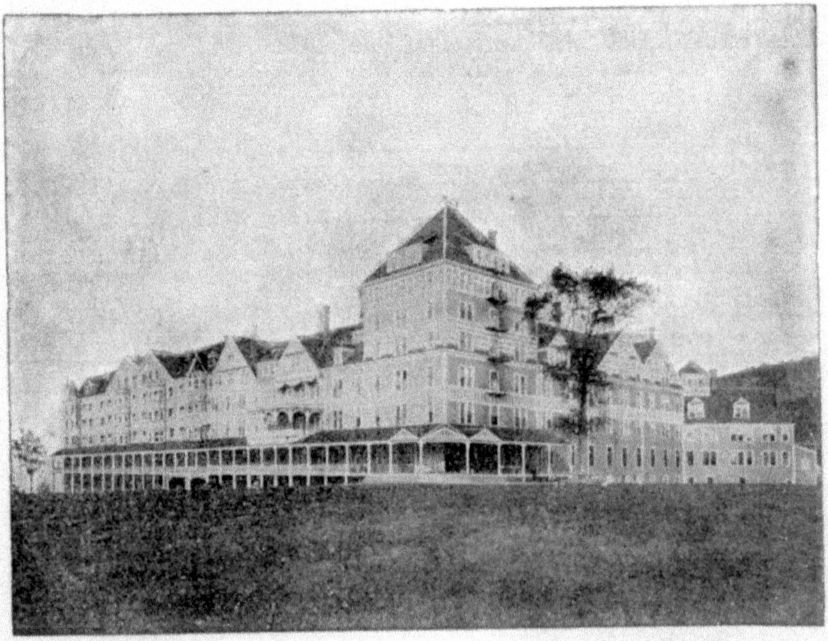

HERE, TOO, IS MT. KINEO HOUSE,

largest inland-water hotel in the country; modern throughout and fitted with steam heat, electric and gas light, baths, telephone, telegraph, post-office, etc.

Every room an outside one.	NO HAY FEVER HERE!	Guides canoes, etc., at hand.	Kineo store has all camp supplies.

Big Kineo booklet sent free on request.

C. A. JUDKINS, Manager. **Mt. Kineo House,** Moosehead Lake, Maine.

11 hours from Boston; 19 from New York.

The Mount Kineo, located across Moosehead Lake from Kineo Station at Rockwood on the Somerset Branch Railroad, was an upscale resort catering to wealthy families, golfers, and yachtsmen. In addition, many anglers and hunters came here and traveled out with their guides to remote locations where they camped. (From *In the Maine Woods*, 1904.)

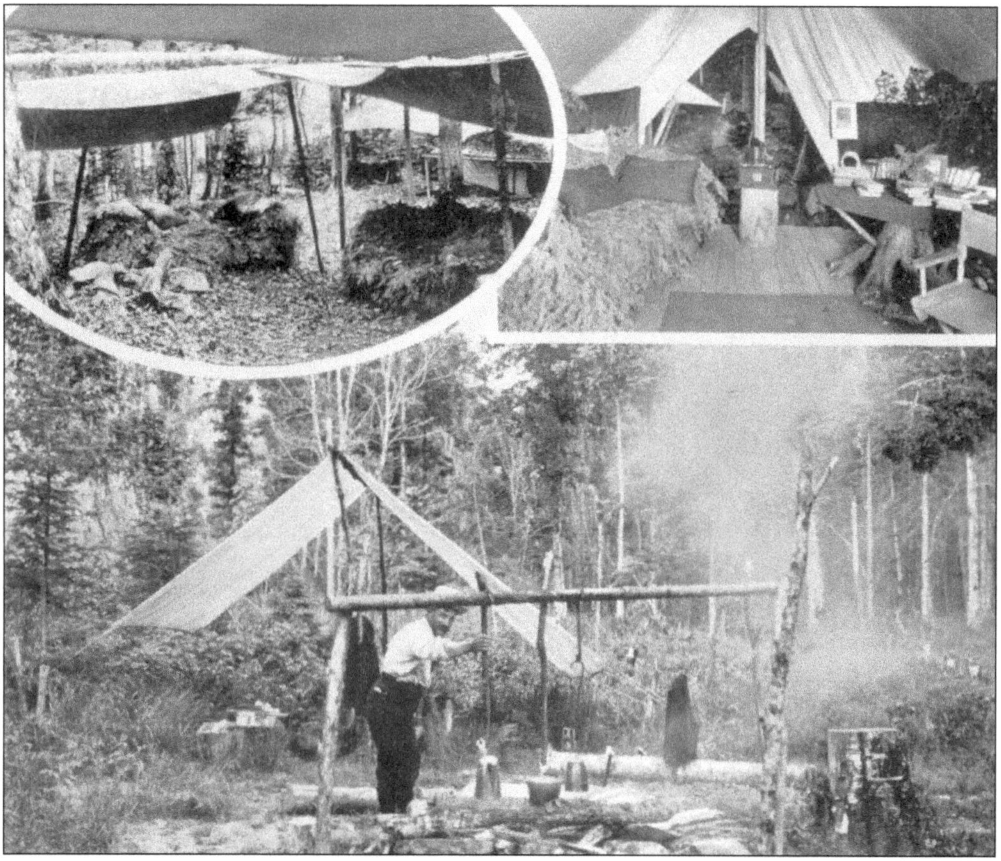

A collage of photographs from Mount Kineo depicts tent life at an outlying location. Note the comforts, especially the beds of hemlock and fir boughs. (From *The New Mount Kineo House*, 1912.)

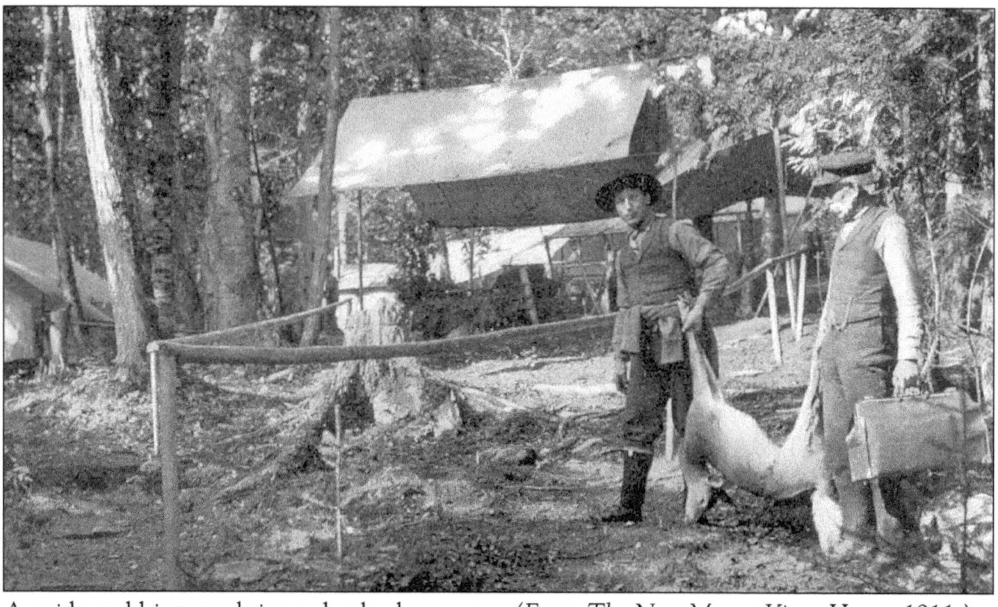

A guide and his sport bring a doe back to camp. (From *The New Mount Kineo House*, 1911.)

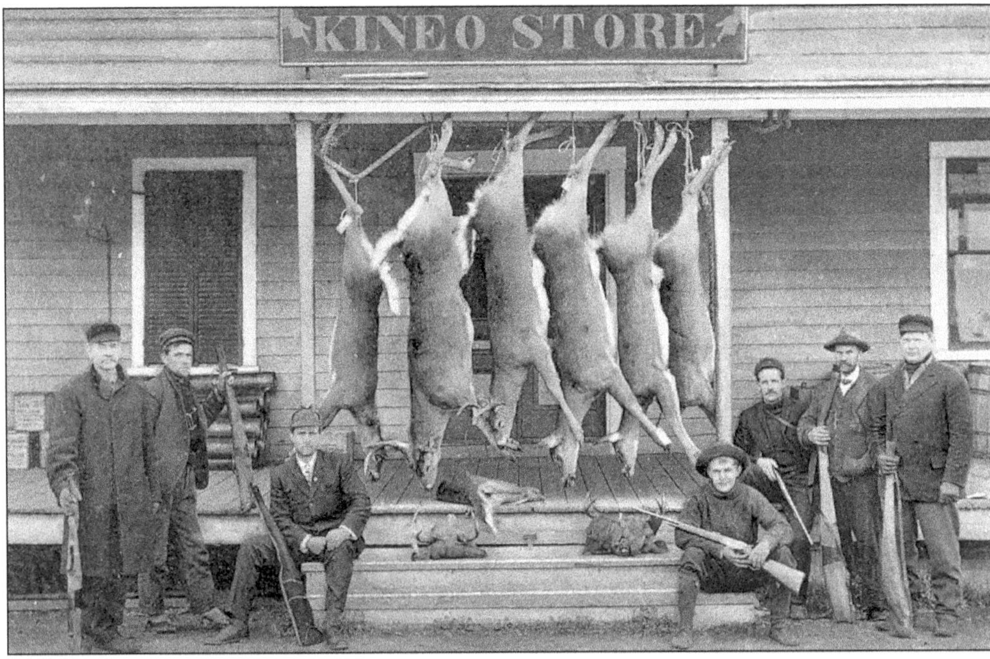

This game, taken near Mount Kineo, is ready to be shipped out by rail to points south. (Steve Rainsford collection.)

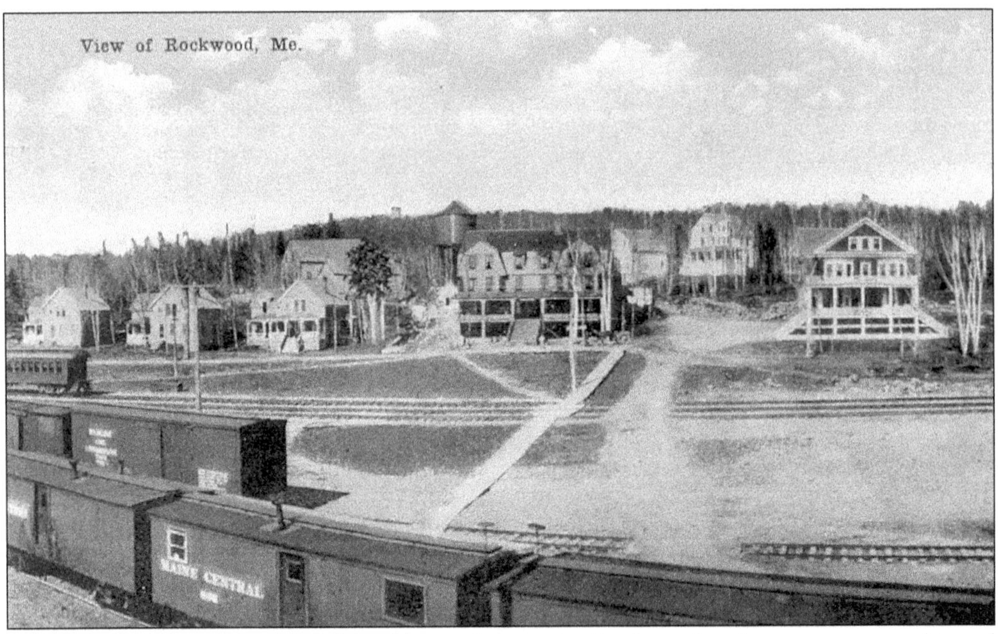

This image shows the railhead at Kineo Station in Rockwood, where game was shipped southward on the Somerset Railroad to the Maine Central Railroad main line. The large building on the left is the Rockwood Hotel and the one on the right is the Rockwood Store, owned by the railroad.

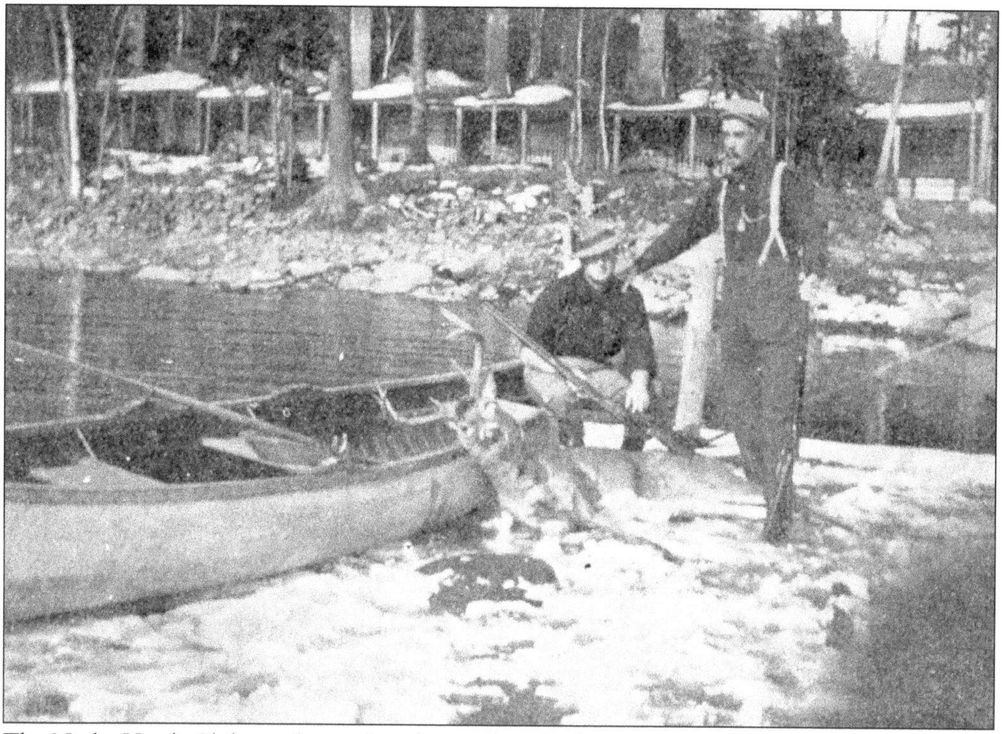

The Night Hawk Club was located at the south end of Moosehead Lake. Here a guide and his sport pose with a real beauty of a buck.

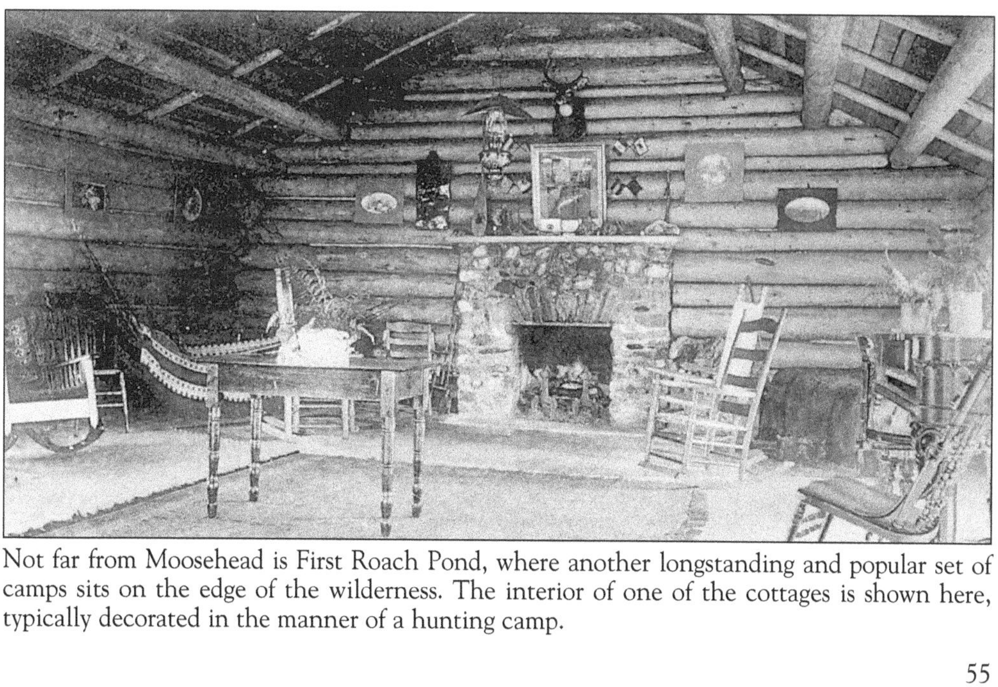

Not far from Moosehead is First Roach Pond, where another longstanding and popular set of camps sits on the edge of the wilderness. The interior of one of the cottages is shown here, typically decorated in the manner of a hunting camp.

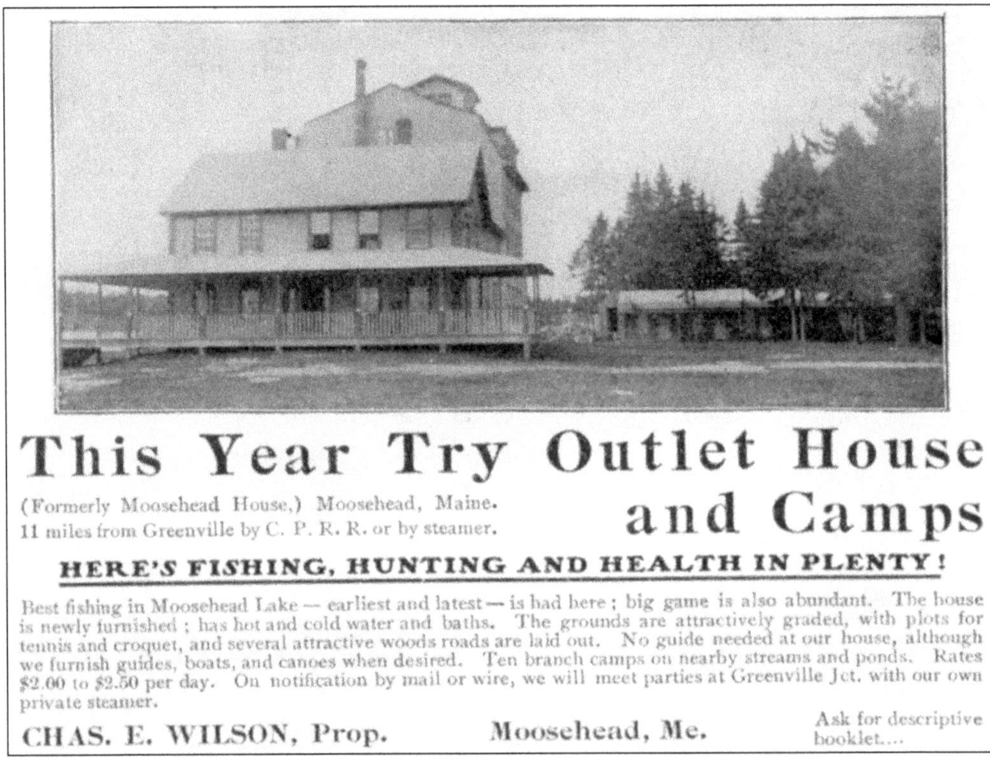

Henry I. Wilson established the Outlet House, now known as Wilsons, in 1865. It is located at the East Outlet of the Kennebec River and, for many years, was reached only by boat or by rail. The hotel is shown here with several camps to the right. (From *In the Maine Woods*, 1904.)

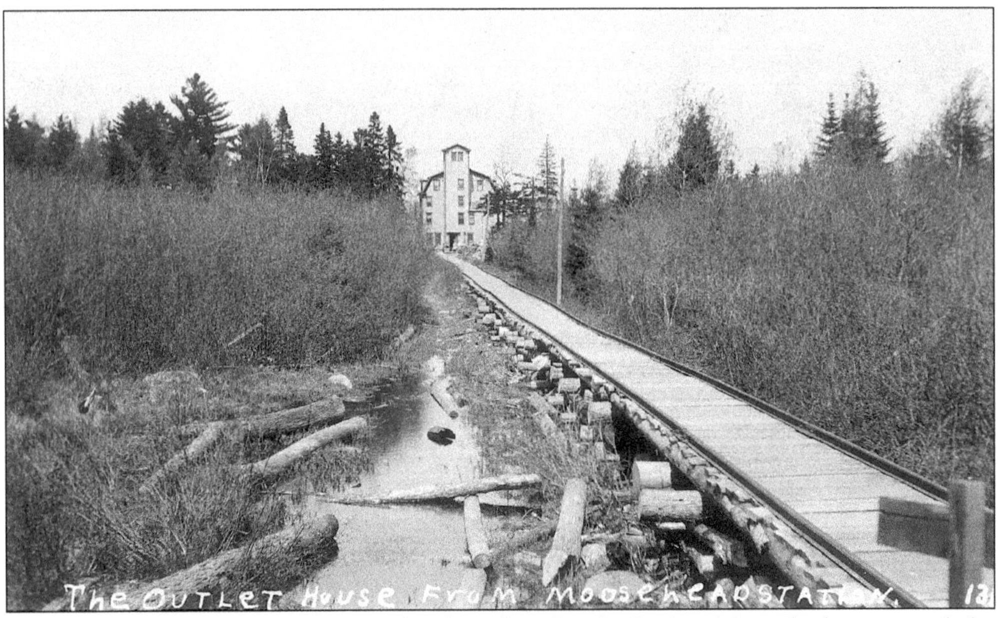

Here is a view from the station on the Canadian Pacific Railroad line, looking toward the Outlet House. A set of rails supported a handcar that moved baggage and large game animals between the hotel and the station.

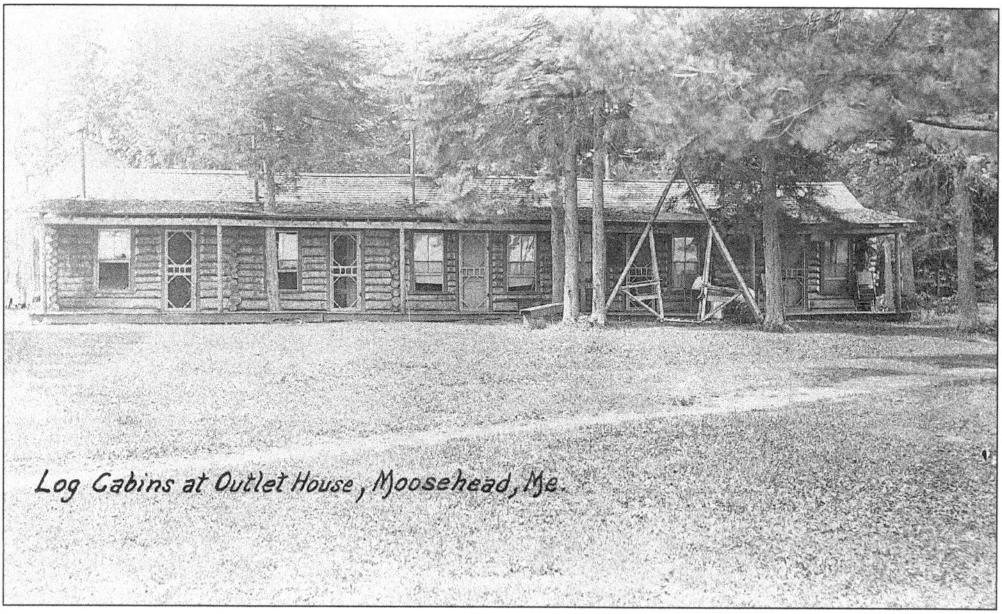

Here is a close-up of the original cabins at what is now Wilsons Camps.

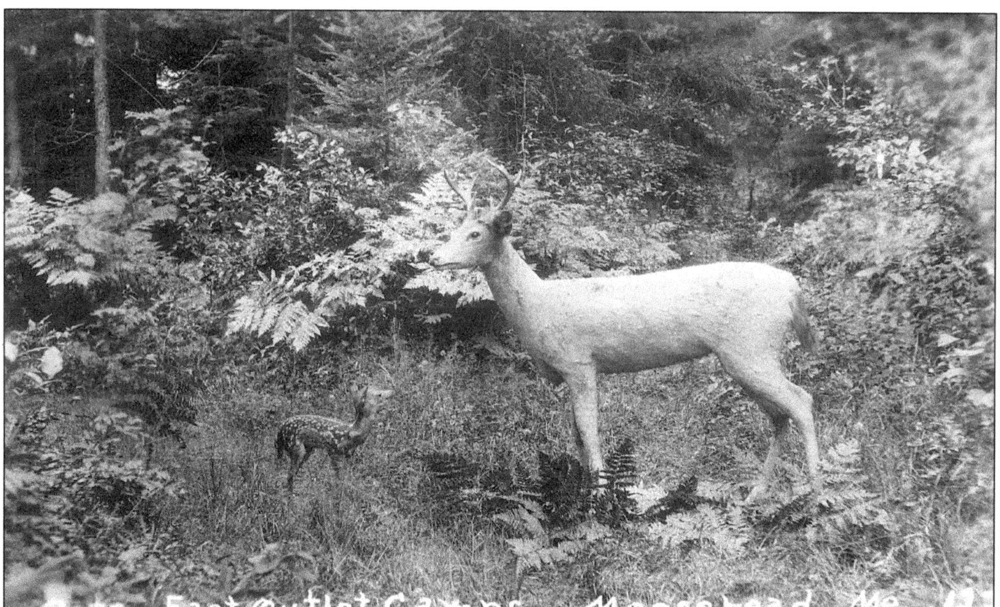

Shown in this photograph are deer mounts. One is of a fawn that died of natural causes at a young age and the other is of a small albino buck. For many years, these mounts were on display at the hotel, and the fawn appeared in several sportsmen's shows around the Northeast.

HUNTING AND FISHING.

The Deer Island House, Situated on Deer Island, in Moosehead Lake, is ten miles from Greenville, terminus of the Moosehead Lake Division, B. & A. R. R.

There are many deer on the Island, and as fine ones are killed here as in any part of the State. As a fishing resort, it is well known. No better fishing in any part of the Lake than here. The steamer "Tethys" is a new boat for the accommodation of guests of the house, and can be engaged to meet parties at Greenville, if desired. For information concerning rooms, etc., address

ED. A. CAPEN, (P. O.) Capen's, Moosehead Lake, Me.

Located on Deer Island in Moosehead Lake, Capens was accessible only by boat. It was a prime location for both hunting and fishing for many years until the hotel burned on November 17, 1953. Capen's brochure advertised, "Deer are plentiful on the island and many fine specimens are taken out during the open season. It is a fact that fully one third of all the deer shipped from Maine comes from the region round and about Moosehead Lake. Hunters in this territory are surest of securing the big game trophies they covet most. Partridge and other small game birds are plentiful." (From *In the Maine Woods*, 1900.)

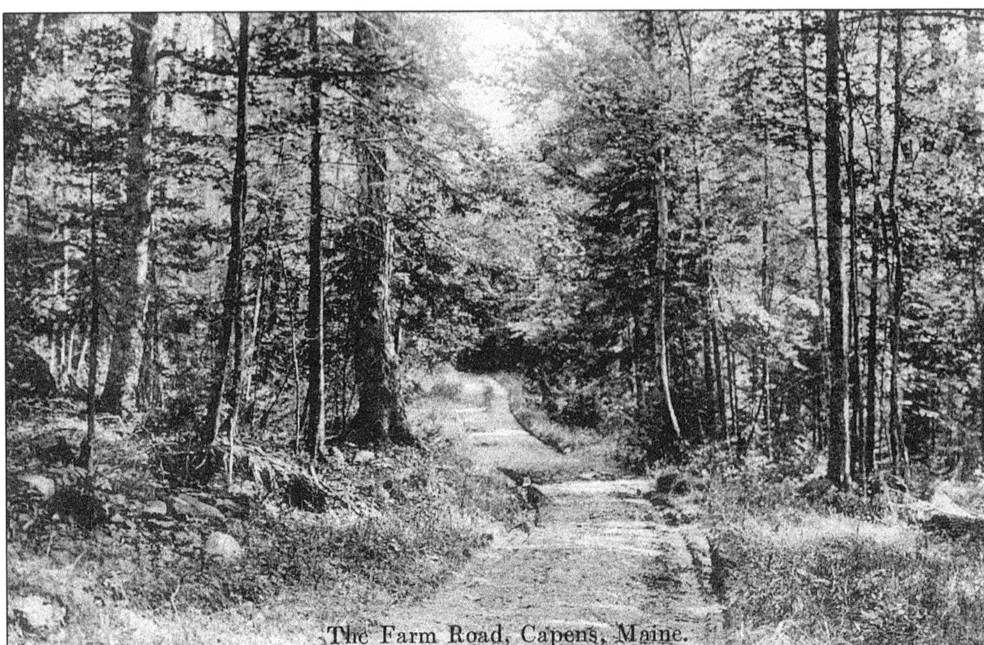

This is the woods road leading from the establishment to their farm near the middle of the island, where there were fields and game in abundance.

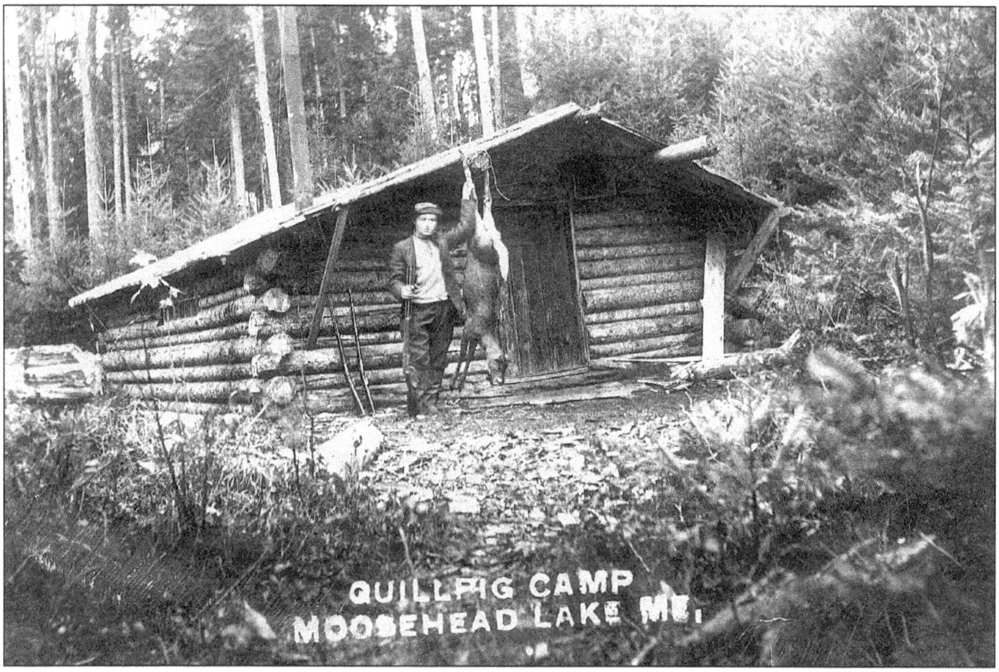

This photograph shows one of several remote camps located in the Moosehead Lake area. This hunter has hung a small doe. The simplicity of a camp of this type provides adequate shelter without a lot to take care of.

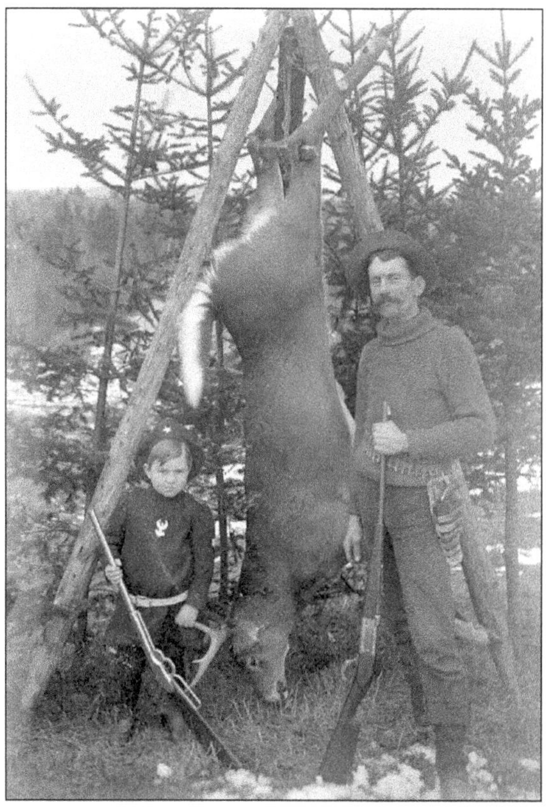

This hunter shows off his trophy. The back of card is marked "Moosehead." (Steve Rainsford collection.)

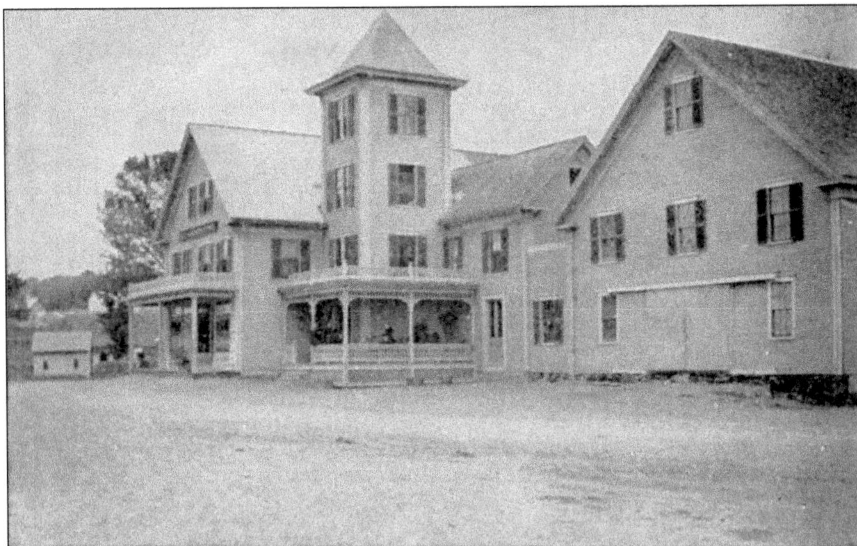

The above is a cut of

D. T. SANDERS & SON'S

Store and Warehouse,

Located at

GREENVILLE VILLAGE, Moosehead Lake, Me.,

Where the business was established 45 years ago.

With the Largest and Best Stocked General Store in the State, and a continuous business connection with Lumbermen and Sportsmen for the above length of time, **we claim to supply everything needed by Sportsmen.**

We Allow No Commission to Guides,— one price to all, and that the lowest consistent with best quality.

Send for complete list of Camp Supplies, with Map of Moosehead Lake and Vicinity on reverse side, free for the asking. We gladly recommend only such guides as we know to be reliable.

Advance orders by mail will be carefully packed, ready for shipment on your arrival.

Our Specialty, Fresh Eggs and Good Butter,— two very necessary articles for Camp.

Direct telephone connection with the Hotel and both Depots at Greenville Junction.

D. T. SANDERS & SON,

Greenville, Maine.

Sanders Store, founded in 1878 by David T. Sanders, sold everything necessary for the angler, hunter, camper, and trapper. For many years, the store outfitted guides, sportsmen, and parties for trips extending from a day to several weeks, whether local or covering many miles. (From *In the Maine Woods*, 1903.)

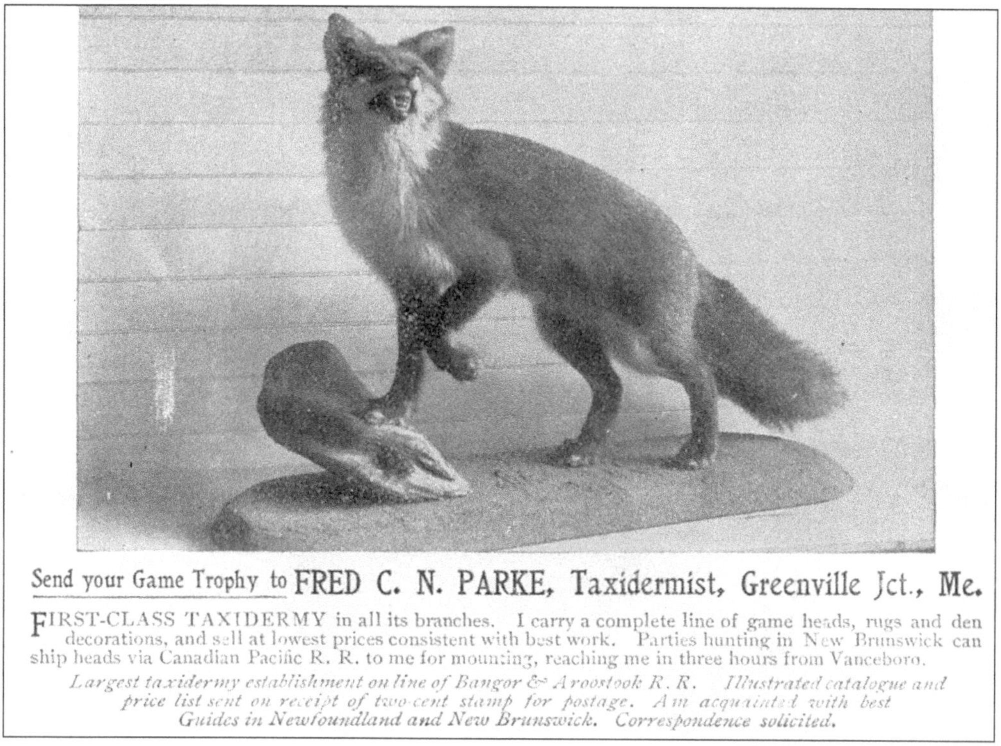

Fred Parke, a very well-known and popular taxidermist, later of Bangor, had a shop in Greenville in 1907. From this mount, one can easily see why his work was very much in demand. (From *In the Maine Woods*, 1907.)

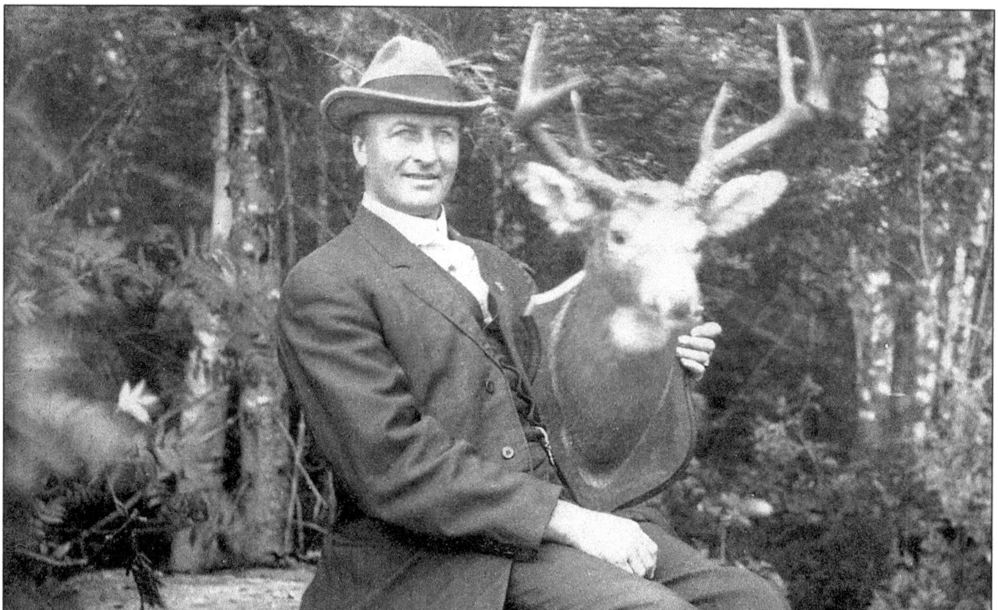

This gentleman had a postal card made from the photograph of his trophy, which was a great buck with a symmetrical rack. The card is postmarked "Greenville, 1913," so this may have been one of Fred Parke's mounts.

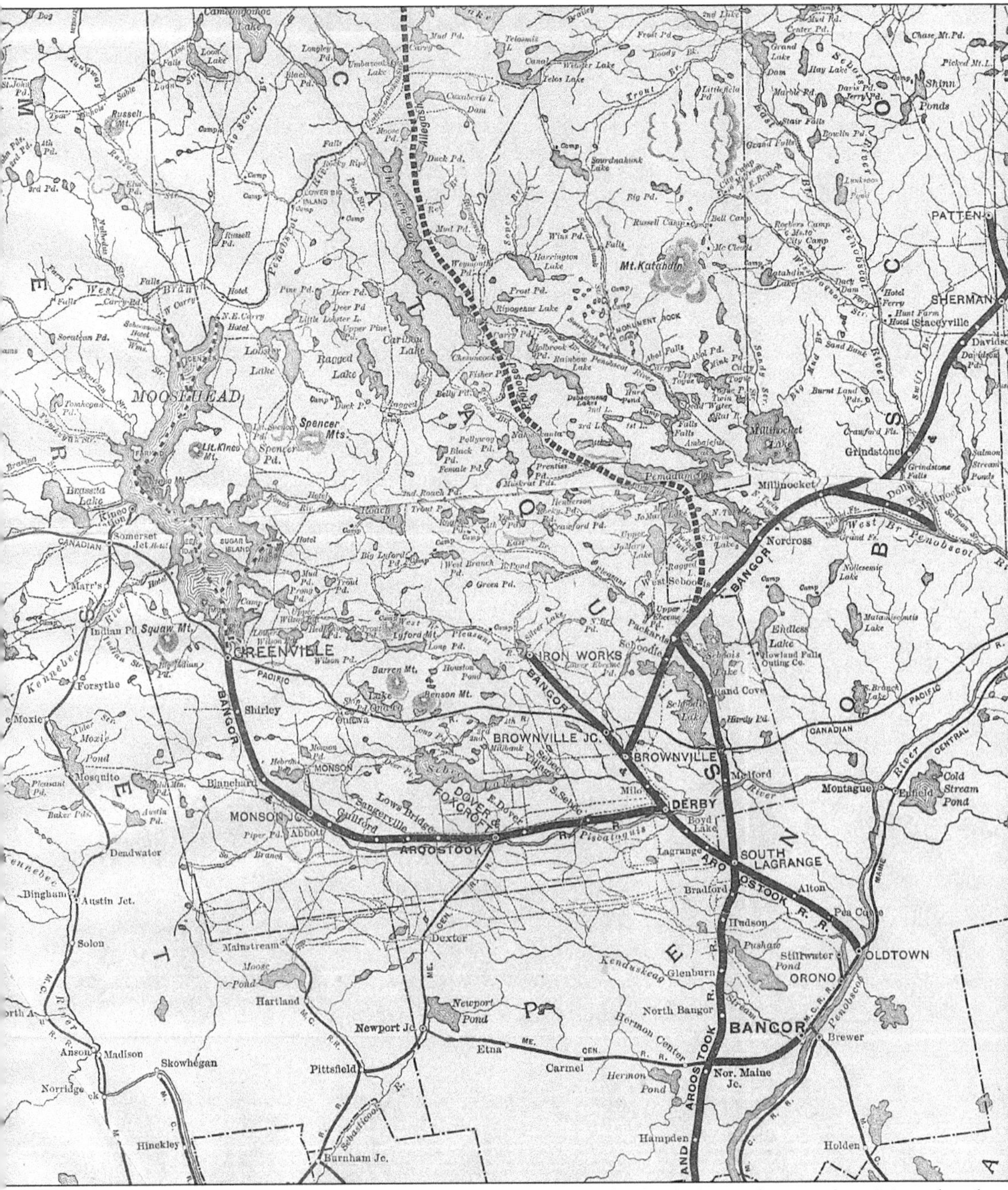

This is a 1915 map of the Bangor & Aroostook Railroad, which shows the area from Moosehead Lake eastward to the Penobscot River drainage.

FOR RESULTS,

FISH AT

Hebron, Onawa, Monson, Greenwood or other nearby ponds, or HUNT in the adjacent forests. A great vacation region, easily reached

Via the Monson R. R.

Many families "summer here." Best of accommodations. Ask for particulars and prices.

CHARLES J. WIER, TREAS. AND GEN'L MGR. — H. E. MORRILL, SUPERINTENDENT.

This narrow-gauge railroad took parties from the Bangor & Aroostook main line to Monson, where they could hunt the remote areas southeast of Greenville and east toward Milo and Brownville. (From *In the Maine Woods*, 1908.)

Most artistic, best furnished, most up-to-date camps in New England.

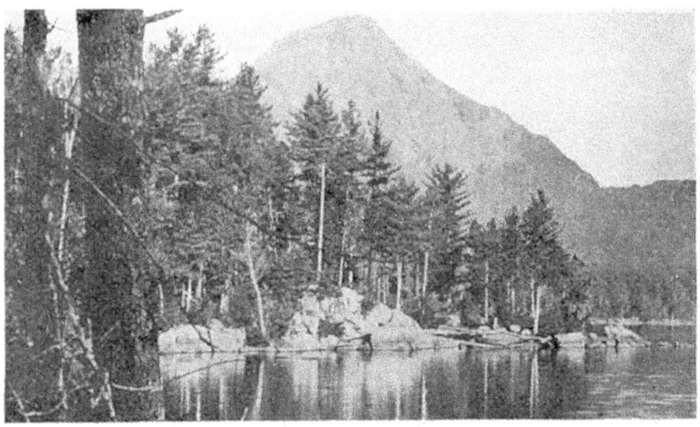

Best hunting, fishing, scenery and "living" in the state.

At Camp Onawa

YOUNG & BUXTON,
Onawa, Maine.

You find first-class moose, deer, bear and small game hunting; hordes of big square-tail salmon, and lake trout, entrancing scenery, accommodations for 40 people; separate camps for each party; beef, lamb, chickens, milk, butter, eggs, etc., from the camp farm; and every possible need and comfort provided for. Free use of boats and canoes. Railroad, express and post office within ten minutes' walk. Thirty trout salmon and togue ponds within a radius of six miles of camp. Rates, \$2.00 a day, \$10.00 a week. Guides, \$3.00 a day; boarded at half price.

Here is one of the more popular locations in the Monson area, which advertised the "best hunting in the state," as many of them did. There were several establishments on Lake Onawa or in the immediate vicinity. This is an advertisement from one of them showing a beautiful view of the lake. Four miles long and two miles wide, Onawa is encircled by bluffs. (From *In the Maine Woods*, 1906.)

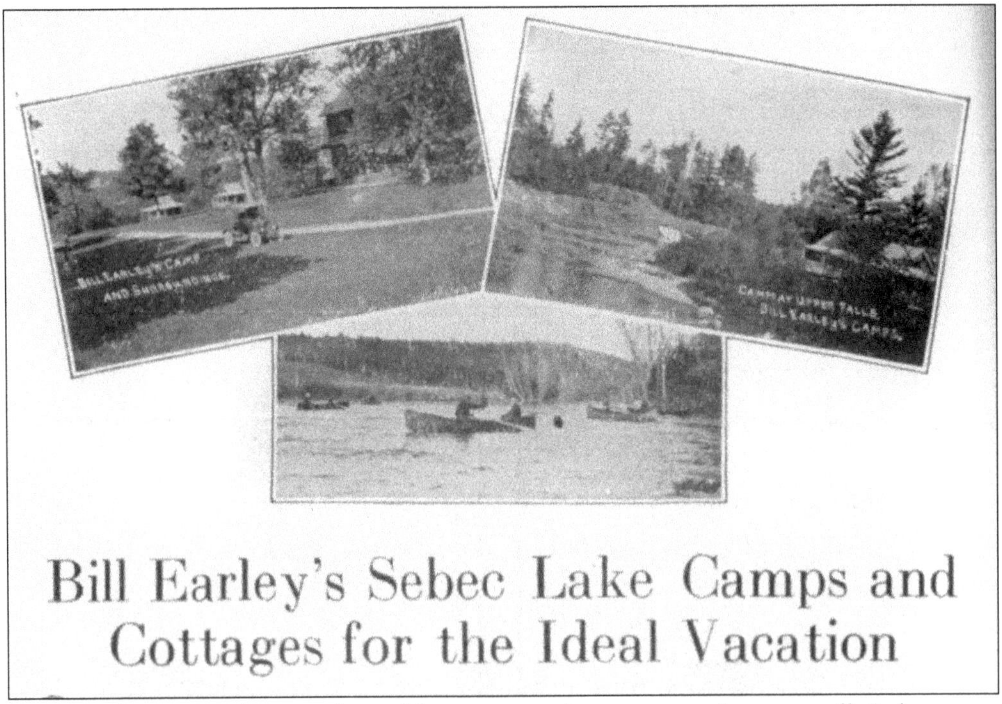

While Earley's catered primarily to fishing parties, hunters came here as well. It became a very famous establishment over the years, known primarily for big salmon. (From *In the Maine Woods*, 1931.)

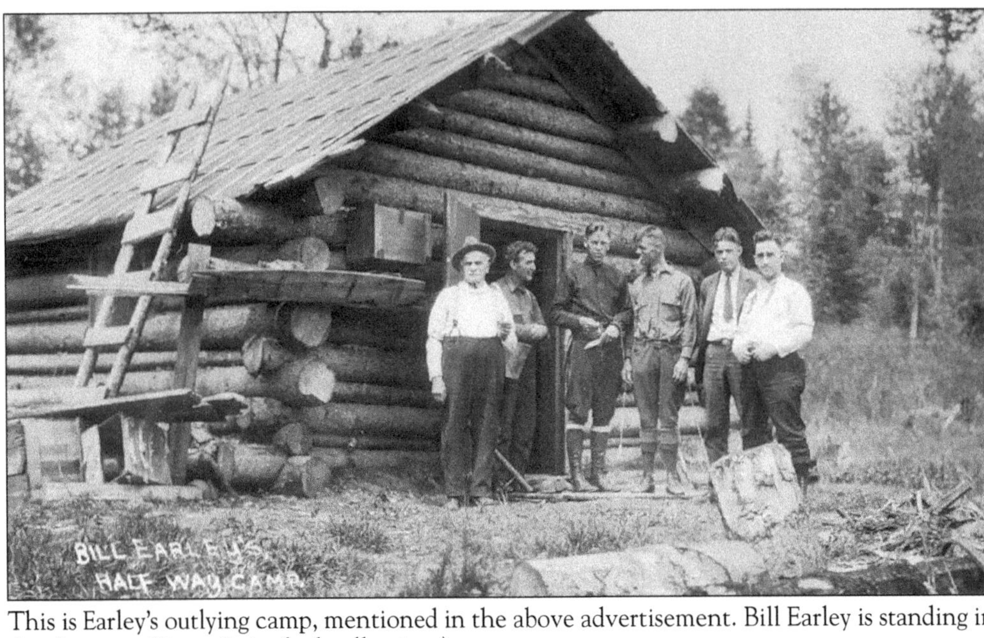

This is Earley's outlying camp, mentioned in the above advertisement. Bill Earley is standing in the doorway. (Steve Rainsford collection.)

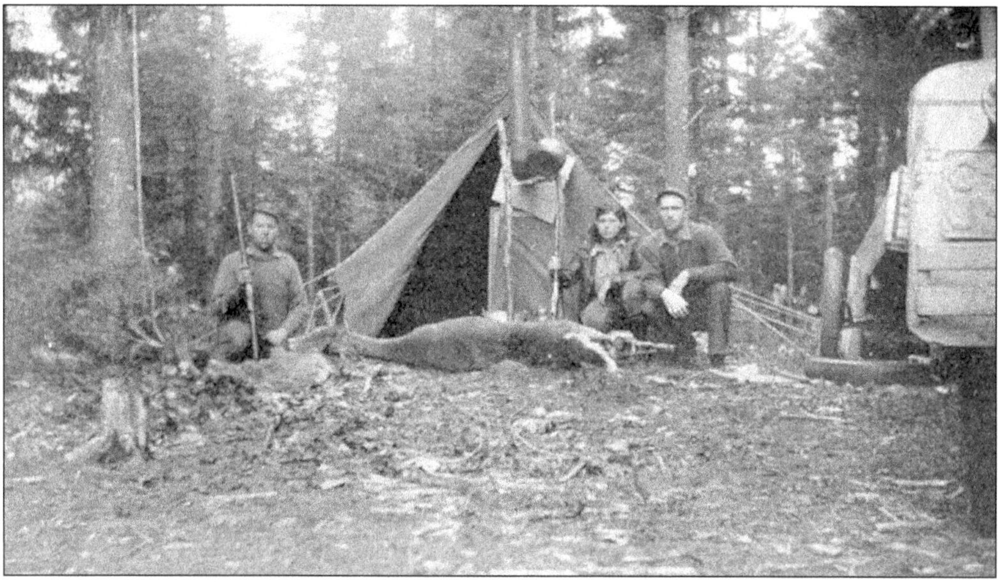

East of Monson and on the spur line of the Bangor & Aroostook Railroad is the Brownville-Katahdin Iron Works Region. These hunters have had success at Ebeeme Pond.

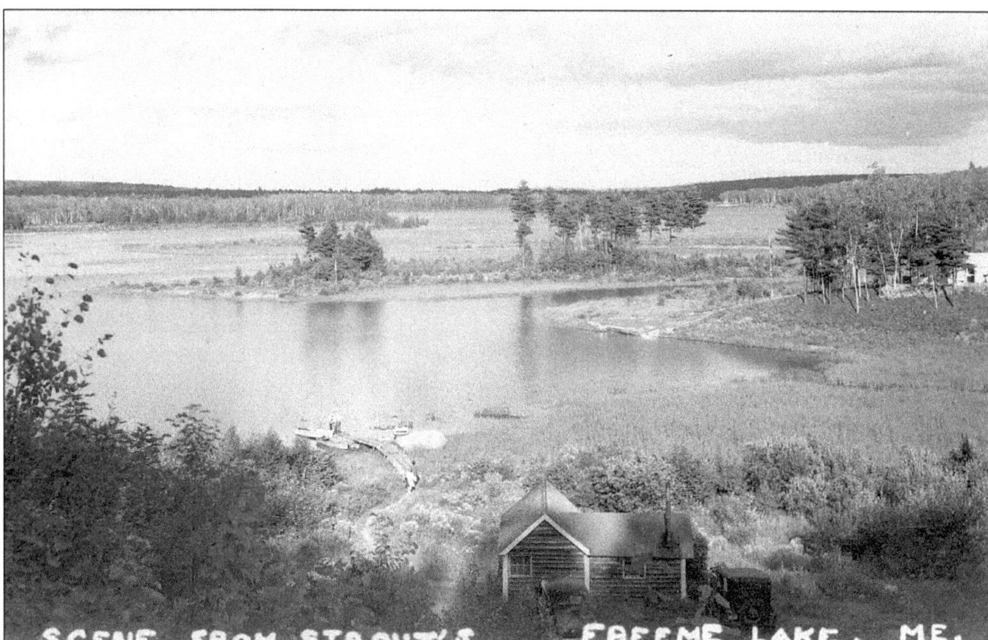

Here is a nice view of Ebeeme Pond and its surrounding wilderness. It is easy to see why this would be a productive game region.

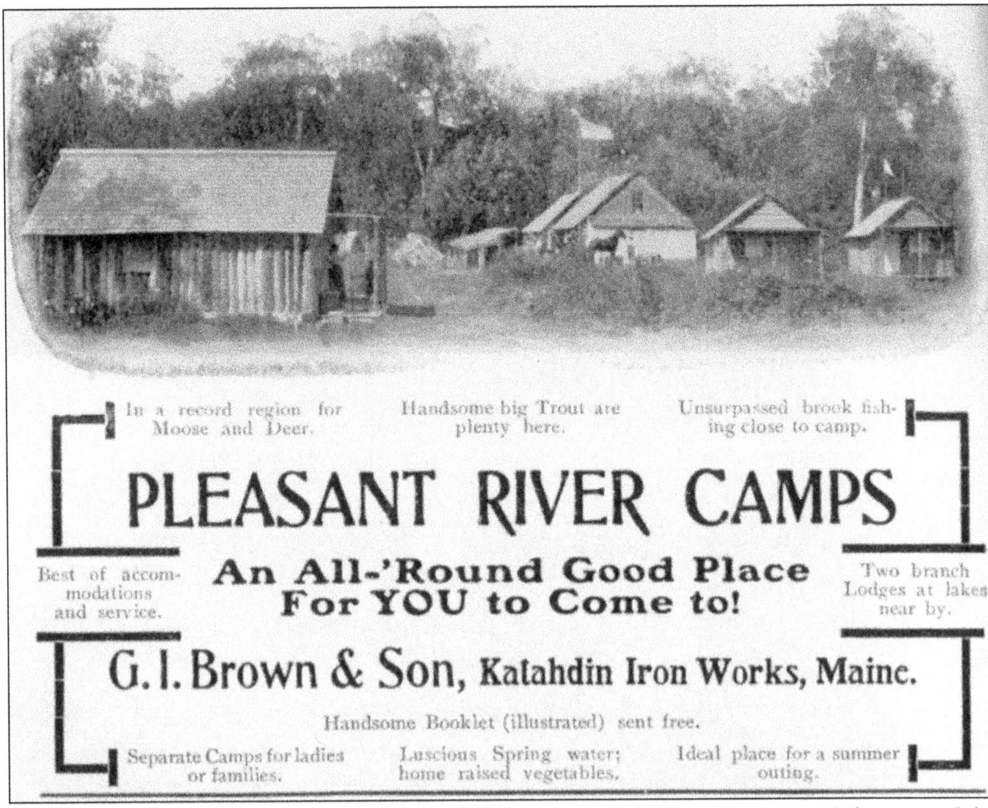

Brown's at Katahdin Iron Works was a popular hunting and fishing camp around the turn of the century. The area was a record region for moose and deer. (From *In the Maine Woods*, 1904.)

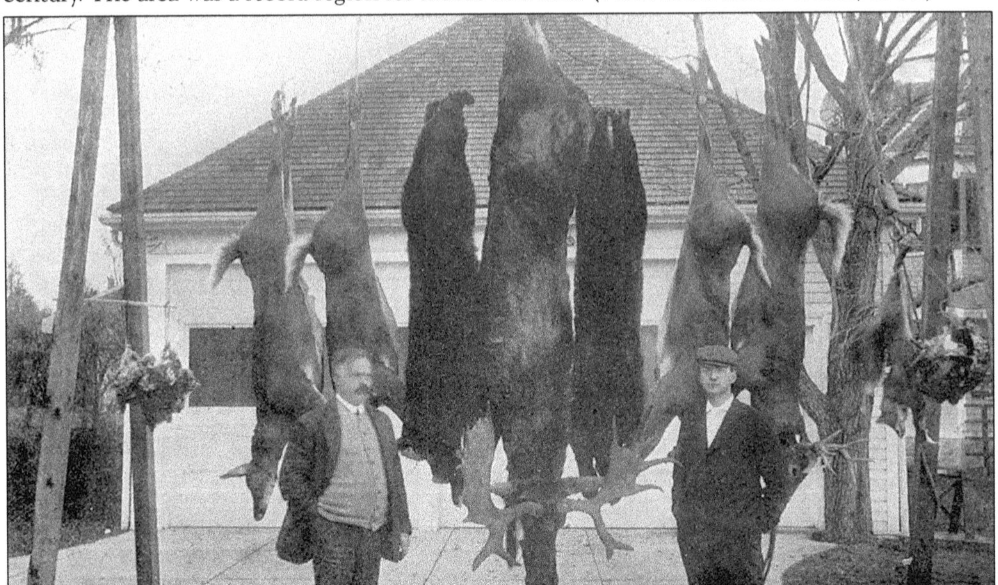

Birds are shown here on the left, small game on the right, and big game in the center. These hunters seem to have come away from the woods with a sample of each. (From *In the Maine Woods*, 1906.)

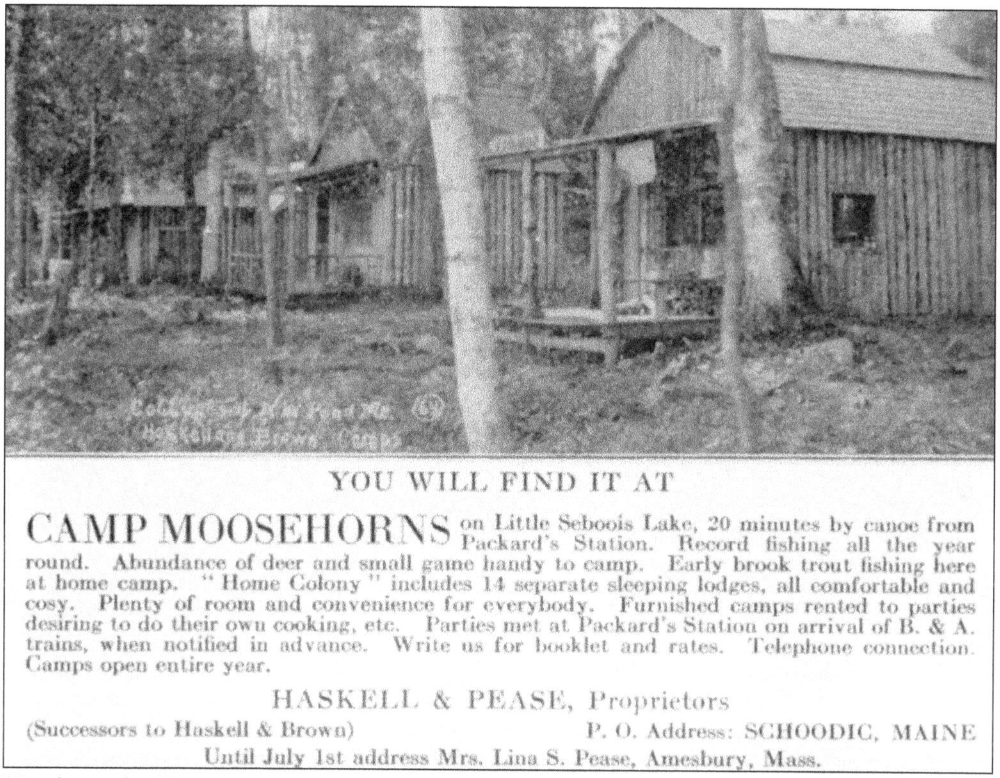

YOU WILL FIND IT AT

CAMP MOOSEHORNS on Little Seboois Lake, 20 minutes by canoe from Packard's Station. Record fishing all the year round. Abundance of deer and small game handy to camp. Early brook trout fishing here at home camp. "Home Colony" includes 14 separate sleeping lodges, all comfortable and cosy. Plenty of room and convenience for everybody. Furnished camps rented to parties desiring to do their own cooking, etc. Parties met at Packard's Station on arrival of B. & A. trains, when notified in advance. Write us for booklet and rates. Telephone connection. Camps open entire year.

HASKELL & PEASE, Proprietors

(Successors to Haskell & Brown) P. O. Address: SCHOODIC, MAINE

Until July 1st address Mrs. Lina S. Pease, Amesbury, Mass.

Handy to the Bangor & Aroostook Railroad, this camp was popular as a base for journeys northward toward Mount Katahdin and remote areas where game was extremely abundant. (From *In the Maine Woods*, 1924.)

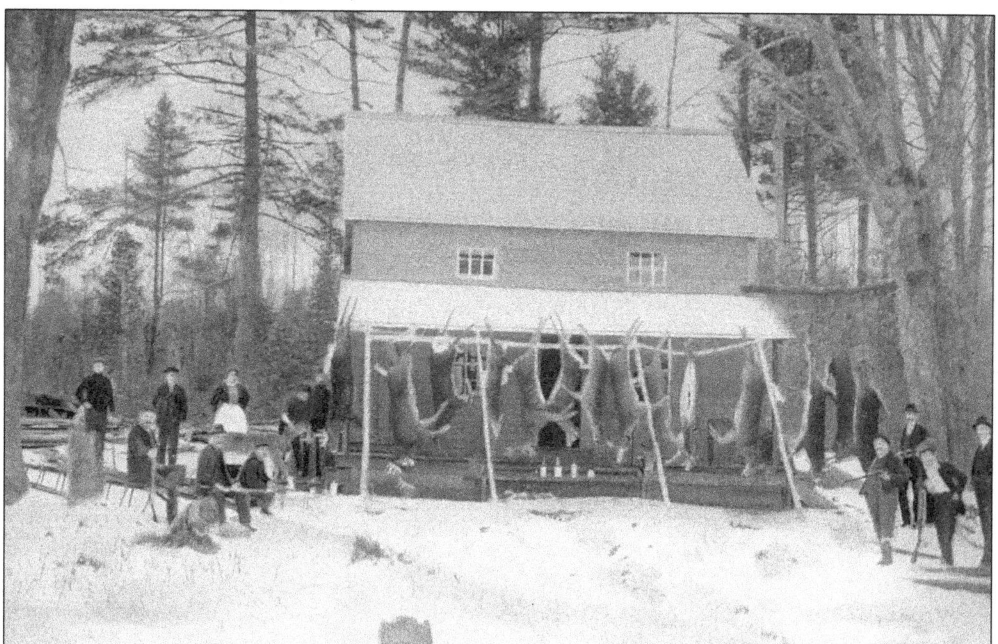

This postcard, used for promotion by the railroad, demonstrates what a great hunting area this was.

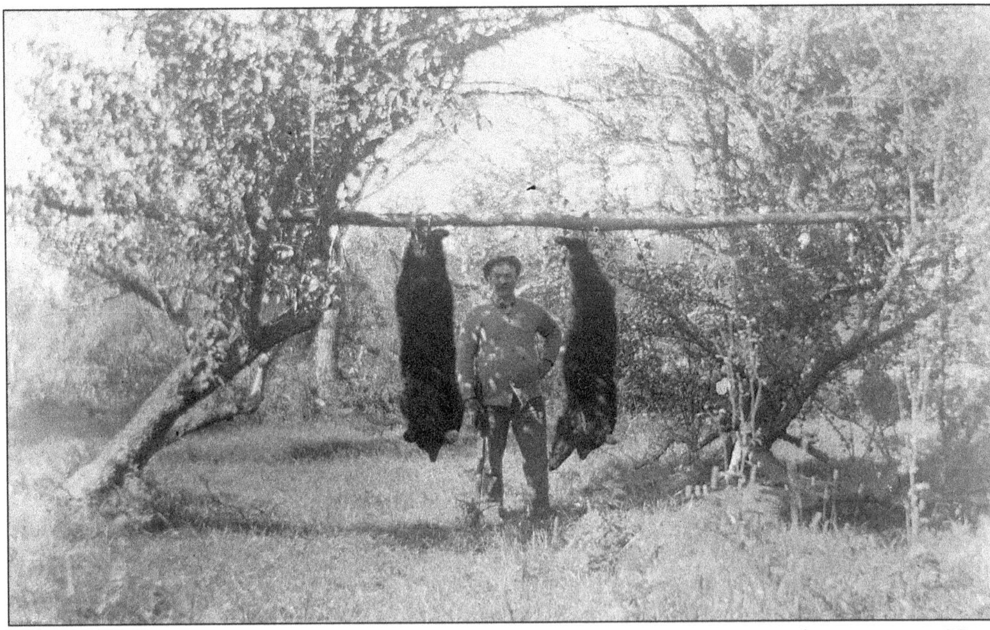

The area between Brownville and Bangor has always been known as great bear country. Here the hunter poses with two bear taken near LaGrange. It was written that "there is something about killing a big black bear which makes the hunter feel better even than if he had killed a big moose but the man who shoots a black bear is lucky, not because bears are scarce, for they are rather plentiful in Maine, but because the black bear is about the smartest animal that travels the woods."

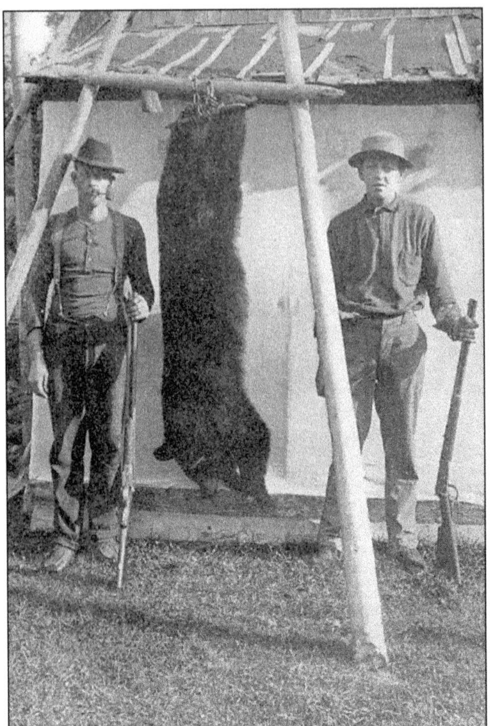

This trophy bear was taken near Milo, further testifying to the productivity of this part of the state as far as bear are concerned. One hunter poses with a double-barreled shotgun while the other has the popular lever-action rifle. Bear, weighing nearly 500 pounds in many cases, have a marvelous sense of sight, smell, and hearing. They usually get out of the way before the hunter sees them, and for all their apparent clumsiness, the black bear will get out of the way with far less noise than a deer that is a quarter the bear's weight. (From *In the Maine Woods*, 1912.)

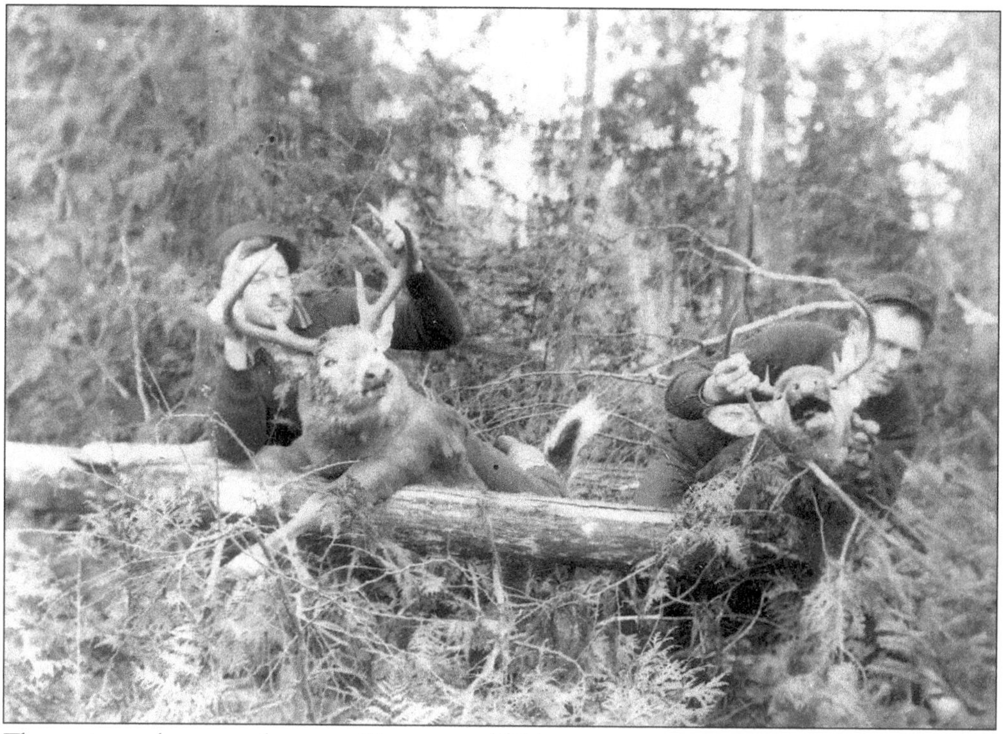

These nice racks were taken near Newport *c.* 1907.

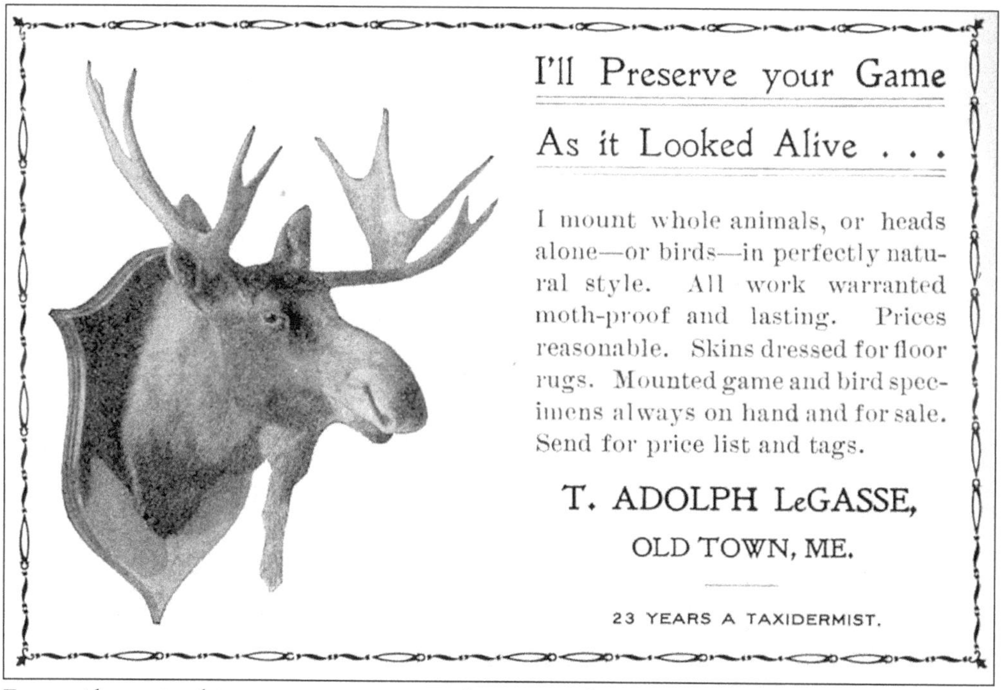

For taxidermy in this area, many went to those specialists in the Bangor–Old Town area, of which LeGasse was one that enjoyed a nice reputation. The moose mount shown here is a testimonial to his ability. (From *In the Maine Woods*, 1906.)

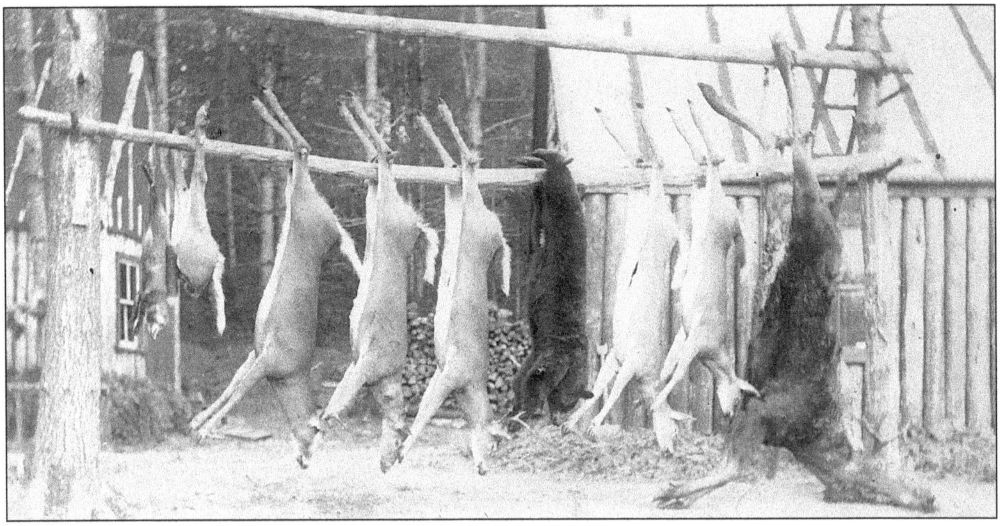

Jordan and Hussey was a well-known establishment in the Seboeis Region. Shown in this 1905 image is an impressive bounty of game animals. (Steve Rainsford collection.)

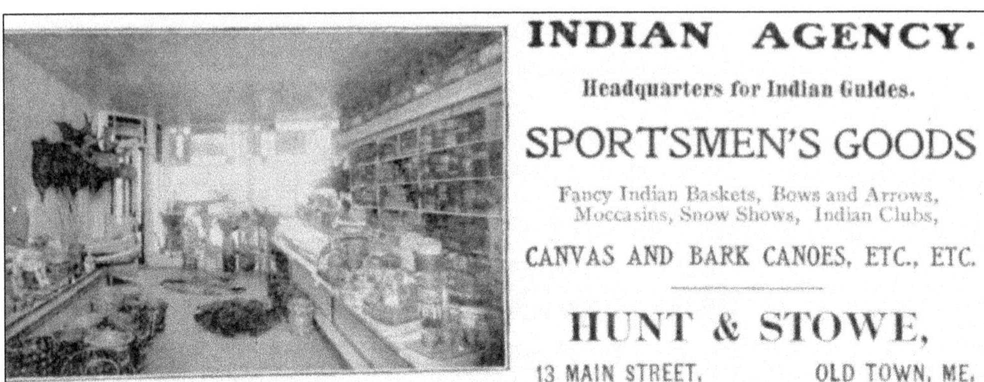

Native American guides were in abundance and in demand during the early part of the century. Hunt & Stowe, located near the Penobscot Indian Reservation, was one of a very few establishments specializing in supplies of this nature. (From *In the Maine Woods*, 1903.)

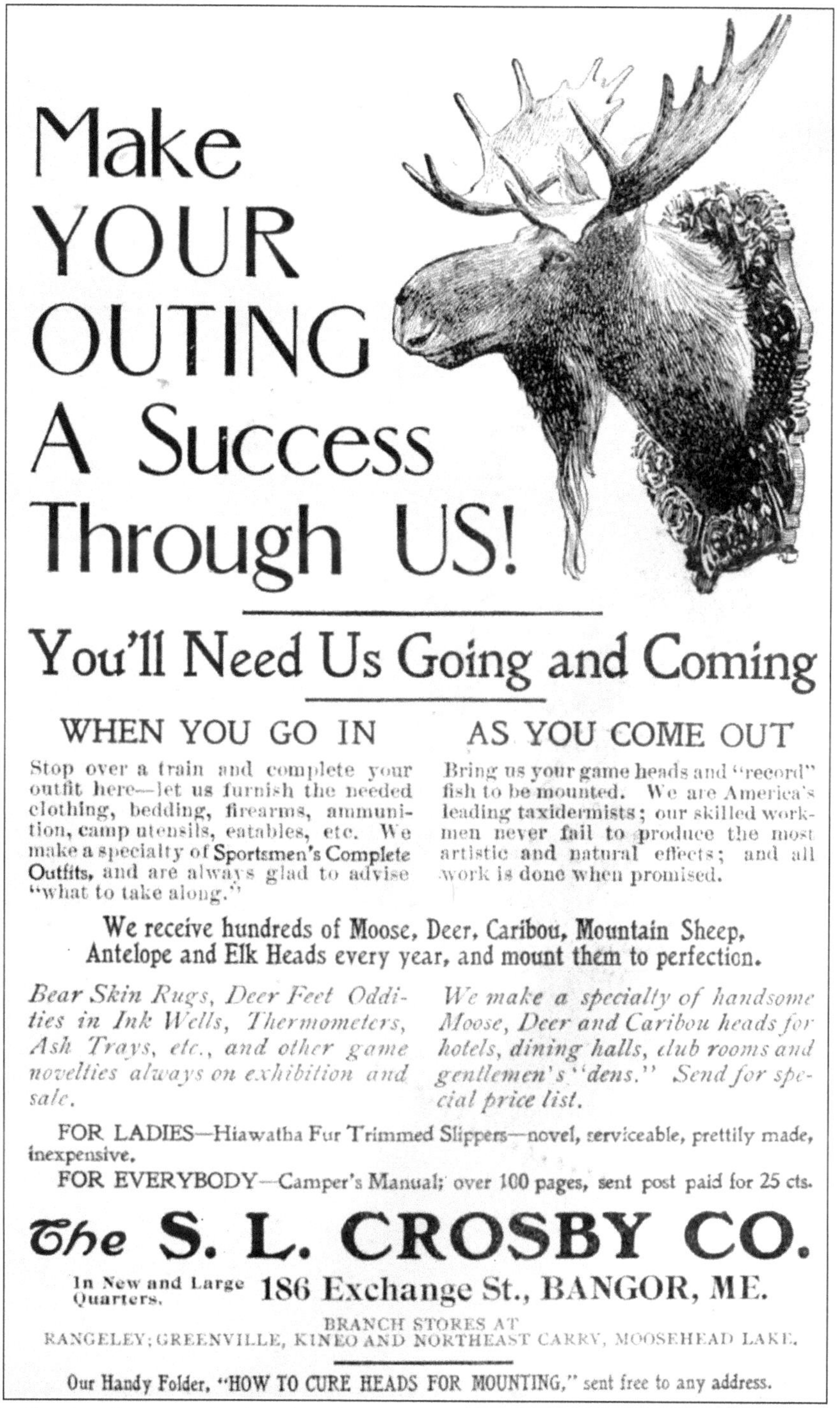

The S.L. Crosby Company had its headquarters at Bangor, but like many others, had branch offices at other locations. Advertised here, they had a location at Rangeley besides three at Moosehead Lake. Sumner Crosby was a personal friend but no relation of Cornelia "Fly Rod" Crosby, having donated taxidermy specimens to her exhibits at the Sportsmen's Show. He passed away in 1899. (From *In the Maine Woods*, 1904.)

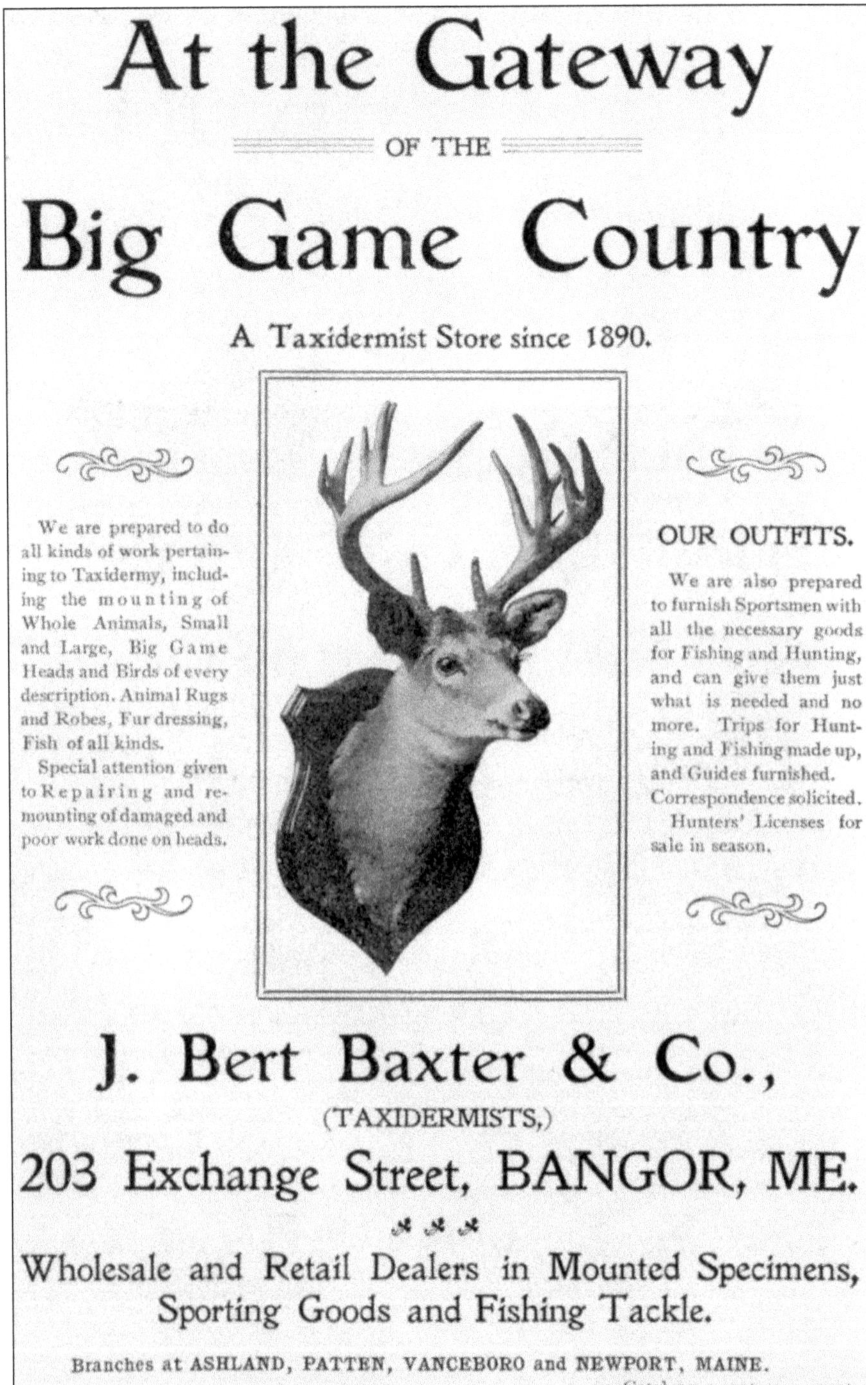

Baxter's Studio was located just a few doors from the S.L. Crosby Company on Exchange Street in Bangor. This location was ideal for sportsmen and was shared with the Thomas Fly Rod Company, along with several logging supply houses. This company had four additional branch offices as well. The abundance of taxidermy studios in the state attests to the popularity of trophies for display. (From *In the Maine Woods*, 1904.)

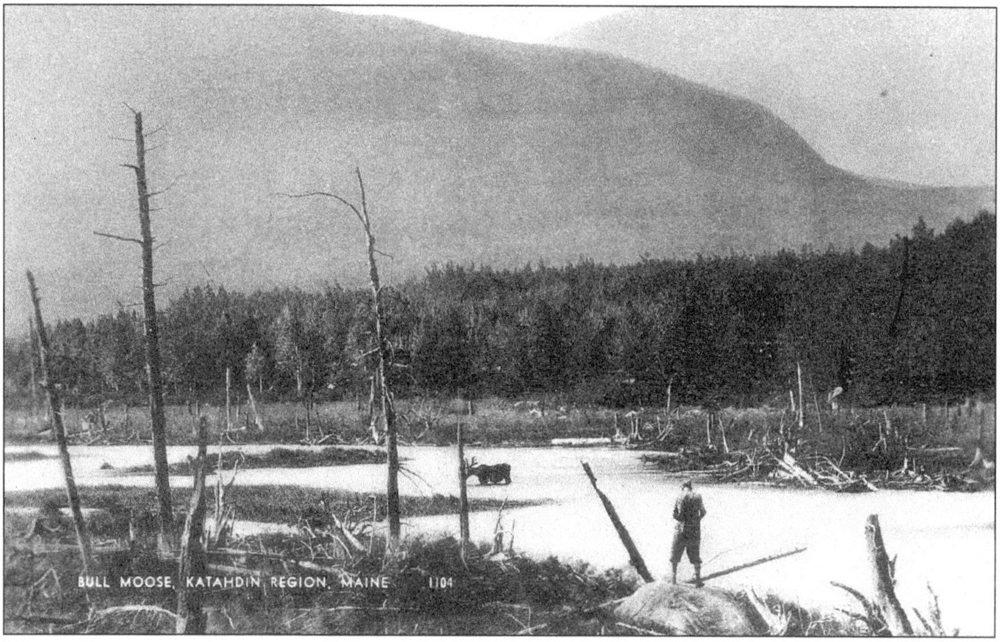

Shown here is another type of hunting: using a camera. Countless visitors have driven by this pond, not far from Ripogenus Dam and near Mount Katahdin, only to witness one or more moose feeding. Many people derive great joy from stalking wild game to get a good picture.

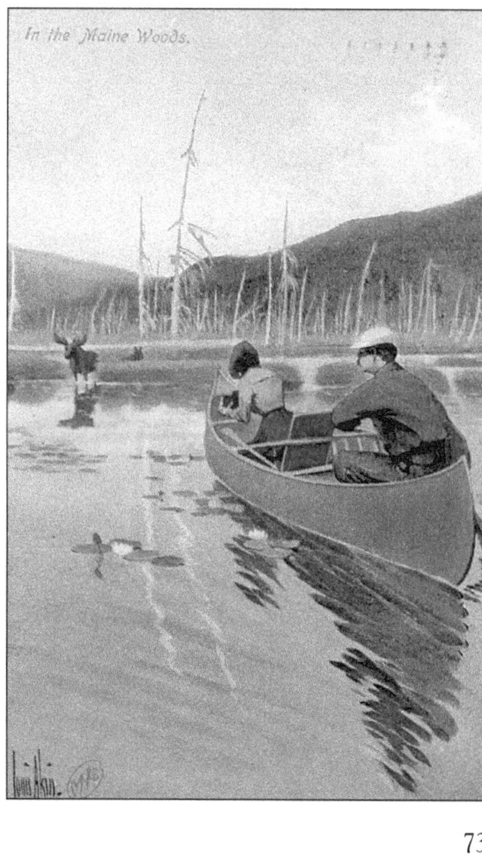

At certain times of year, it is possible to get very close to moose in order to take prizewinning photographs. Here, the canoeist attempts to get as close as possible for the photographer. These moose are shown in a typical setting for the summer months.

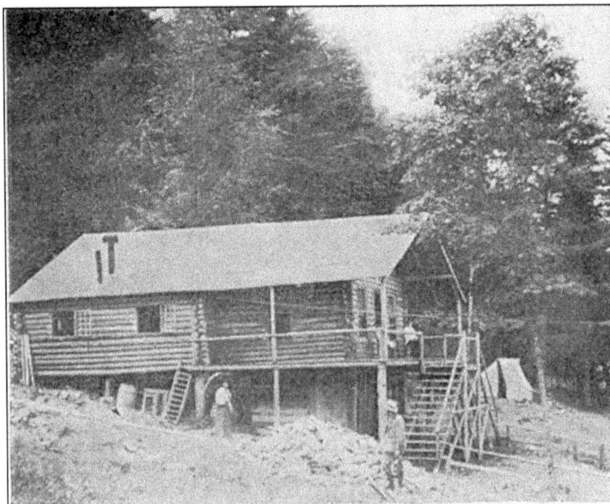

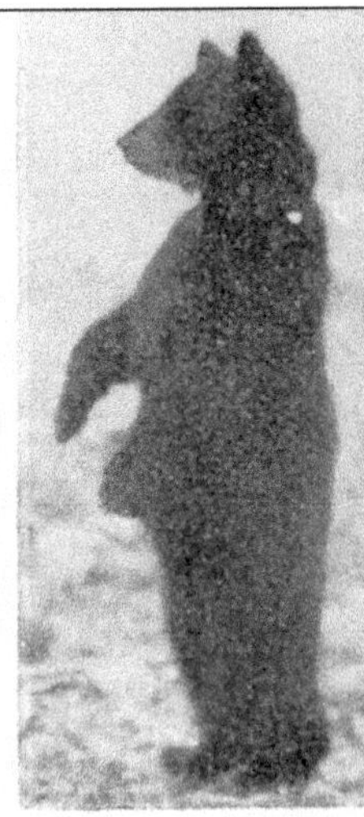

Ripogenus Lake Camps

HUNTING ——— FISHING ——— CANOEING

One of the best and largest localities in Maine. 80 miles from Greenville, (nearest R. R. station), 60 miles by steamer—20 by canoe—an easy two days trip. HOME CAMPS are new and well furnished—Spring beds, etc. A good place for sportsmen and their families. BACK CAMPS and LEAN-TOS are rough and wild, and though comfortable, are not strictly intended for ladies. Good living everywhere. RATES for Sportsmen $2 per day, guides $1.50 per day, guides wages $3 per day including canoe. Not a better chance in the Country for **Trout Fishing** or for **Moose, Deer and Bear** in the Fall. Write early, asking for circular and map.

REG. C. THOMAS, - - Chesuncook P. O. Maine

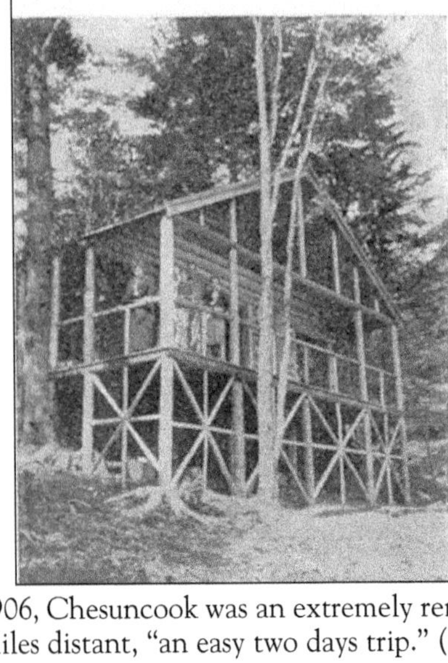

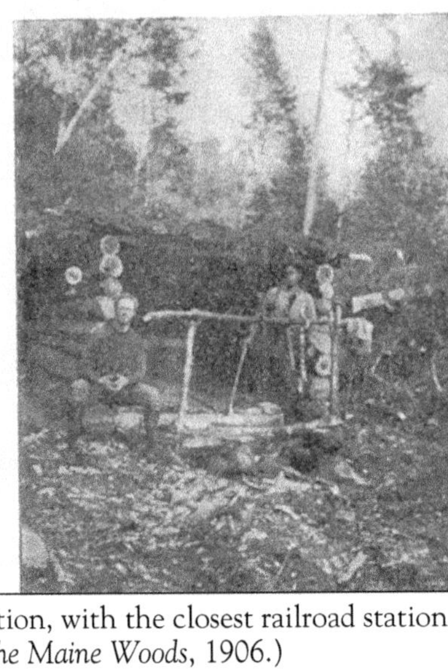

In 1906, Chesuncook was an extremely remote location, with the closest railroad station being 80 miles distant, "an easy two days trip." (From *In the Maine Woods*, 1906.)

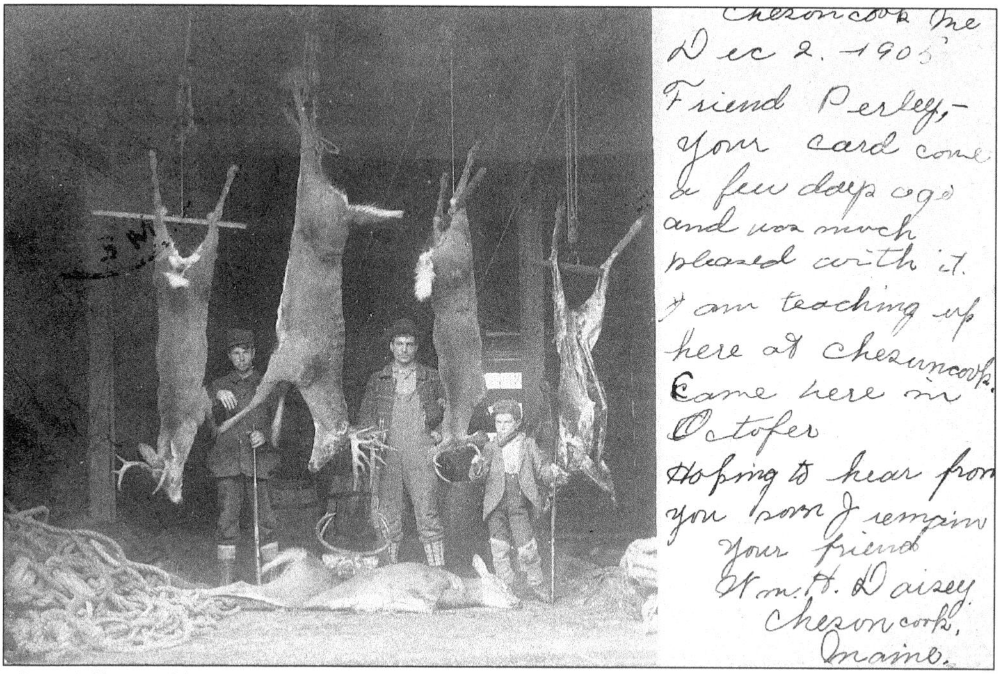

These folks would attest to the foregoing advertisement about excellent hunting. The large deer is easily a 10-pointer.

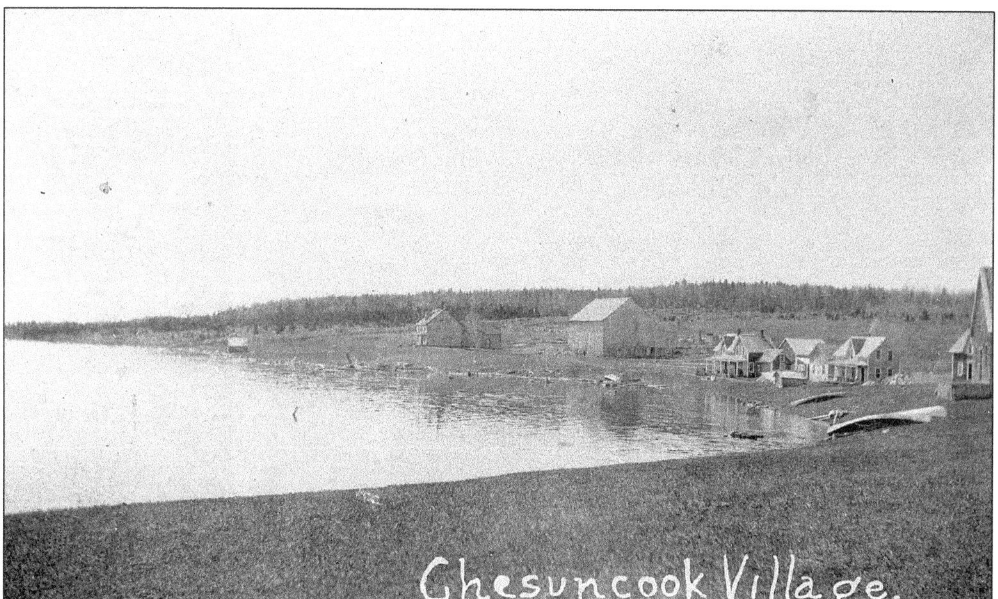

Shown here is part of Chesuncook Village, where the author of the above card was teaching in 1905. The village is located on the water of Chesuncook Lake and has no road to it. It is reached, even today, by either plane or boat.

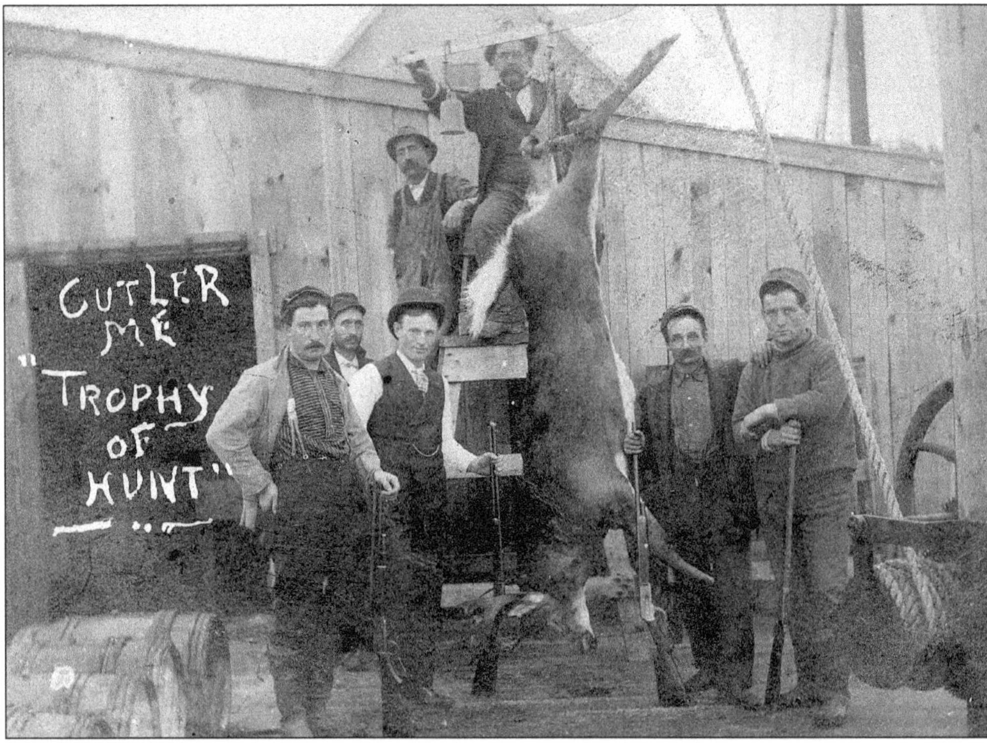

Down East, the Machias-Washington County Region, has long been known for an abundance of game. Its reputation has spread widely, and the fall season witnesses an influx of hunters seeking all types of game, particularly large deer.

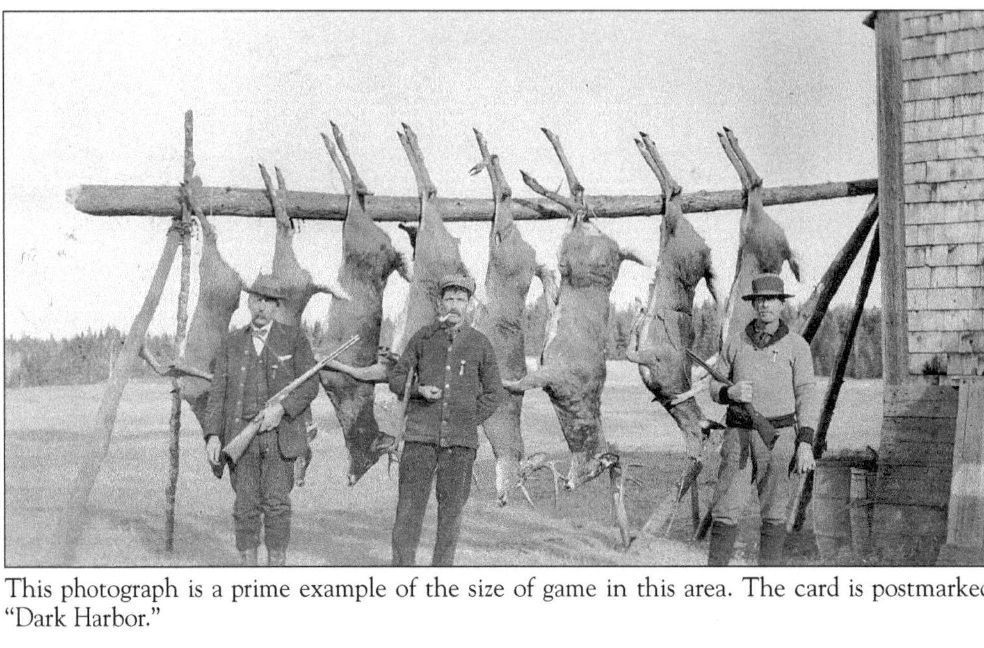

This photograph is a prime example of the size of game in this area. The card is postmarked "Dark Harbor."

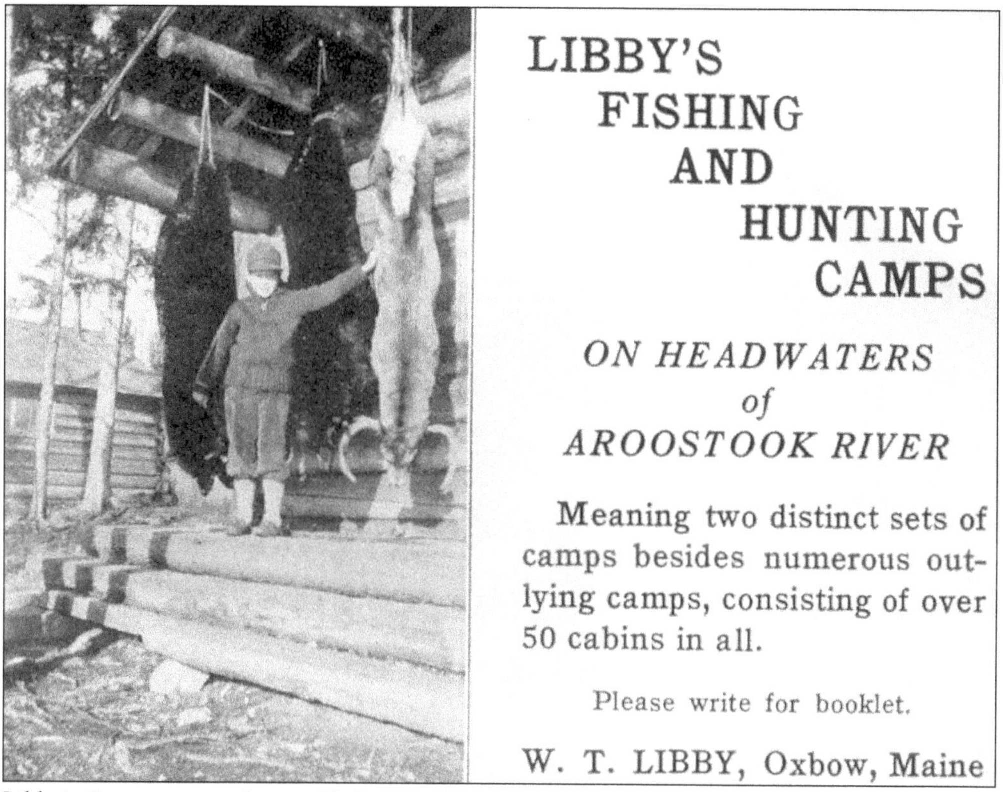

Libby's Camps, a popular establishment for many years, advertised an extensive operation in 1935. Two sets of camps consisting of more than 50 cabins gave the sportsman plenty of choice of location or accommodation. (From *In the Maine Woods*, 1935.)

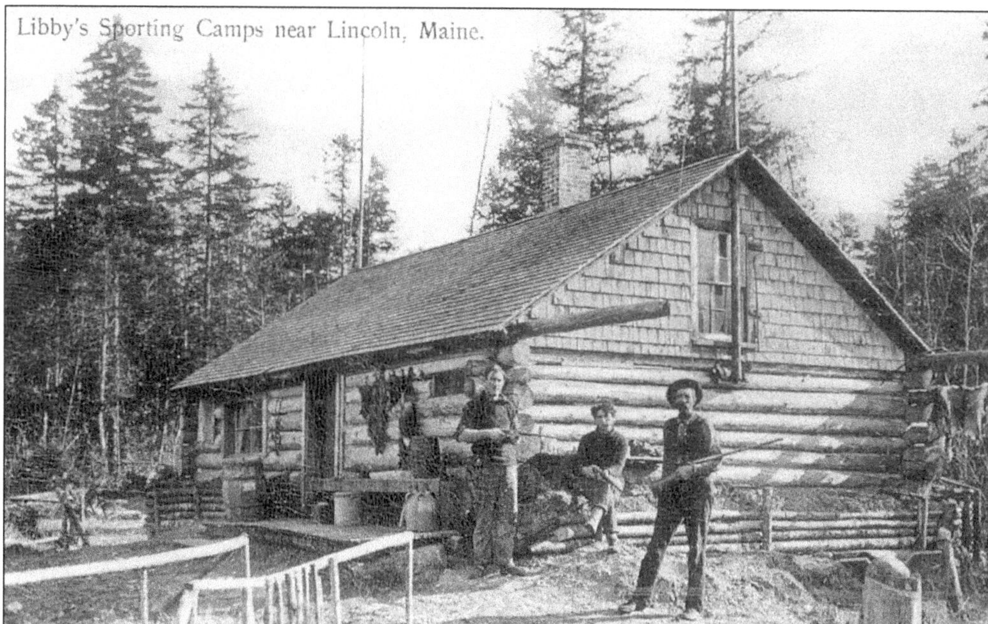

Here is a nice shot of one of the camps at Libby's Millinocket Camps, with hunters posing in front.

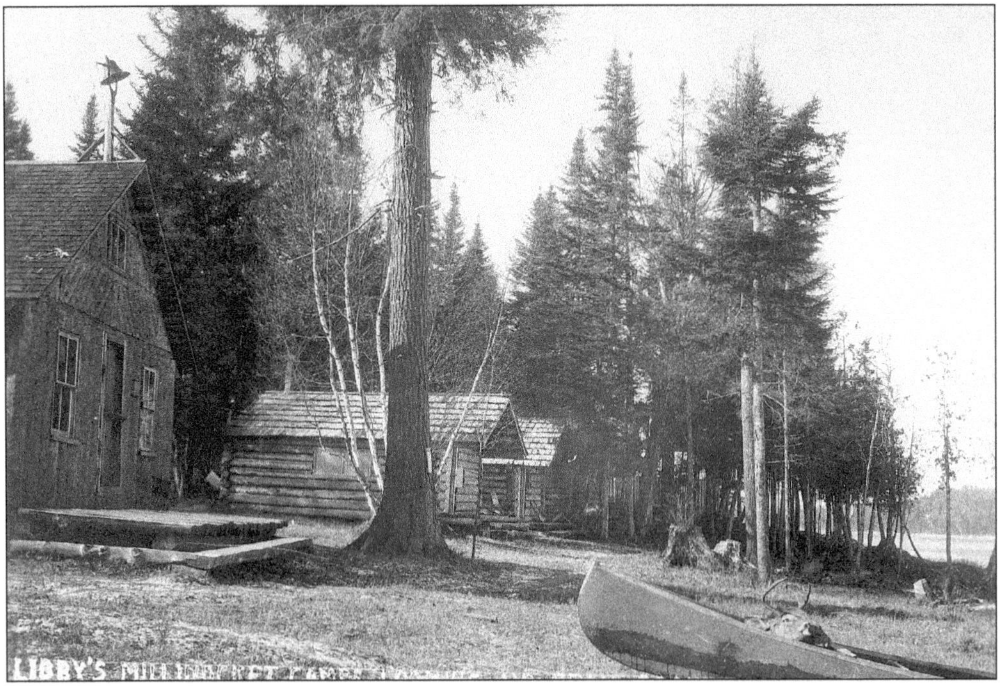

This is a nice shot of Libby's Millinocket Camps and their location near the lake. Note the large buck in the bow of the canoe. The Libby family has had camps in this area for more than 100 years, consolidating their operation and relocating on the shore of Millinocket Lake in 1938.

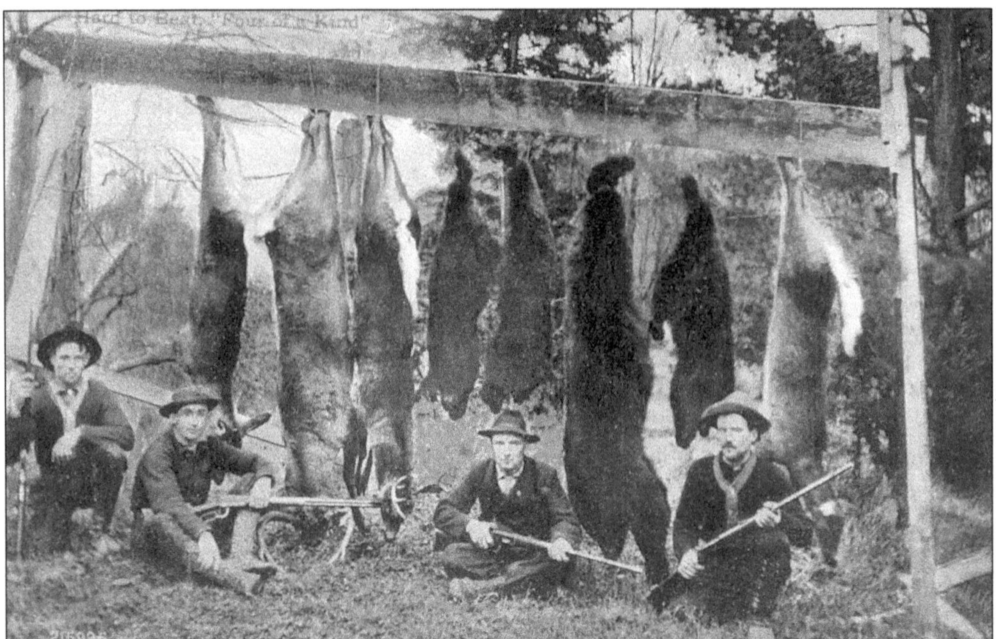

Four hunters pose with four deer and four bear, a relatively easy accomplishment in the north woods during the early part of the century. Each man is holding a lever-action Winchester or Stevens rifle.

Women were successful with lever-action rifles as well as men. It is likely that this big buck is this woman's prize. The card is postmarked "West Brooksville, 1910." (Steve Rainsford collection.)

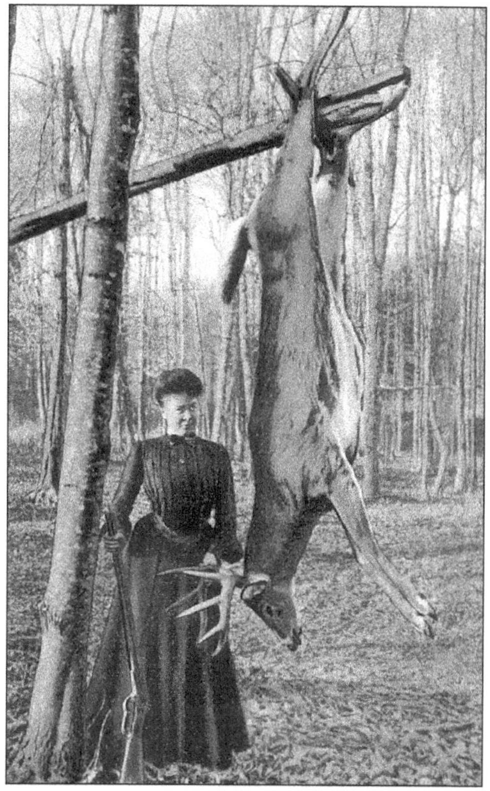

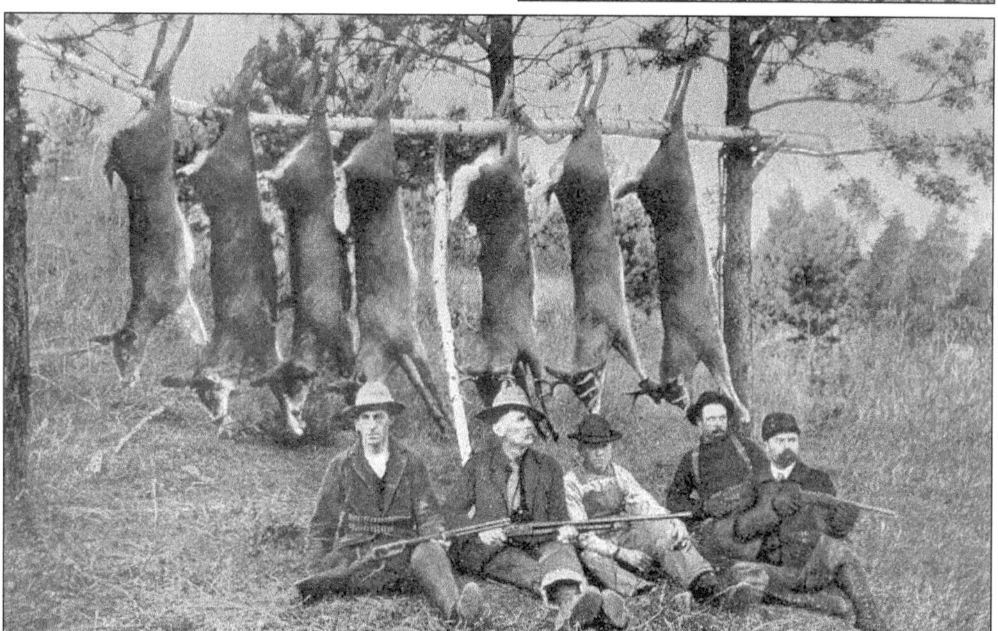

Hunters and a guide are shown here with seven impressive animals. Lever-action rifles are the weapons of choice here as well, and judging from the ammunition on hunter's belts, at least some of the rifles are probably .44 or .45 caliber. Among the most popular guns were 44-40 and 45-70 for deer, bear, and moose hunting.

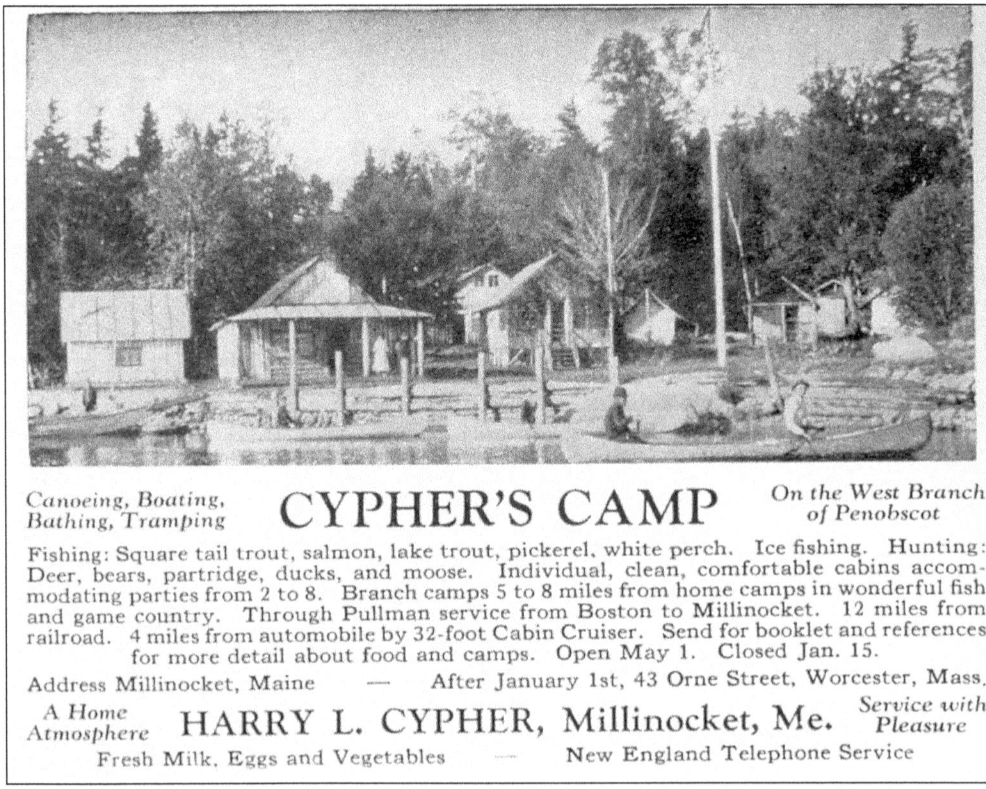

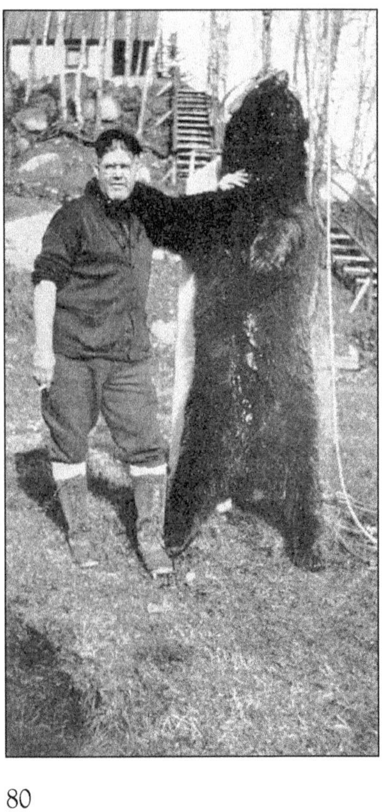

Located 12 miles from the railroad, Cypher's had a longstanding record of big game hunting as well as fishing. It was another establishment of several that had "branch camps." (From *In the Maine Woods*, 1932.)

This photograph attests to the type of game found in this region. E.W. Hicks of Holden, Massachusetts, shot this black bear, weighing 465 pounds dressed. At the time, it was the largest bear recorded by the Maine Department of Inland Fisheries and Game. (From *In the Maine Woods*, 1932.)

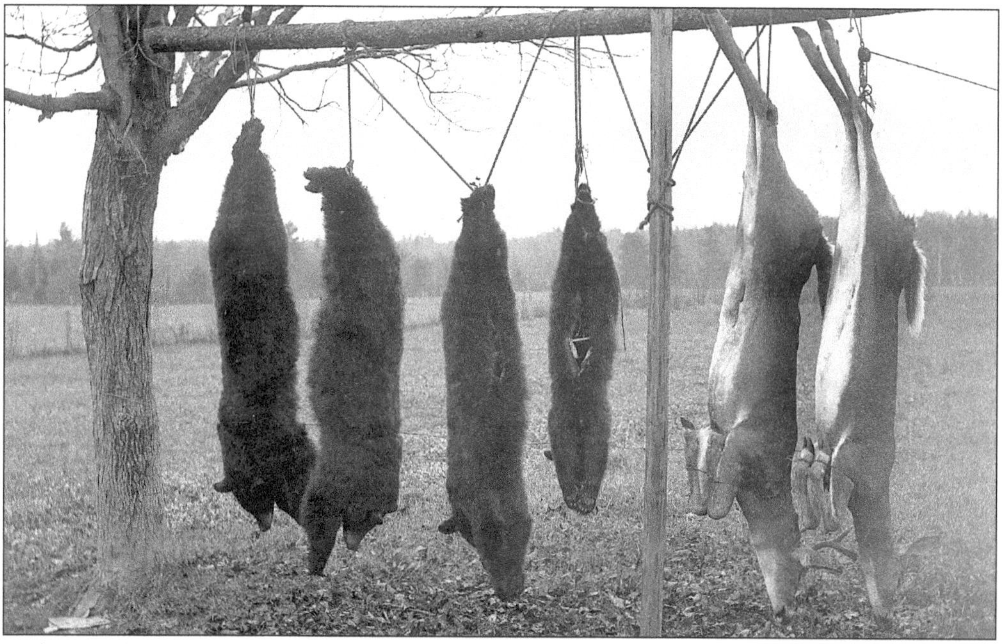

Walter Bartlett killed this rack of game in the Mattawamkeag area the week of October 27, 1917.

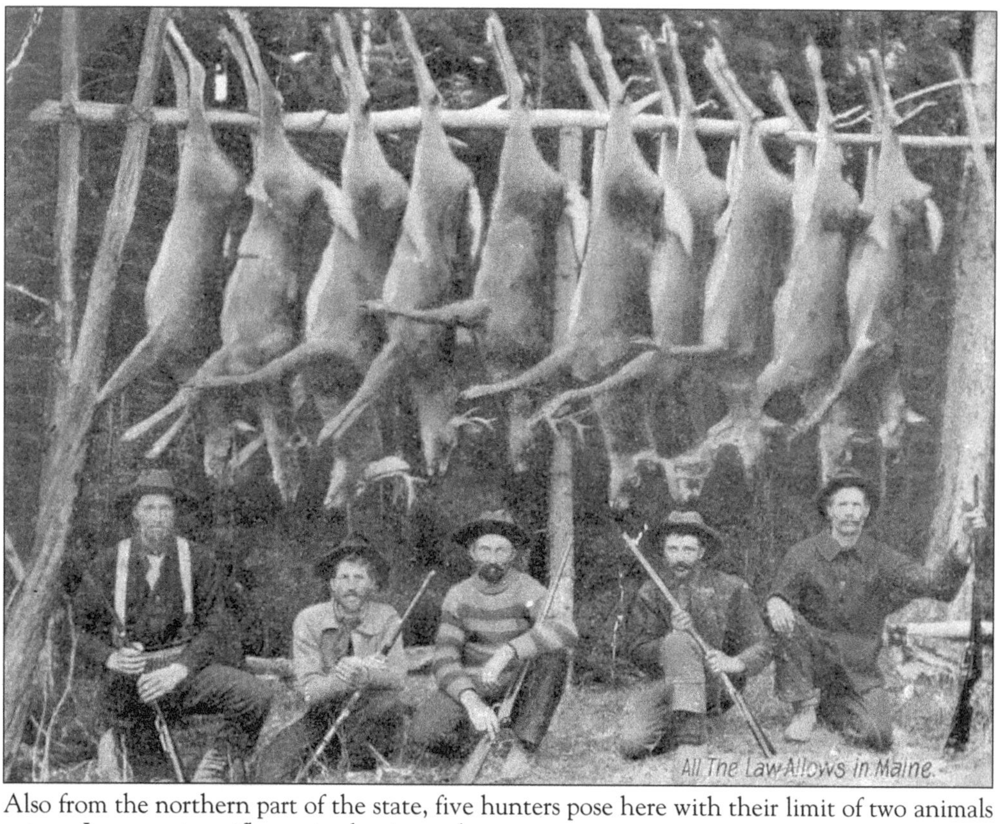

Also from the northern part of the state, five hunters pose here with their limit of two animals apiece. Lever-action rifles again dominate the scene.

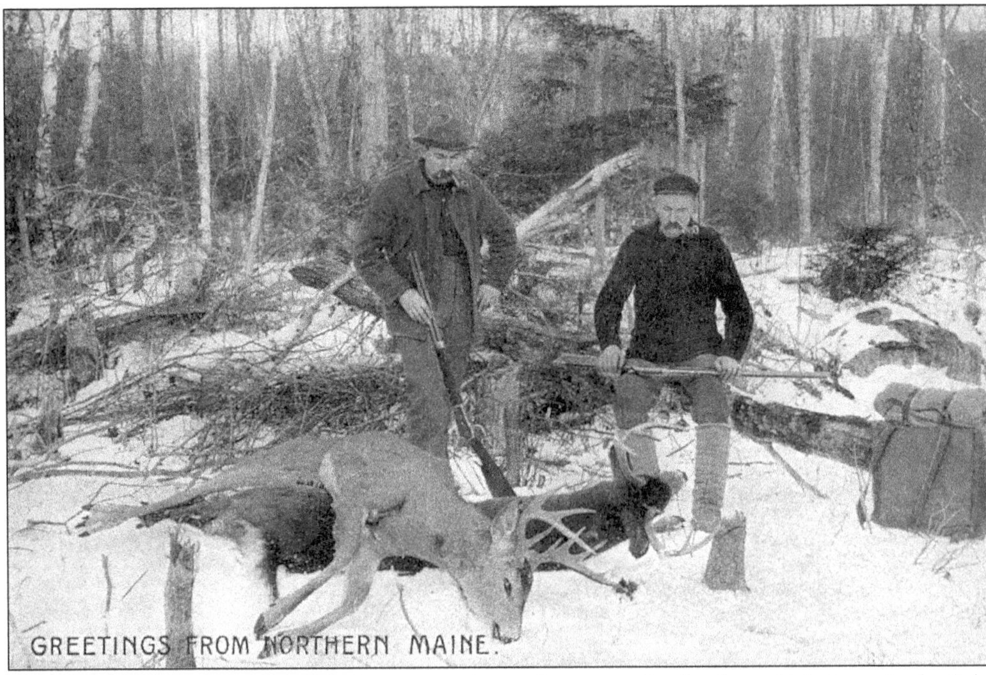

In this scene, these two hunters have just downed two trophy bucks, which is typical of the northern Maine woods. Note the dress and their rifles.

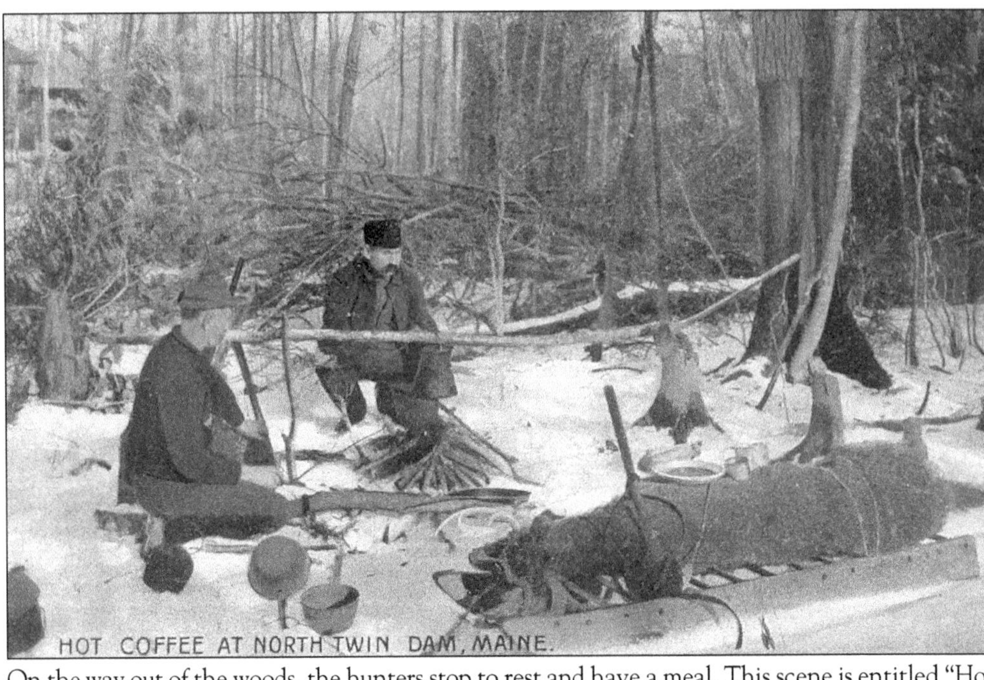

On the way out of the woods, the hunters stop to rest and have a meal. This scene is entitled "Hot Coffee at North Twin Dam, Maine." More than likely their drink of choice is hot tea, which is much more rejuvenating and satisfying in the outdoors than coffee, particularly in cold weather.

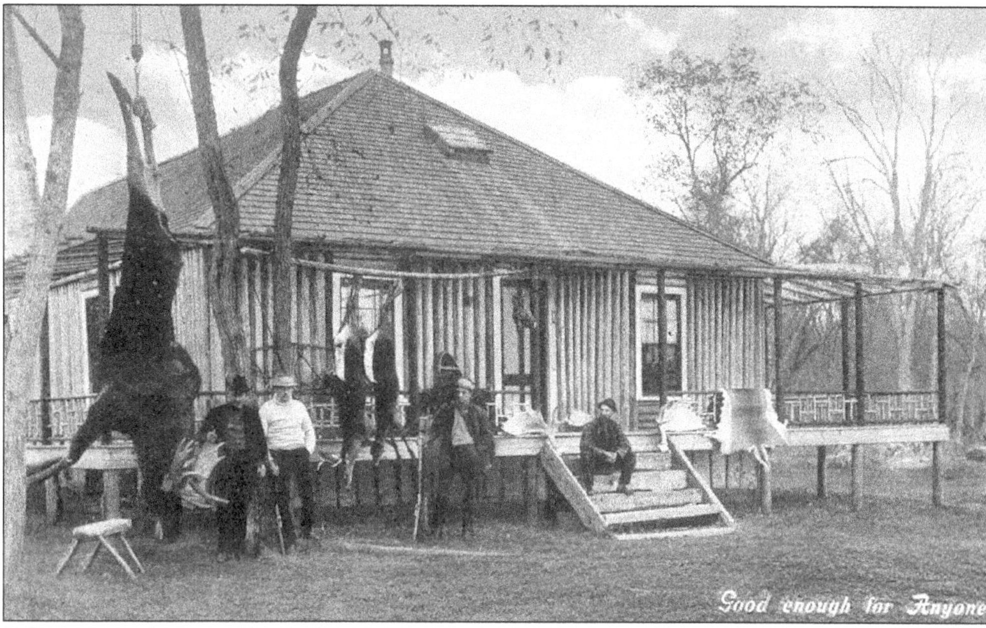

Debscogneag Camp was located at Norcross on Debscogneag Deadwater on the West Branch of the Penobscot River. This camp was located within a few miles of Mount Katahdin. Several trophies are shown here, but in particular, one of the hunters has bagged an extremely large moose.

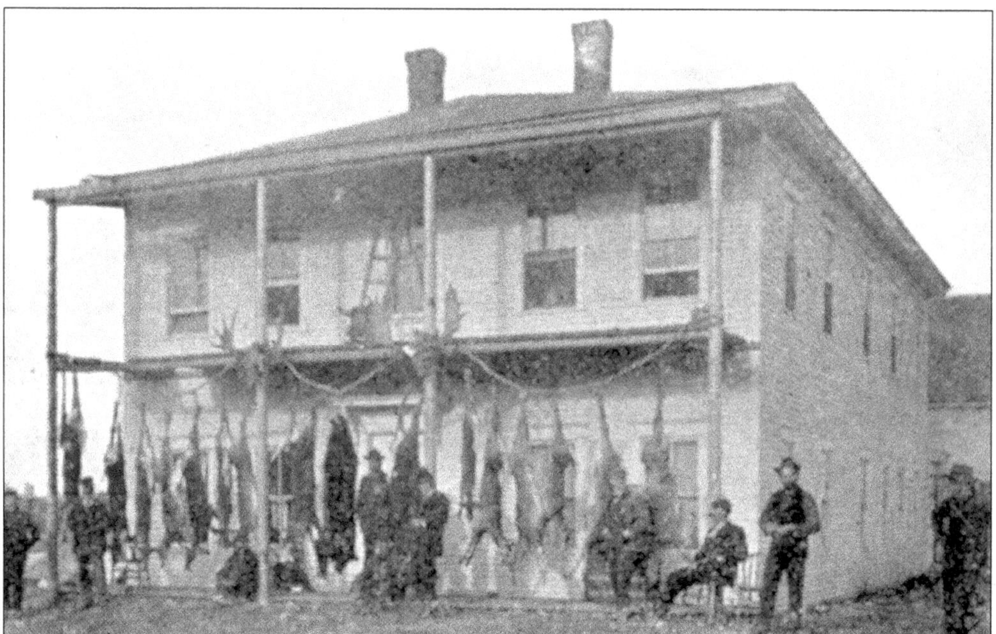

Also at Norcross, the Norcross House was the only hotel in the area, calling itself "the leading sportsmen's resort" in this part of the region. Folks at Norcross were in a fortunate location, having service by both rail and steamer, unlike many of the remote locations. Hunters did very well in this area, as shown by the display of animals in this advertisement. (From *In the Maine Woods*, 1900.)

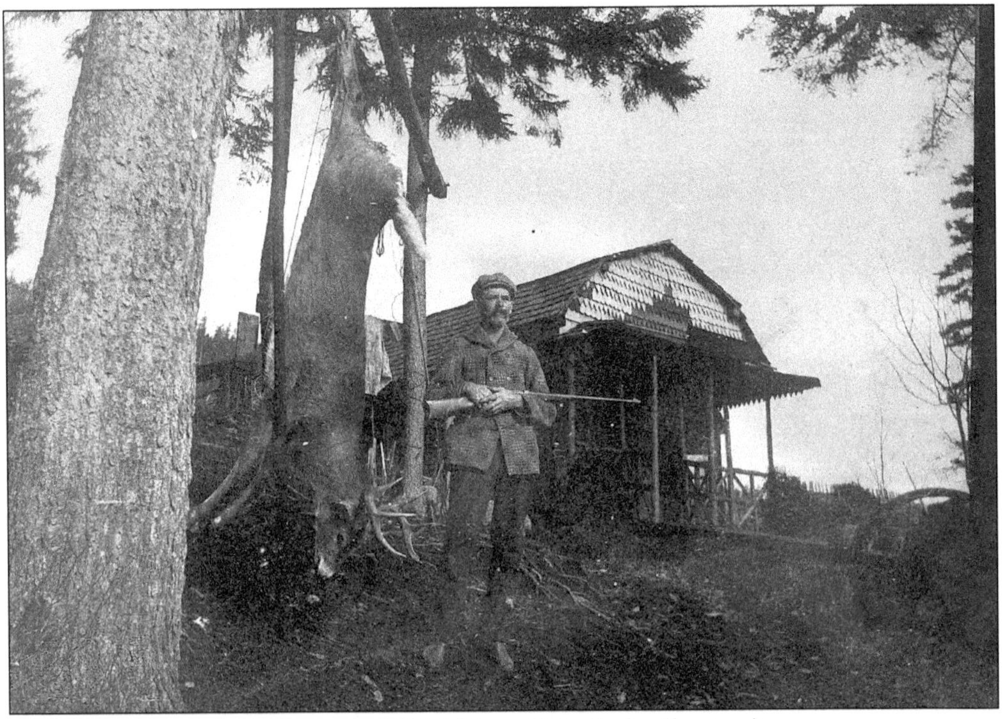

This card is postmarked "Norcross, 1915." (Steve Rainsford collection.)

KATAHDIN LAKE. Sporting camps. Moose hunting a specialty. Years of experience. Results guaranteed. Write JOHN CUSHMAN, *Guide*, SHERMAN, ME.

GUIDE FOR MOOSE or Deer. Fishing parties guided. LOUIS BELL, ST. CROIX, ME.

ON EAST BRANCH. Hunting and fishing camps, sixteen miles from Stacyville. Parties met. Address W. E. CUSHMAN, P. O. SHERMAN, ME.

GUIDE FOR MOOSE or deer hunting, or for fishing, from the Ashland Branch. C. B. ANDERSON, SMYRNA MILLS, ME.

GUIDE FOR MOOSE. Camps on Lepomkeag Stream, eleven miles from Oxbow. U. G. SWETT, OXBOW, ME.

GUIDE FOR MOOSE. Hunters taken to home of the moose. Make engagement with E. H. CURRIER, OXBOW, ME.

Here is a typical advertisement for hunting guides. Early on, it was written, "Maine guides as a class are good-hearted, genial companions. When camping they do the cooking for the entire party, clear the tenting grounds and make all things snug and comfortable, in addition to carrying the heavy burdens and doing a tremendous amount of hard work." In addition, it was said, "There are no better big game hunters in the world than the guides. They know not only the habits of the animals they hunt, but they are as familiar with the woods as with their own dooryards. They explore for lumber, trap fur-bearing animals in it, gather spruce gum in it, lumber in it, until they know its every feature. These men of the forest are always studying the ways of the great animals inhabiting the north woods. They know the runways, or ranges, of the bull moose, and at what time the animals may be expected at a certain place." (From *In the Maine Woods*, 1900.)

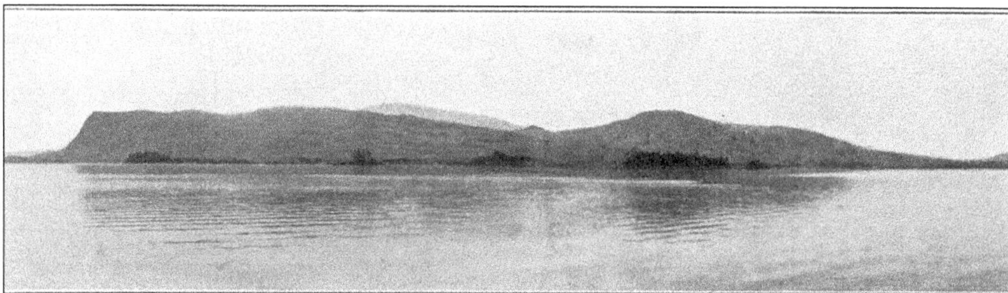

GRAND LAKE, MATAGAMON MAINE

AS SEEN FROM MYRICKS SPORTING CAMPS, TRAVELER RANGE OF MOUNTAINS IN DISTANCE

Grand Lake, Matagamon, the Sportsman's paradise is situated on the head waters of the East Branch of the Penobscot River. It is reached by stage from Patten, Maine, (Bangor and Aroostook R.R.). Good Automobile roads to Shin Pond.

Practically virgin country, waters alive with trout, salmon and togue. Wonderful fishing. Deer, Moose, Bear, Partridge, Duck are plentiful. Comfortable Camps, good beds. Wholesome food. Detached Camps. Come and Invite your friends. No disappointments. Fish and Game are here.

Full particulars by writing IRVING B. MYRICK, Proprietor.

This postcard advertisement says and shows it all. The Matagamon area is one of the region's first wild sections encountered as one journeys north. No doubt there were few disappointments.

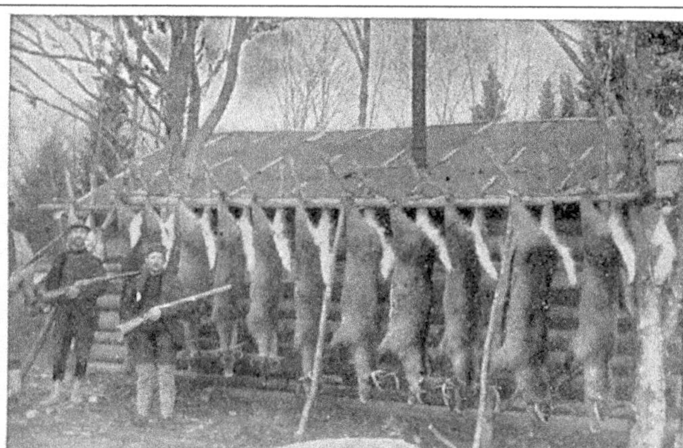

HARVEY'S at Matagamon, Grand Lake, Penobscot East Branch. Twenty-eight miles from Patten by stage over a good road. Fine trout fishing in Grand Lake and in the East Branch below Grand Lake dam. The greatest hunting region in the state. The largest moose heads taken out of the Maine woods in the last decade have been taken out of this region. The fishing, partridge shooting and big game hunting here can't be equalled in Maine. Motor boats and canoes on Grand Lake; experienced guides. Accommodations are of the best. Separate sleeping camps. The best of table fare, fresh vegetables, eggs, milk and butter. You can have a good time here, get rested or get your fill of sport. Long distance telephone. Mail every other day. Parties met at Patten by team. Supply store for sportsmen. Write, telephone or telegraph. Send for circulars.

ZENAS L. HARVEY, Matagamon, Maine

Harvey's was located at Matagamon and boasted that the "largest moose heads taken out of the Maine woods in the last decade" were from this region. This photograph supports the descriptions. (From *In the Maine Woods*, 1909.)

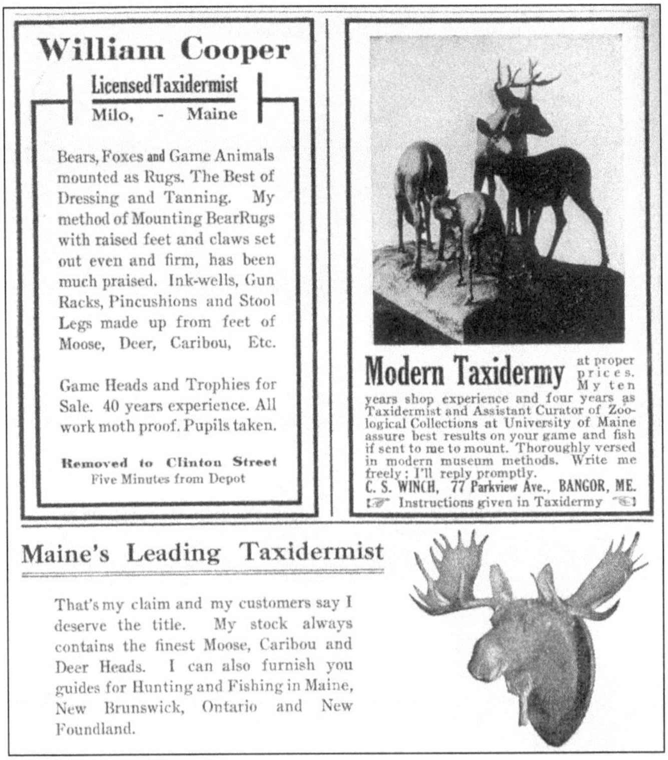

With so many trophy animals being taken from the Aroostook Region, there was a tremendous demand for taxidermists. Three of the prominent ones for this region are described in these advertisements. (From *In the Maine Woods*, 1912.)

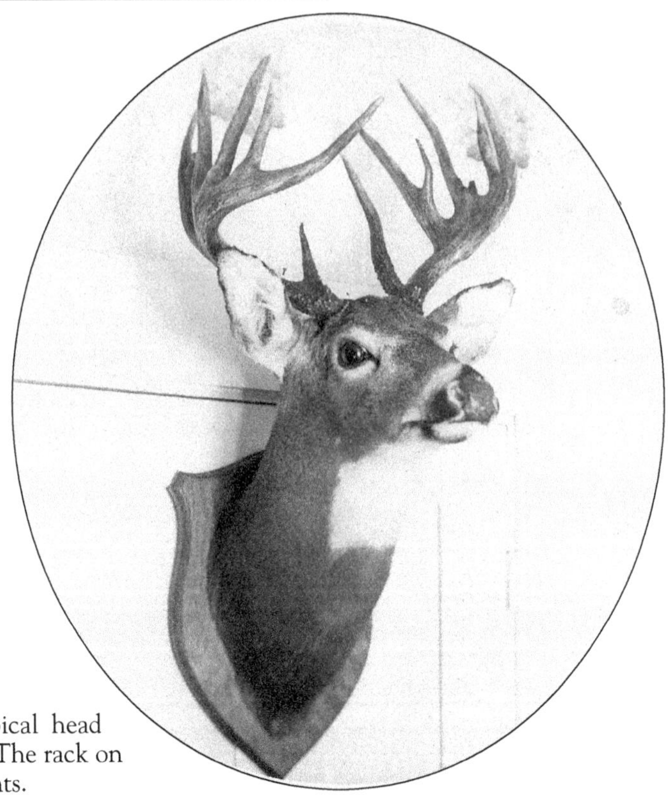

This photograph shows a typical head mount of a large trophy buck. The rack on this animal has at least 12 points.

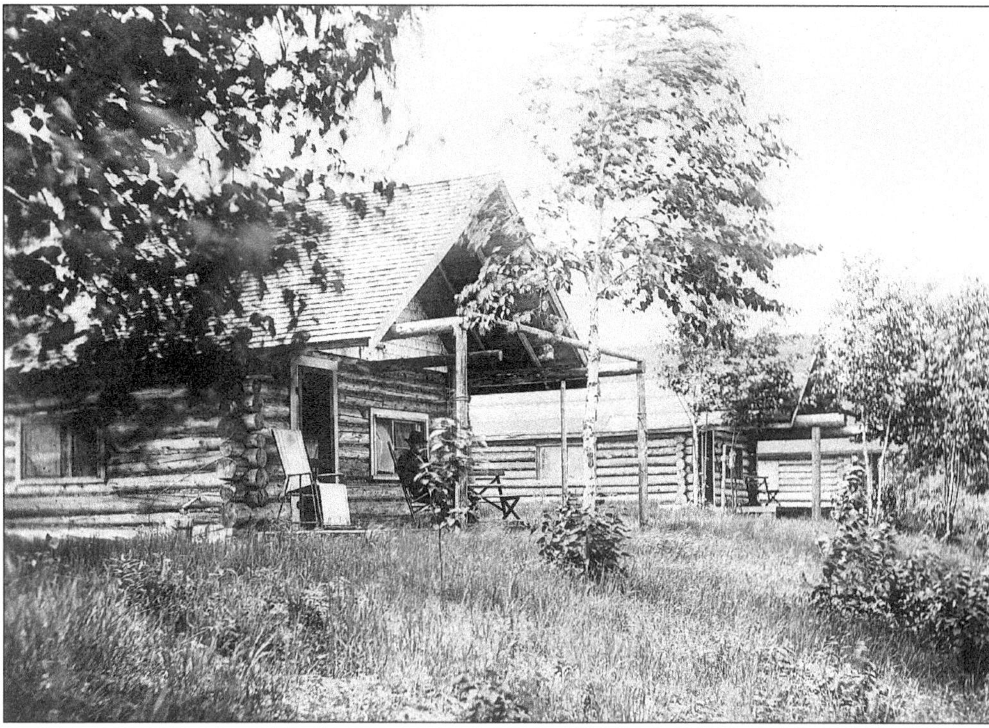

Well-known guide, sportsman, and raconteur William Wingate Sewall operated Hook Point Camps on Mattawamkeag Lake in Island Falls. Sewall was the first white child born at Island Falls and he spent the better part of his life there. The camps were located "four miles by buckboard from Island Falls."

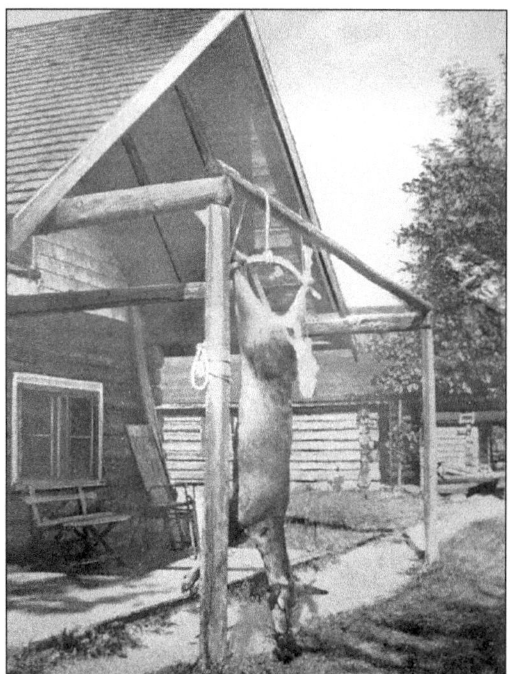

A fair-sized doe hangs in front of one of the Hook Point camps. It was typical of hunting camps such as this to have permanently erected game poles on site to hang up the animals.

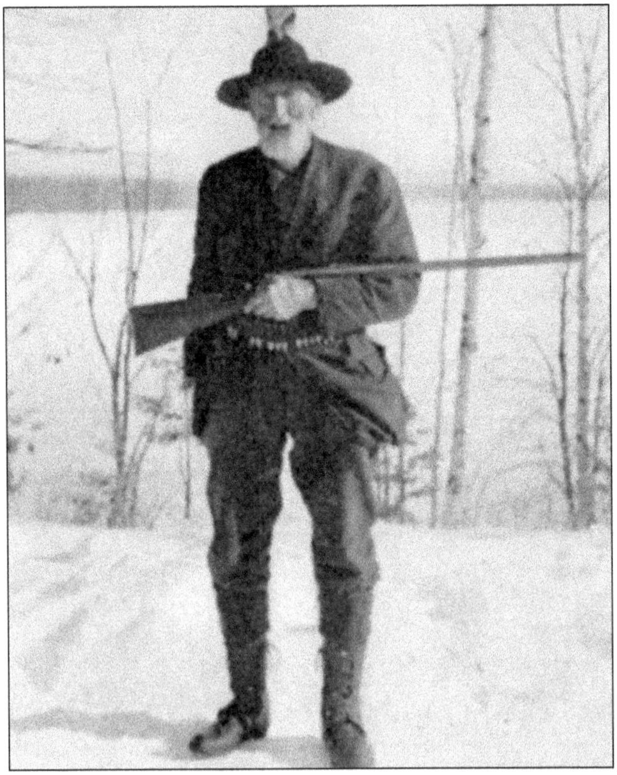

Bill Sewall was a friend of Pres. Theodore Roosevelt, having guided him and introduced him to both the Maine woods and hunting when the Roosevelt was an 18-year-old boy. The friendship lasted a long time, and Sewall even visited the president when he was in office. He also served as foreman for a while on Roosevelt's western ranch. Sewall is shown in this photograph at the age 77. (From *In the Maine Woods*, 1923.)

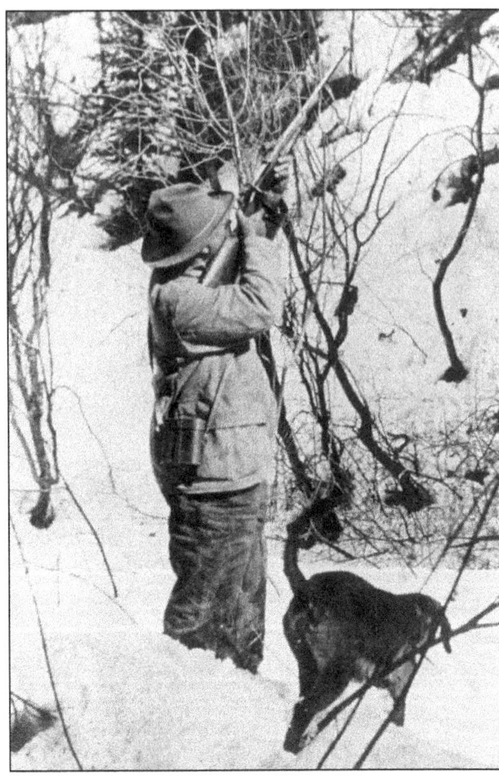

While there are numerous photographs of Theodore Roosevelt in hunting dress and with wild game, there are few pictures of him in Maine. He visited his friend Bill Sewall many times over the years and stayed at Hook Point Camps. Roosevelt also camped at Munsungun. Sewall spent time with the fish and game department erecting a game warden's camp at this site, which they named Roosevelt Camp.

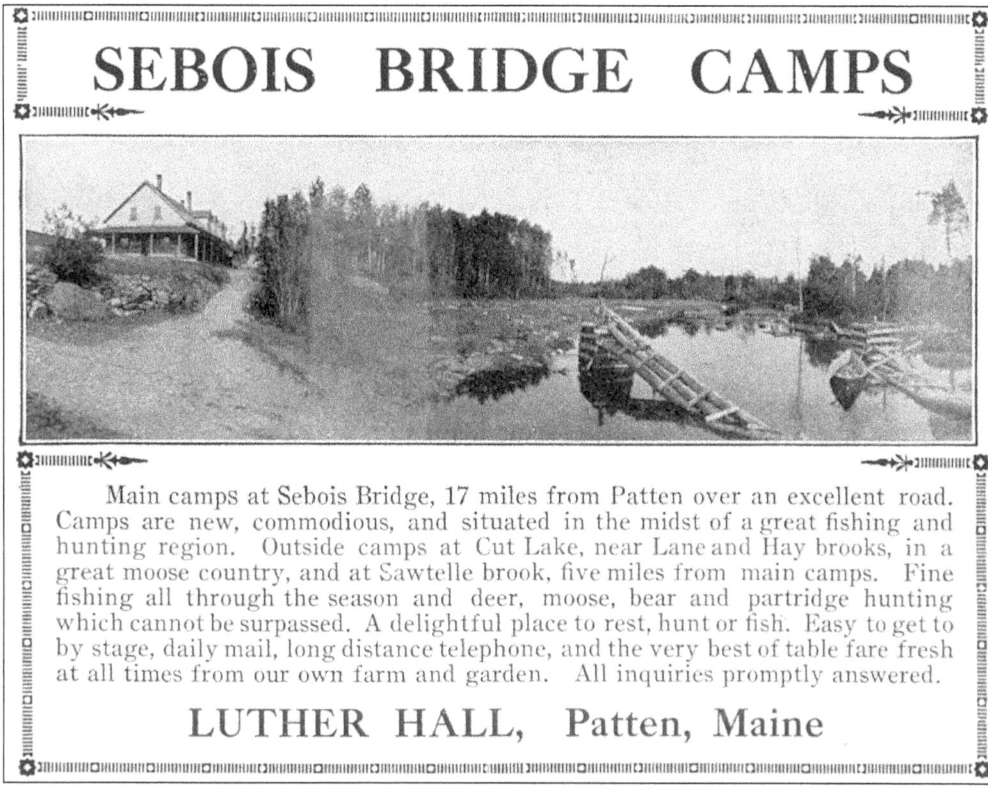

Near Munsungun Lake is Sebois, the site of another popular remote camp located 17 miles from Patten. Outside camps at several locations allow the hunter to cover quite a bit of territory. (From *In the Maine Woods*, 1909.)

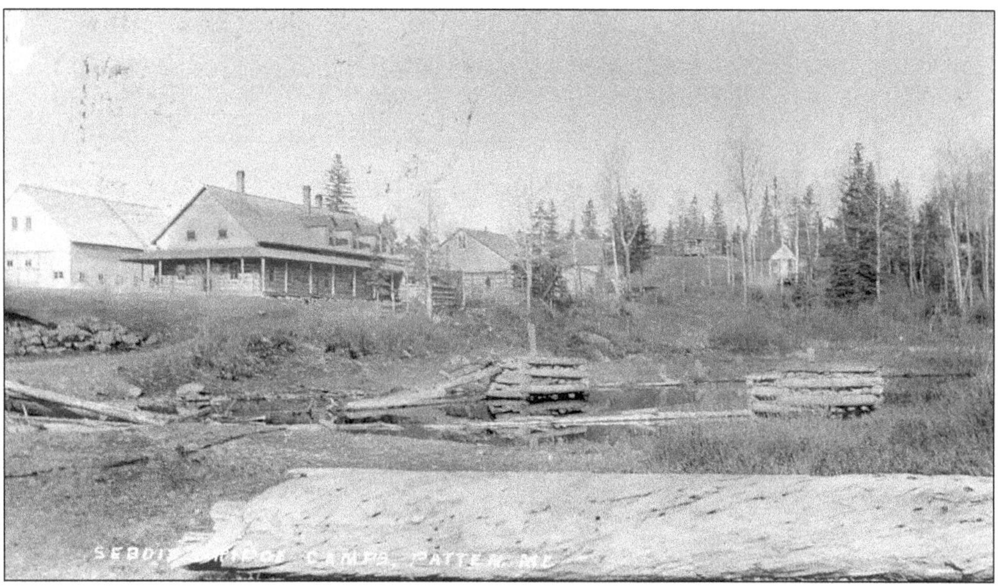

In this early photograph of the camps at Sebois, we can see that it was quite an establishment for such a remote location.

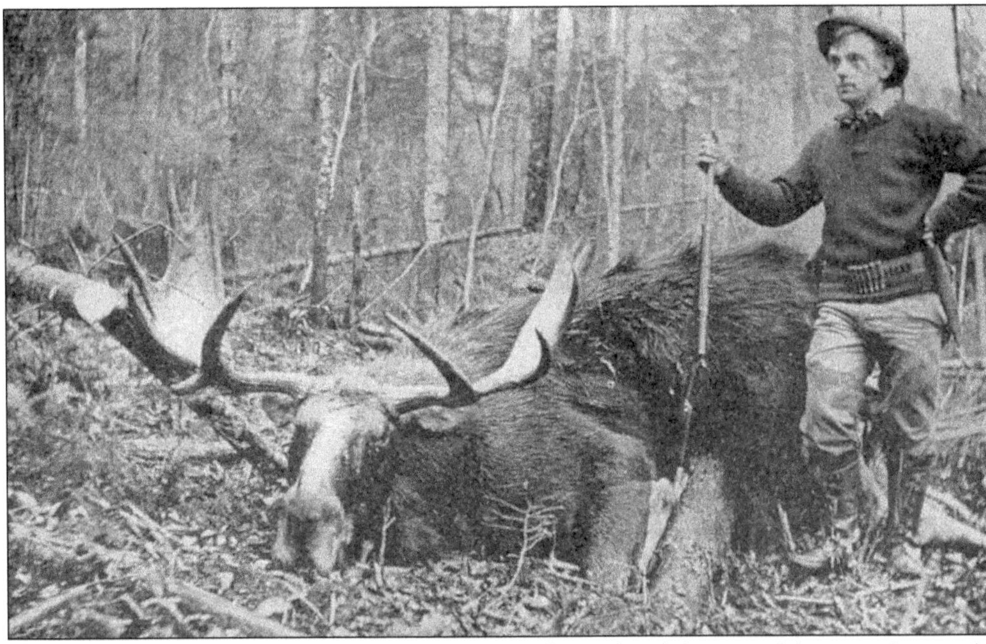

This hunter has downed a huge moose. Note the rifle used and the size of the cartridges in the hunter's belt. Now the hard work begins by getting the animal out of the woods. (From *In the Maine Woods*, 1912.)

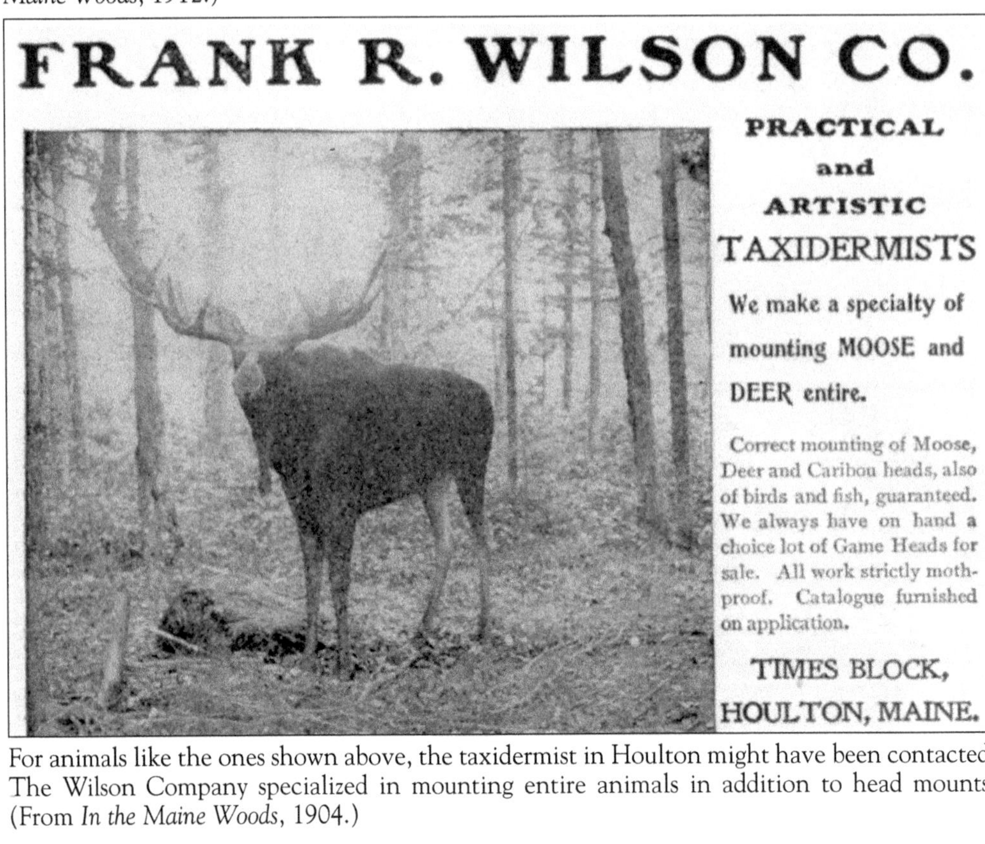

For animals like the ones shown above, the taxidermist in Houlton might have been contacted. The Wilson Company specialized in mounting entire animals in addition to head mounts. (From *In the Maine Woods*, 1904.)

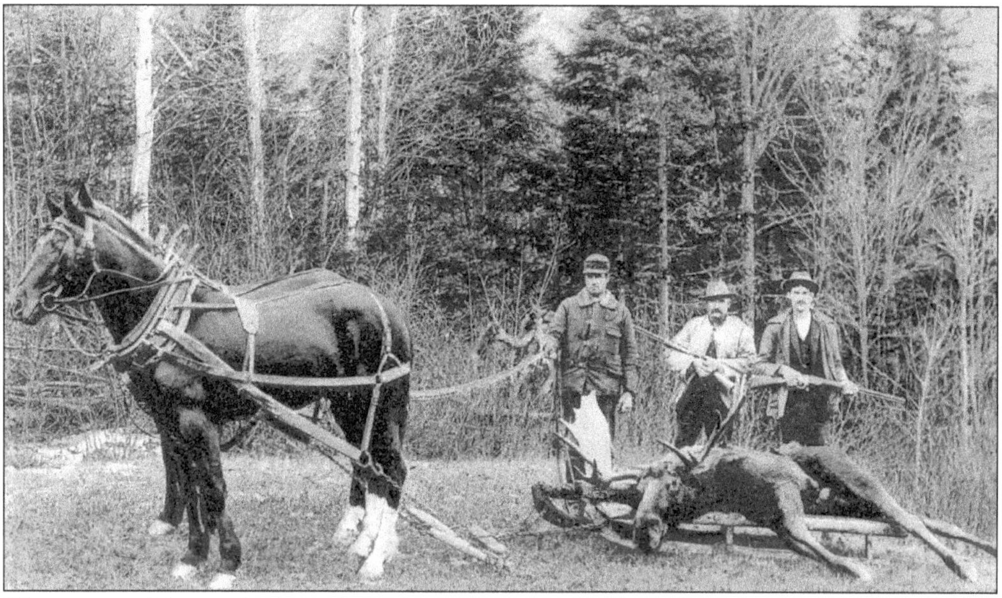

This is one of the methods used to take an entire animal out of the woods, probably the best way. A team of horses with a sled could move a very large moose, such as the one shown in this picture taken in the Houlton area.

HORACE B. KELSO

LICENSED TAXIDERMIST

Mounting Game Heads a Specialty
All Work Guaranteed True to Life and Moth Proof
Game Heads Always on Hand for Sale

Houlton, - - - - Maine

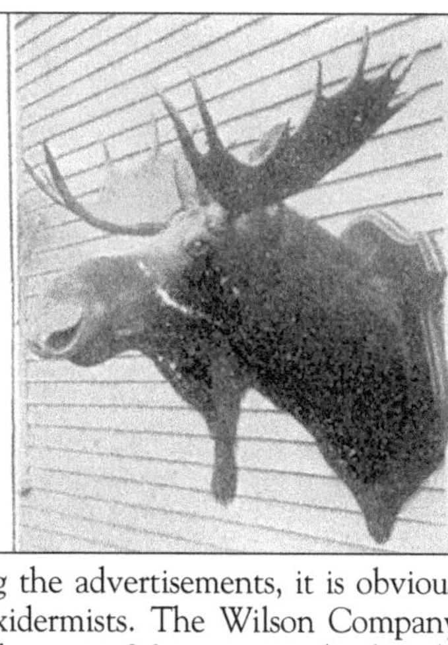

Kelso was another taxidermist located in Houlton. By reading the advertisements, it is obvious where the trophy animals came from by the demand for taxidermists. The Wilson Company specialized in entire animals, but Kelso specialized in doing head mounts. Mounts were also for sale for those hunters who were unable to shoot their own trophy. (From *In the Maine Woods*, 1907.)

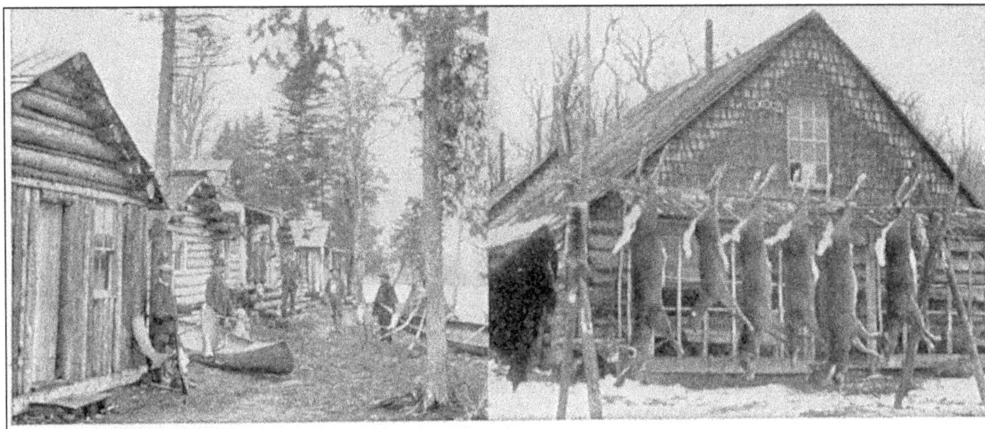

ATKINS' CAMPS, Reached from Masardis and Oxbow.

Leave Boston in evening, arrive at Masardis next noon, and at first of camps that evening. Distance from railroad 25 miles, made by team and canoe.

String of twelve camps on lakes, ponds, and streams of **the famous Fishing and Hunting Region at the headwaters of the Aroostook.** Home camps at Millnockett Lake consist of twelve cabins made of peeled logs; open fireplaces, spring beds, A1 table. Privacy and home comforts for women. Sportsmen can come here with their families and get the very best of sport, as well as comfortable living. No better summer fishing in Maine. Moose hunting unexcelled. Deer plenty. Write for circular and map.

William Atkins, P. O. Address, Oxbow, Me.

Atkins' Camps were located pretty well back from civilization, about 35 miles from the railroad. Twelve camps spread out through the area provided the hunter with plenty of opportunity to take advantage of the "unexcelled moose hunting." Today, Atkins' Camps are known as Libby's Camps. Even though there has been relocation of cabins and a reconsolidation, the establishment continues with a lodge, seven guest camps, and eight outpost camps that are very similar to what they were a century ago. (From *In the Maine Woods*, 1900.)

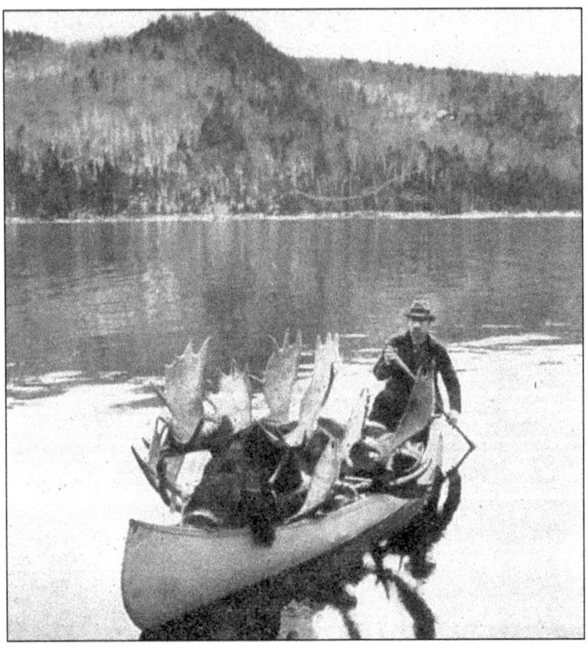

A hunter, probably a guide, transports several moose heads across the lake in his canoe. Judging from these racks, some real trophy animals were taken in this area. In 1903, it was written, "No sportsman should attempt to hunt for moose in Maine's great wilderness without a guide; if he does, he is most likely to come home empty-handed. Even the best of moose guides sometimes fail to come up with the game after tracking it for hours, and yet the Maine guides have no superiors in all the world as hunters of big game."

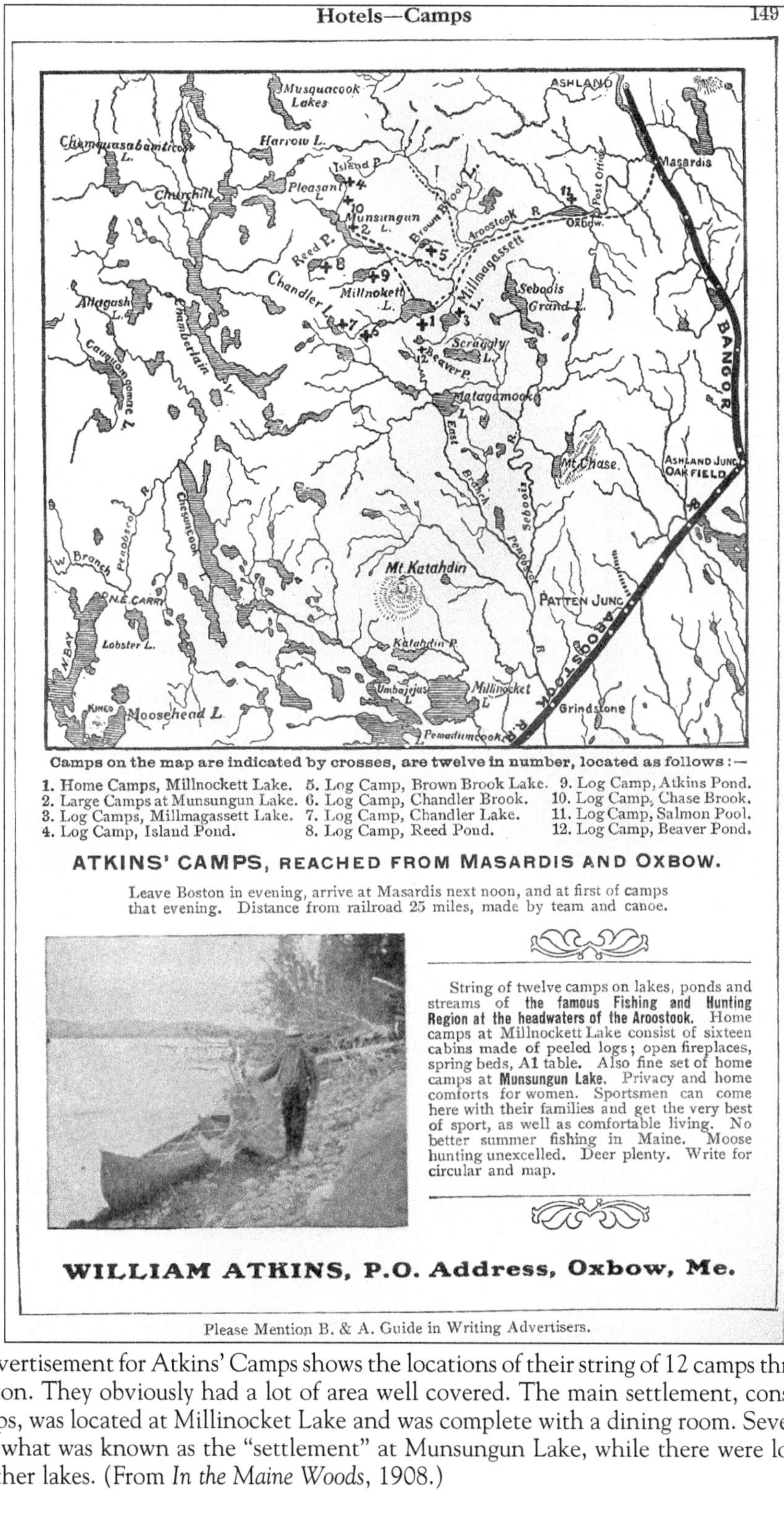

Camps on the map are indicated by crosses, are twelve in number, located as follows:—

1. Home Camps, Millnockett Lake.
2. Large Camps at Munsungun Lake.
3. Log Camps, Millmagassett Lake.
4. Log Camp, Island Pond.
5. Log Camp, Brown Brook Lake.
6. Log Camp, Chandler Brook.
7. Log Camp, Chandler Lake.
8. Log Camp, Reed Pond.
9. Log Camp, Atkins Pond.
10. Log Camp, Chase Brook.
11. Log Camp, Salmon Pool.
12. Log Camp, Beaver Pond.

ATKINS' CAMPS, REACHED FROM MASARDIS AND OXBOW.

Leave Boston in evening, arrive at Masardis next noon, and at first of camps that evening. Distance from railroad 25 miles, made by team and canoe.

String of twelve camps on lakes, ponds and streams of **the famous Fishing and Hunting Region at the headwaters of the Aroostook.** Home camps at Millnockett Lake consist of sixteen cabins made of peeled logs; open fireplaces, spring beds, A1 table. Also fine set of home camps at **Munsungun Lake.** Privacy and home comforts for women. Sportsmen can come here with their families and get the very best of sport, as well as comfortable living. No better summer fishing in Maine. Moose hunting unexcelled. Deer plenty. Write for circular and map.

WILLIAM ATKINS, P.O. Address, Oxbow, Me.

This advertisement for Atkins' Camps shows the locations of their string of 12 camps throughout the region. They obviously had a lot of area well covered. The main settlement, consisting of 18 camps, was located at Millinocket Lake and was complete with a dining room. Seven camps formed what was known as the "settlement" at Munsungun Lake, while there were log cabins at 10 other lakes. (From *In the Maine Woods*, 1908.)

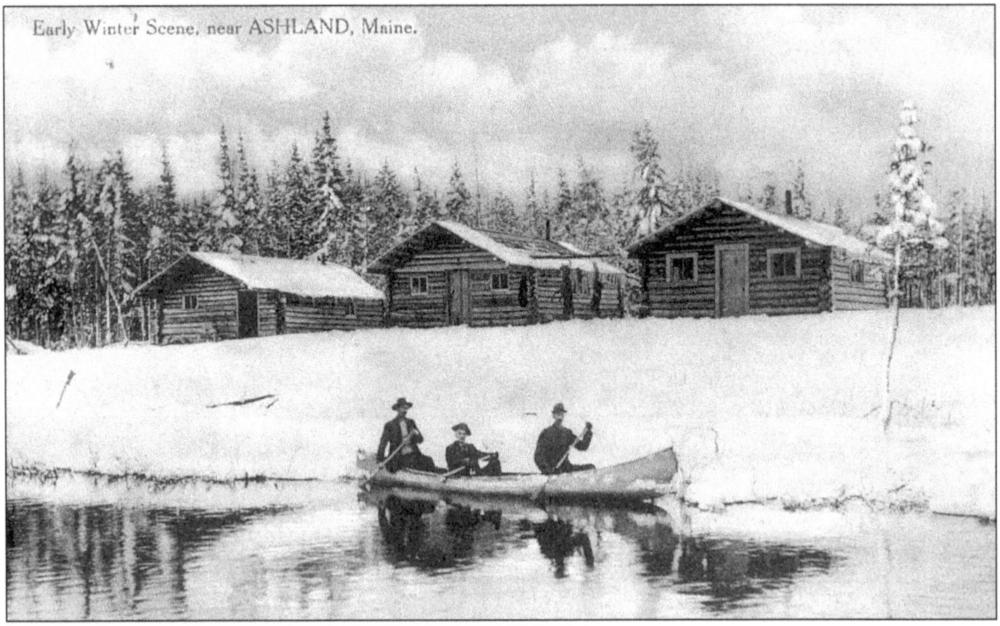

Here is one of many scenes in the Ashland area showing hardy hunters traveling by canoe well after the snow has arrived, which, according to many, makes for much better hunting. Note the deer hanging at the camps.

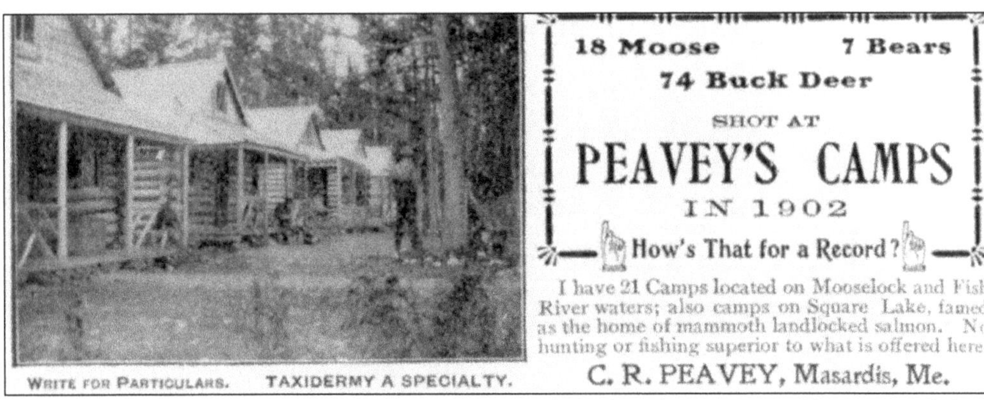

Peavey's Camps were another that had a large number of outlying camps. Theirs spread from Masardis to nearly the north end of the state. A record of this number of animals is worth advertising. Apparently, they took care of their own taxidermy. (From *In the Maine Woods*, 1903.)

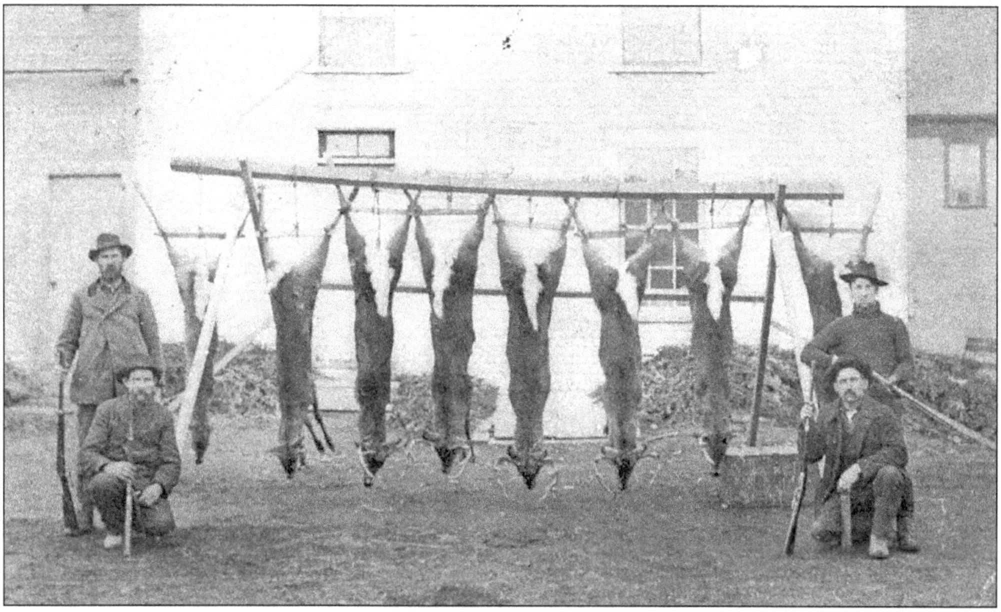

This photograph, taken in Washburn, demonstrates what could be accomplished in a three-day trip—four hunters with eight deer, filling the limit of two animals per person. (Steve Rainsford collection.)

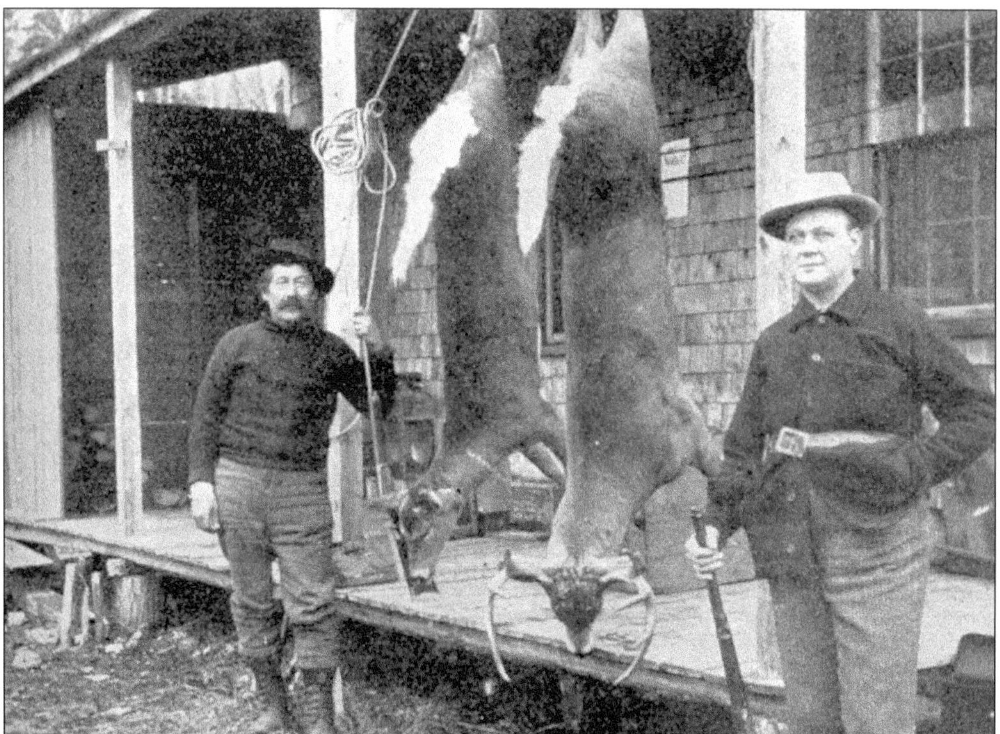

Besides numbers, large trophy deer were frequently taken. These two hunters proudly display two very nice animals. (From *In the Maine Woods*, 1906.)

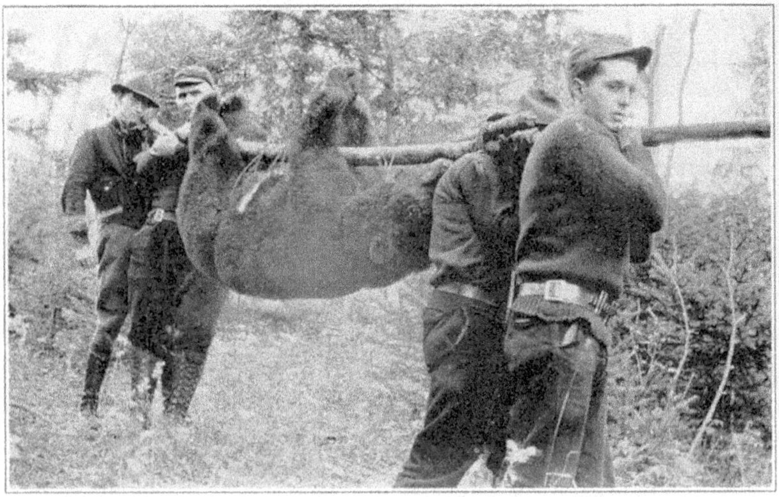

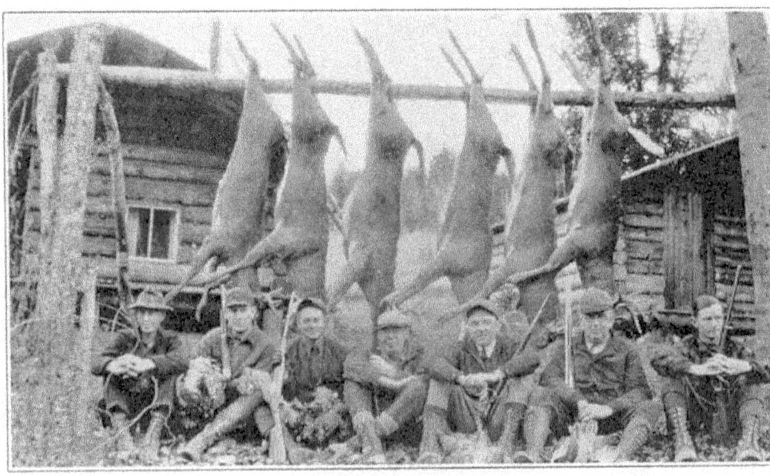

SPORTSMAN !

Ever feel your hair raise or had a great thrill run up your spine? You will if you hunt with me or one of my guides at my chain of camps in the great virgin wilds of Aroostook County and have a big bear or lordly buck pointed out to you. My camps are located in a virgin forest which runs back for more than 200 miles without a single break and here is bear and deer for all. I also have some of the finest lake and stream fishing that can be found.

Before making reservations elsewhere see what I have to offer. Write for my free, 40-page illustrated camp booklet; its worth seeing, and let me refer you to people in your own State or City who have fished or hunted at my camps. The above photos will show you the sport that awaits you. These were taken season of 1931.

Address - - - - V. E. LYNCH, ASHLAND, MAINE

One of the most famous of all hunters and guides was V.E. Lynch. He heavily advertised, was often written about, and wrote a lot of material of his own. Besides numerous articles in popular magazines, Lynch was editor of the *National Sportsman* magazine. Here he offers a 40-page booklet describing his operation. Lynch was a real promoter and a successful hunter and trapper. He published many photographs of animals and successful hunters. (From *In the Maine Woods*, 1932.)

Mrs. Lynch was a hunter in her own right, shown here with a large bear she has taken. (From *In the Maine Woods*, 1934.)

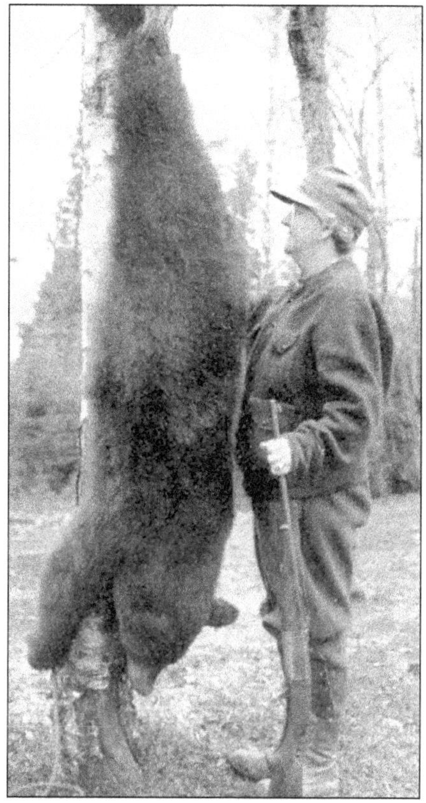

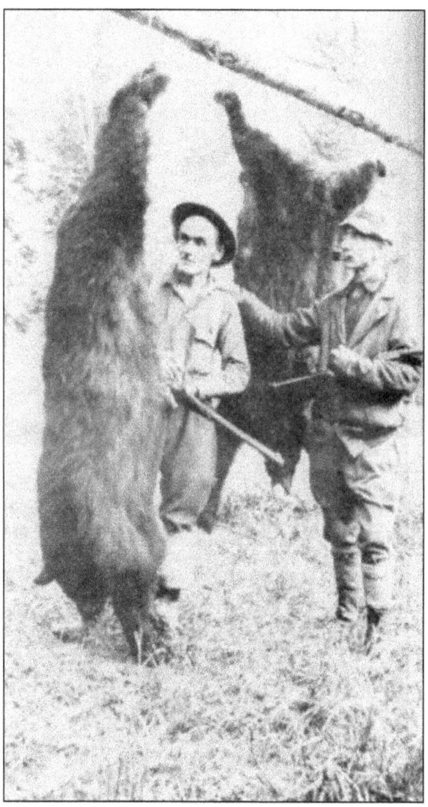

Two more bear shot at Lynch's Camps are shown here with a Dr. Wilfoury of Richmond, Virginia, and his guide. (From *In the Maine Woods*, 1931.)

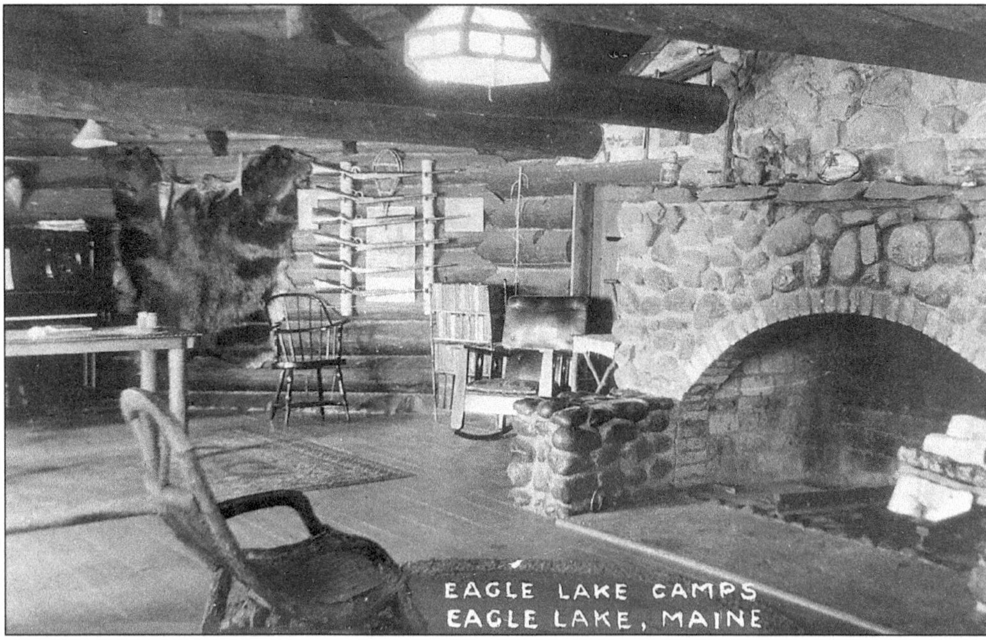

Here is the well-adorned lobby of the Eagle Lake Camps. Many of these lodges had large fireplaces like the one shown here. If it were a hunting camp, it would have frequently displayed guns along with trophies of all types.

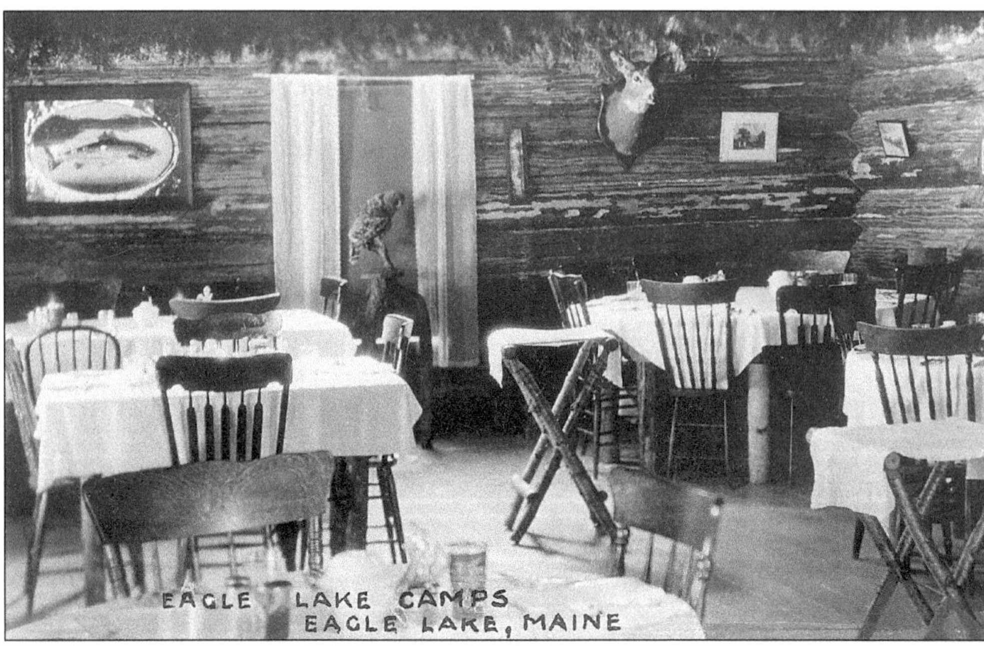

The dining room at Eagle Lake Camps also displays trophies and pictures to entice the sportsman. Typical of camps such as this, dining rooms were set in formal fashion.

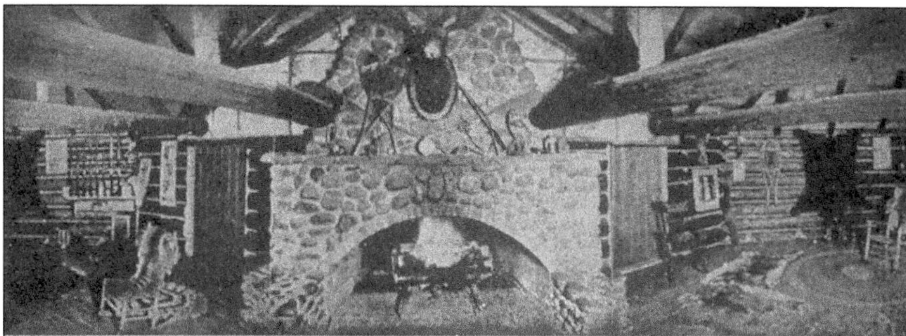

EAGLE LAKE CAMPS—ASSEMBLY ROOM

There is no better spot in Maine for fishing and hunting. Waters are famous for record trout and salmon; fly fishing all summer. Surrounding country abounds in deer, bears, few moose and game birds.

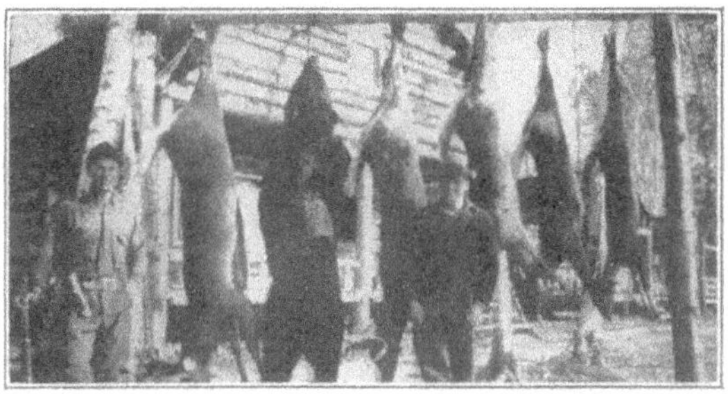

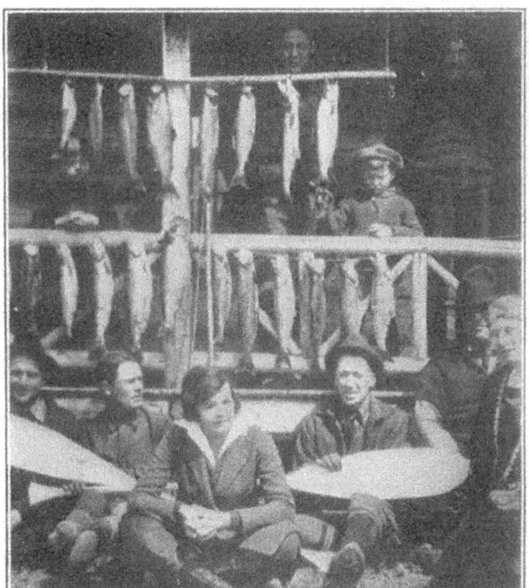

Eagle Lake Camps are a model woods resort. Electric lights and running water in all cabins. Eleven cabins with baths. All conveniences are provided without the loss of real Woodsy Rustic Charm. Two large motor boats and canoes for the use of guests. Camps are reached by motor boat six miles from Eagle Lake railroad station.

Northern Maine is famous for its cool nights, dry and invigorating atmosphere, laden with health-giving qualities from the pine and balsam forest. Private cabins with baths; also large, spacious dining room and office.

HUNTERS!

For eleven years I have been with these camps. Every hunter who has spent a week to ten days with us has taken his deer allotment home. We have five outside camps in different directions from the main camp. Our camps command 100 square miles of hunting ground.

Eagle Lake is 18 miles long and as deep as 125 feet. Big Fish, Portage and St. Froid Lakes, and all Red River lakes flow into it from one side. Long Lake, Mud Lake, Cross Lake and Square Lake flow into it from the other side. It is screened, and we claim as good early fishing as any place and better Summer fishing than any place for Salmon.

Mrs. Saul Michaud
Director and Manager
EAGLE LAKE, ME.

The camps were proud of their reception area, judging from what they place in their advertisement. They also had all of the modern conveniences by the 1930s, something not everyone had. Those that did have modern facilities, including long-distance telephone, did not hesitate to tell the world about it. This is another facility with outside camps. (From *In the Maine Woods*, 1932.)

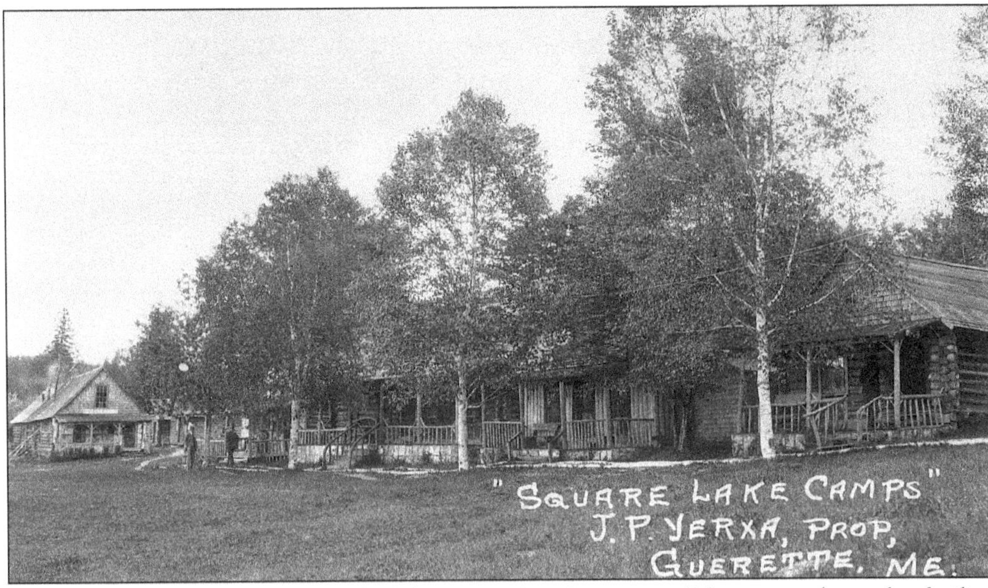

Located at the extreme north end of the state, Yerxa's was a well-known and popular facility. It was on Square Lake, a boat trip from the railroad. Jack Yerxa and his wife, Jennie, ran the camps from about 1912 until Jack Yerxa's death in 1950.

Abundance of Game at Square Lake

Deer, Bear, Partridge and Duck

THE PHOTO BELOW SPEAKS more highly than words. You may rest assured of your legal allowance of game at Square Lake Camps and vicinity. The region is positively unexcelled for hunting as well as fishing and statistics from this section will show that more game is procured in this section than in any other when put on a comparative basis of the number of hunters in the different sections. The country is high, mostly hardwood growth and very open, making easy walking. There are many trails cut through the surrounding woods enabling the hunter to move about without giving the game any warning.

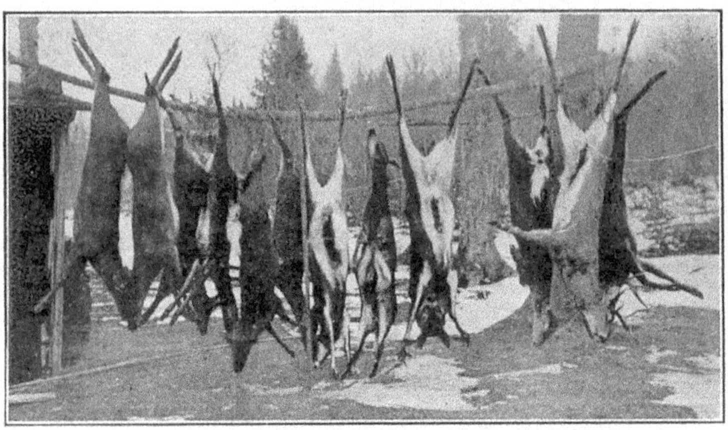

There is no section in New England where game is found more plentiful. Don't be misled, come to Square Lake Camps.

There are two outlying hunting Camps of Big Goddard stream reached by canoe in hunting season.

Yerxa's brochure contains lengthy descriptions of the camps, their patronage, and the offerings of game and fish. This page shows and describes the hunting that is awaiting the sportsmen. The statistics rated this region as one of the very best.

Three

GAME FURRED AND FEATHERED

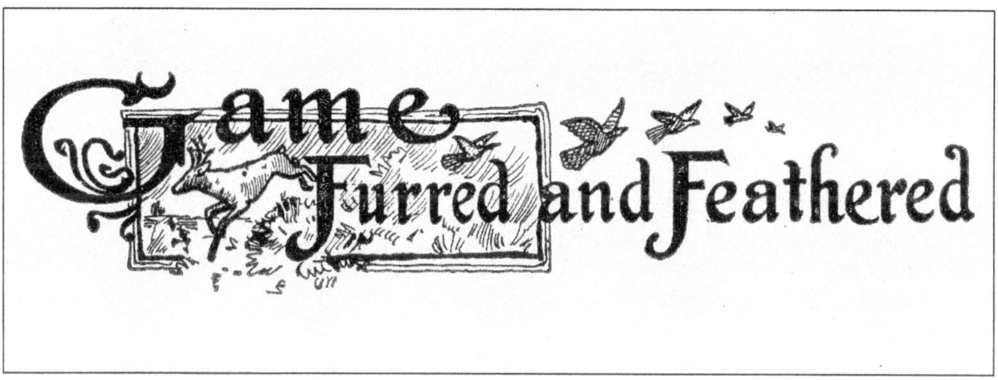

While Maine has generally been promoted as a big game area, and the available literature and photography is spectacular from that standpoint, it also has provided excellent sport and hunting for other types of game animals. Several areas—Down East, parts of Aroostook County, and the farm-forest regions of the central part of the state—provide great upland game shooting. Hunting with dogs, whether for upland game or waterfowl, provides a very rewarding sport. In other areas, with so many small ponds, rivers, and streams, fur-bearing animals are in abundance, and for many years, trappers have made a decent living collecting furs. Early traplines were tended on snowshoes. Today, they are visited by snowmobile and are lengthier and contain more sets than in times past. Trappers used to have temporary housing along their traplines, overnighting in "line camps." Today, they mostly return home at the end of the day. Both the demand for fur and the prices paid are significantly less than they used to be. As a result, there are fewer trappers, resulting in an overabundance of some animals. (From *In the Maine Woods*, 1909.)

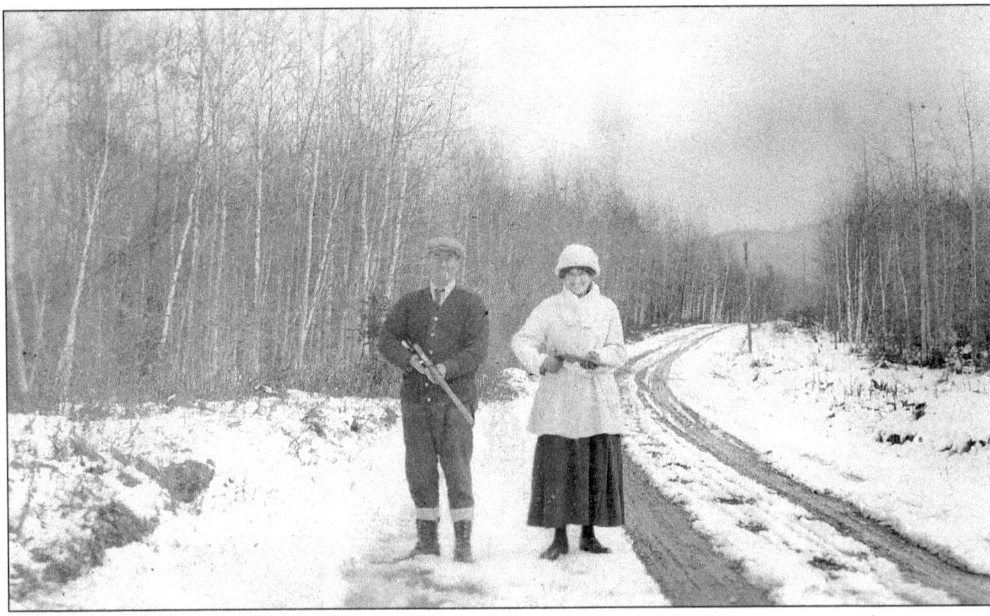

Two hunters take to the tote roads after a recent snowstorm. Tracking is easy, and it is a good time for rabbit hunting. Judging from the background vegetation and the type of guns in this photograph, these folks are probably looking for rabbits, or more accurately, snowshoe hares.

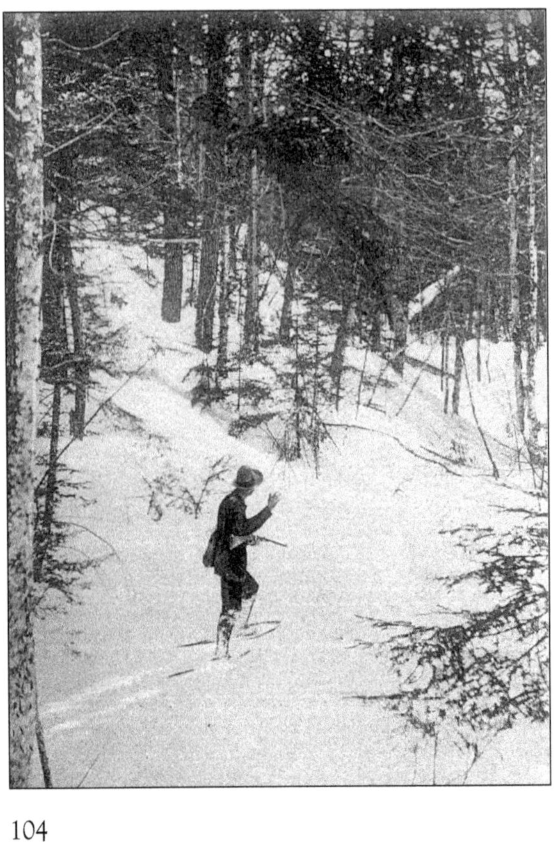

Here is another photograph of a hunter on snowshoes taking advantage of tracking snow. He is ready and expecting to see something emerge from the woods beyond.

V.E. Lynch, of Ashland, is setting out his traps as he travels the waterways in his canoe. He has already taken a fox and a bobcat, two animals he was particularly known for being very successful in getting. Lynch depended on trapping during the winter months, along with his sporting camp operation. (From *In the Maine Woods*, 1930.)

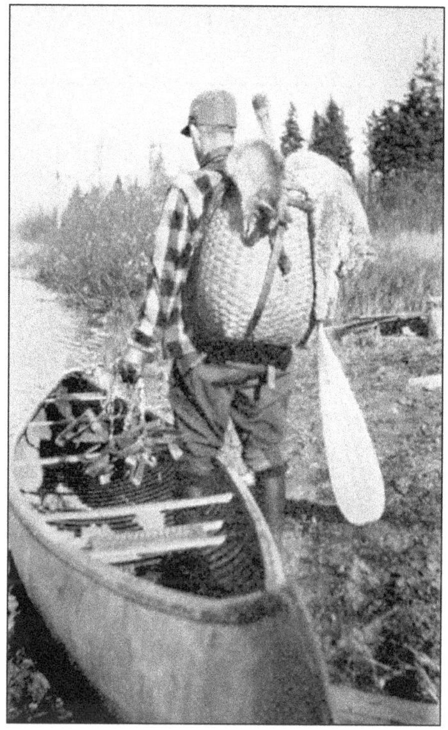

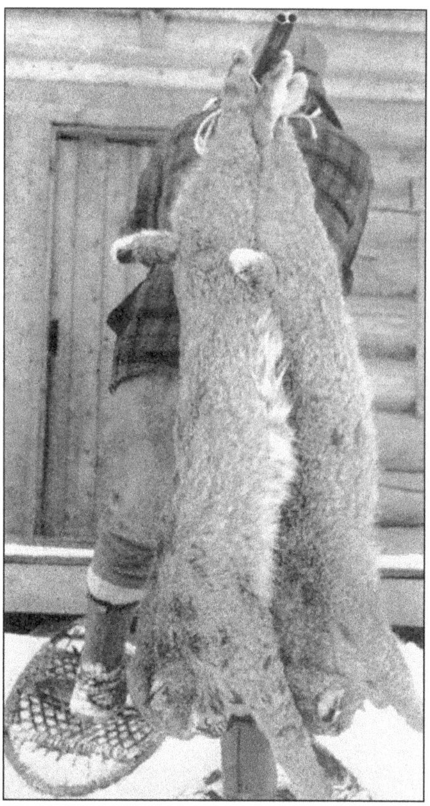

Lynch is back at his camp with two large bobcats. Notice the shotgun over his shoulder, which he used on these cats after they were treed by his hound. He wrote in 1931, "The lynx cat here in Northern Maine grows to weigh 50 pounds and more. They are very destructive to our deer. The writer has known of five deer being killed in one night by a single bobcat. Cat running not only offers good sport to our many sportsmen but killing them saves the lives of many deer." For many years, there was a handsome bounty on bobcat. (From *In the Maine Woods*, 1934.)

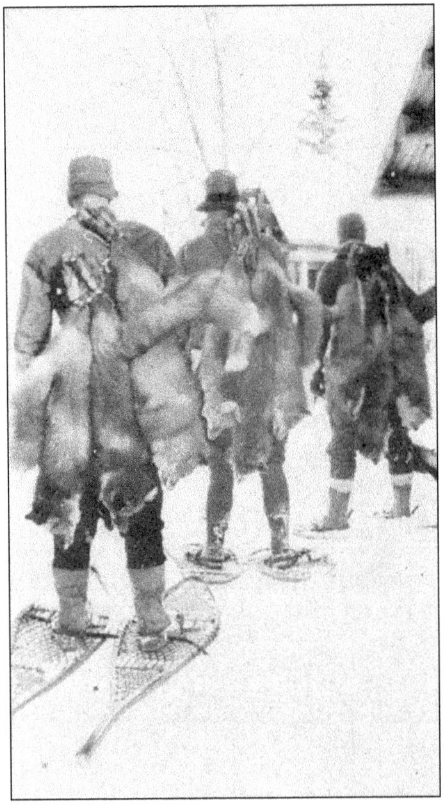

V.E. Lynch and two helpers are running a wilderness trapline. They have obviously been very successful with foxes. The red, gray, and black varieties of foxes have been found in Maine in considerable numbers. (From *In the Maine Woods*, 1931.)

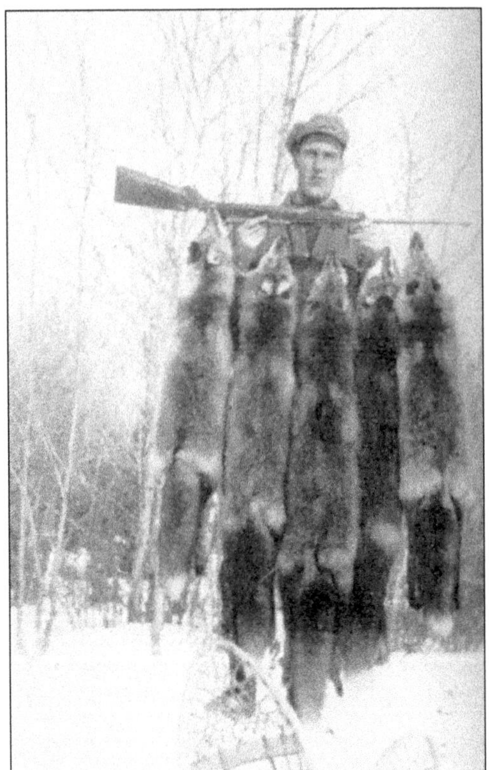

This photograph shows a hunter with his prizes of five prime fox shot in the vicinity of Patten. (From *In the Maine Woods*, 1934.)

This photograph, taken by Lynch, shows hunters with bobcats and one of the dogs used to chase them. Lynch wrote, "Bobcat running, with the aid of dogs and on snowshoes, makes excellent winter sport." (From *In the Maine Woods*, 1934.)

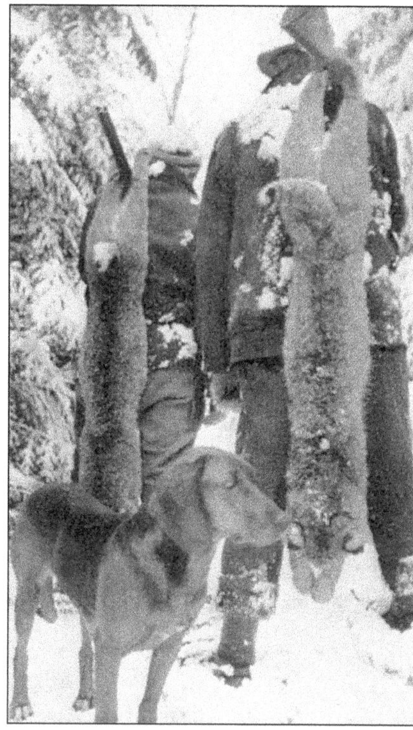

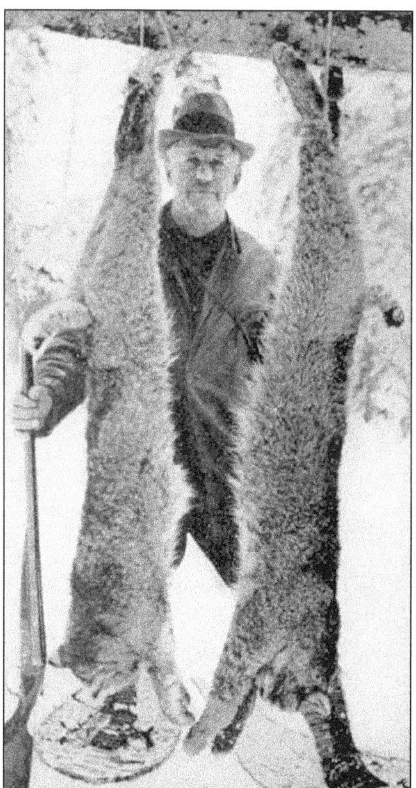

Lynch poses here with two huge bobcats that he bagged ahead of his hound. Although he wrote of long shots with high-powered rifles to get bobcats, most of his photographs show hunters with shotguns such as this one. (From *In the Maine Woods*, 1935.)

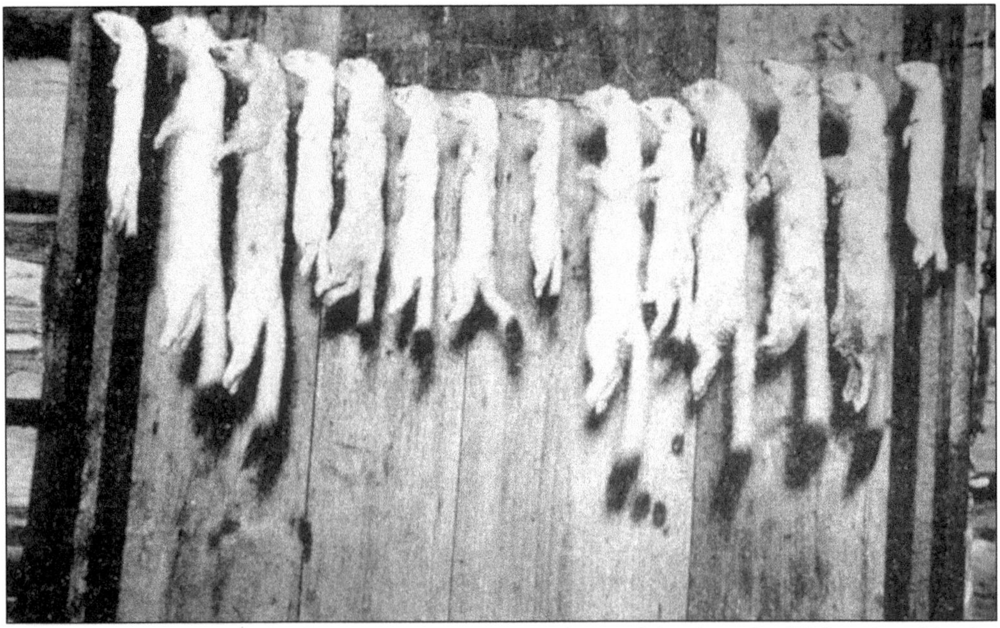

Shown here is a fine catch of Maine ermine, or weasel, prized for their fur. Walter Arnold, who was likely the trapper of these animals, took this photograph. (From *In the Maine Woods*, 1935.)

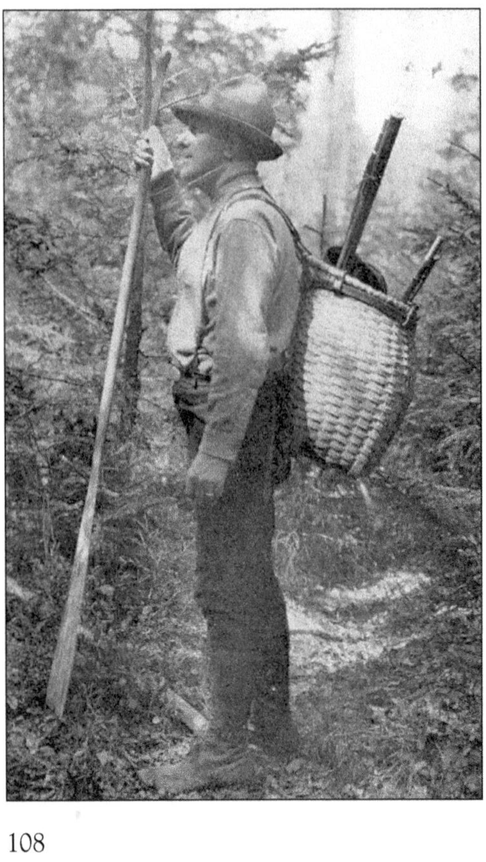

Walter L. Arnold was another famous trapper, who was well known for his books on trapping techniques and his mail-order sales of all sorts of trapping supplies that included animal scents. Born in 1894, Arnold grew up in the Sebec-Katahdin Iron Works Region, was superintendent of the Borestone Fish Hatchery 1917–1918, and was one of the original founders of the Maine Trappers Association. He served as its president, secretary, and treasurer. He hunted, trapped, and guided with his father, who was a market hunter in the 1870s, when such was legal. (From *In the Maine Woods*, 1930.)

In 1959, Arnold sold his business and went back into the woods to live at a location where the only way in or out was to fly or go by snowmobile during the winter. His wife having died in 1968, Arnold lived alone in this fashion until his illness in 1980, when he died. Walter was nationally known, having published articles in such places as the *Boston Globe* and *National Geographic*. For the last 10 years of his life, he was known as the "Dean of Mountain Men." Shown here is a trapper's cabin similar to what Walter Arnold lived in for more than 20 years.

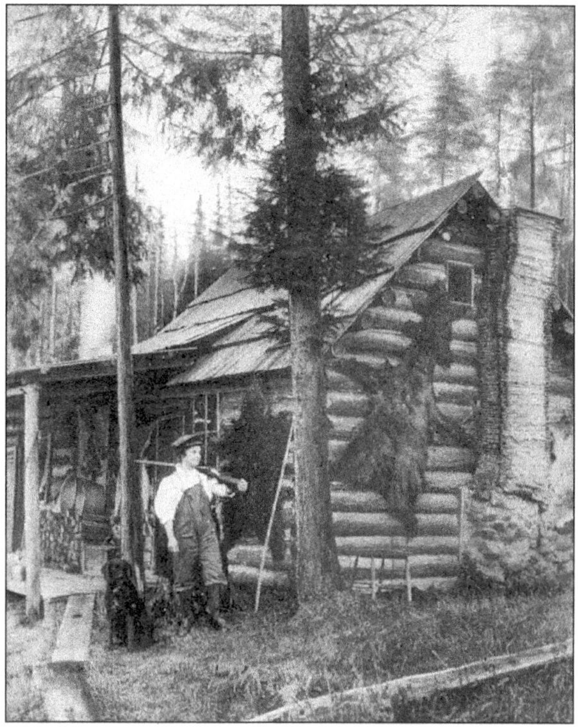

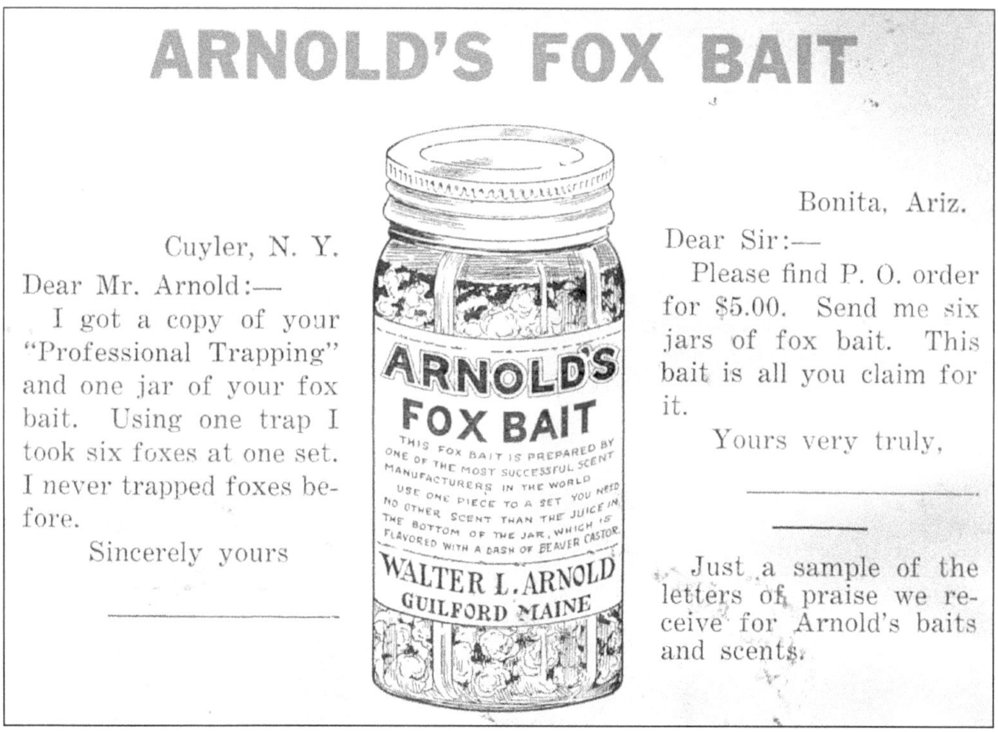

Here is an advertisement from Arnold's brochure *Trapping Equipment, Season 1937–38*. He is believed to be the first man to advertise and market lure-making ingredients, and his catalog was sent across the country. (Steve Rainsford collection.)

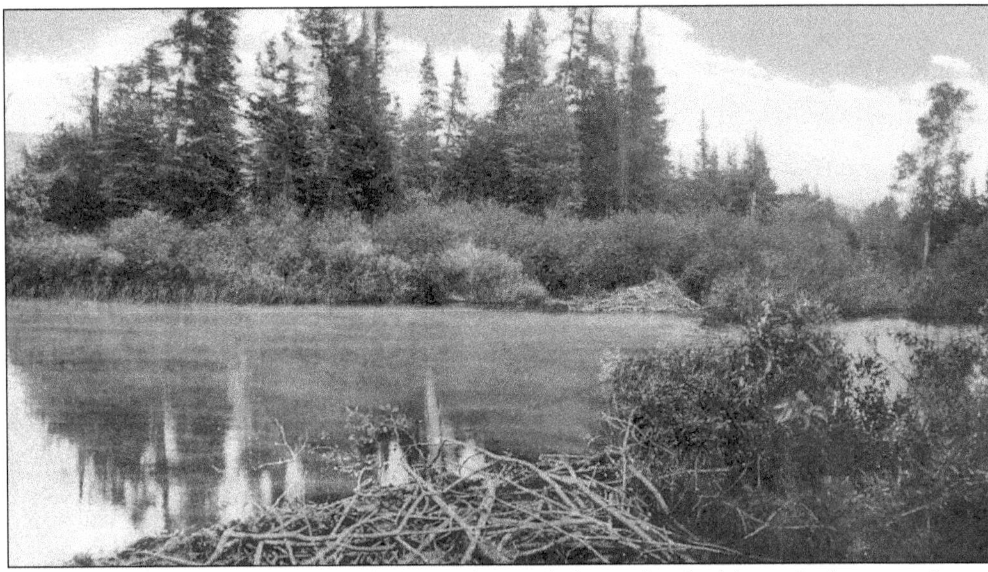

This is what the beaver trapper looks for—a beaver lodge with a freshly made dam, signifying a family of beavers for him to trap. Beavers were trapped so heavily nationwide in the 1800s that, by 1900, they were nearly extinct. Protected and stocked in many areas, they are now extremely abundant. Since they are no longer heavily trapped, beavers have become a nuisance in many areas by plugging up culverts, felling trees, and creating unwanted flooding. However, their fresh ponds provide great habitat for waterfowl and trout.

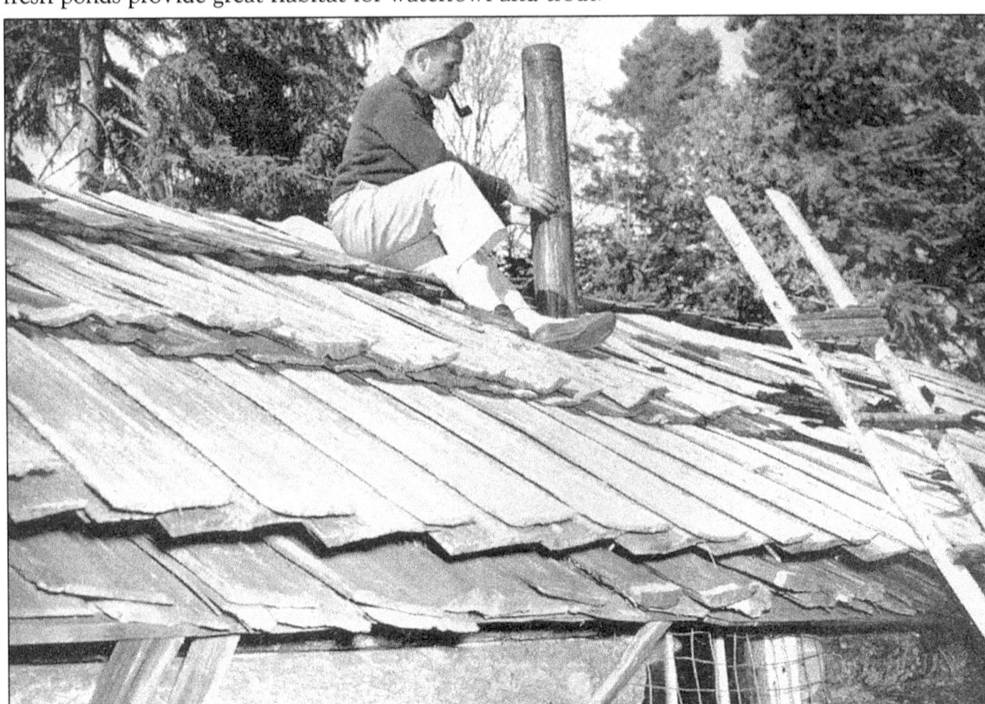

Here is a trapper's cabin located at Allagash Lake. The owner is providing yearly maintenance, this time to the stovepipe, an item needing frequent attention. Note the wire in the window to discourage bears. (From *In the Maine Woods*, 1952.)

The Howe Fur Company, established in 1918, was well known nationwide for its supplies and services. Its 1951 catalog was 72 pages and offered hunting and trapping supplies—from clothing and footwear to taxidermy supplies, guns, and canoes.

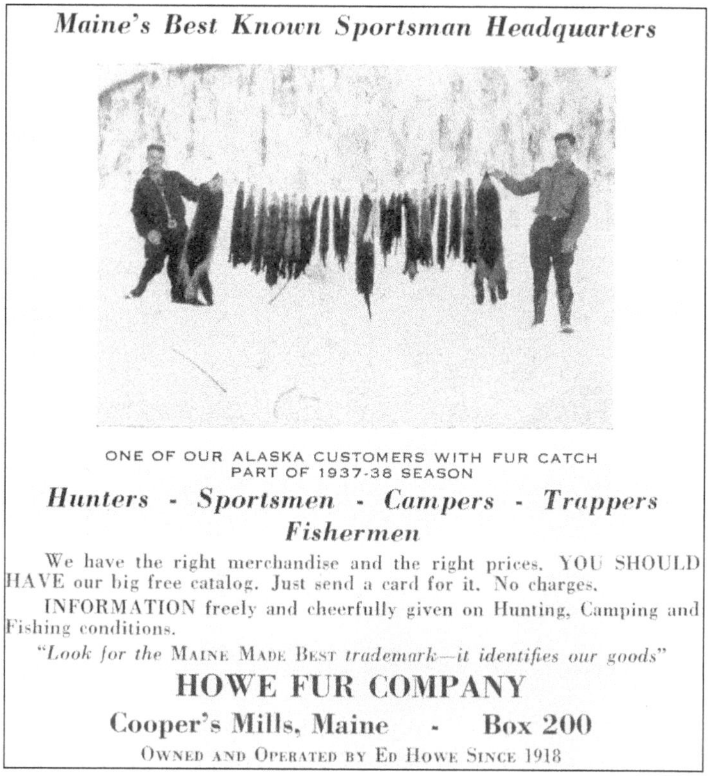

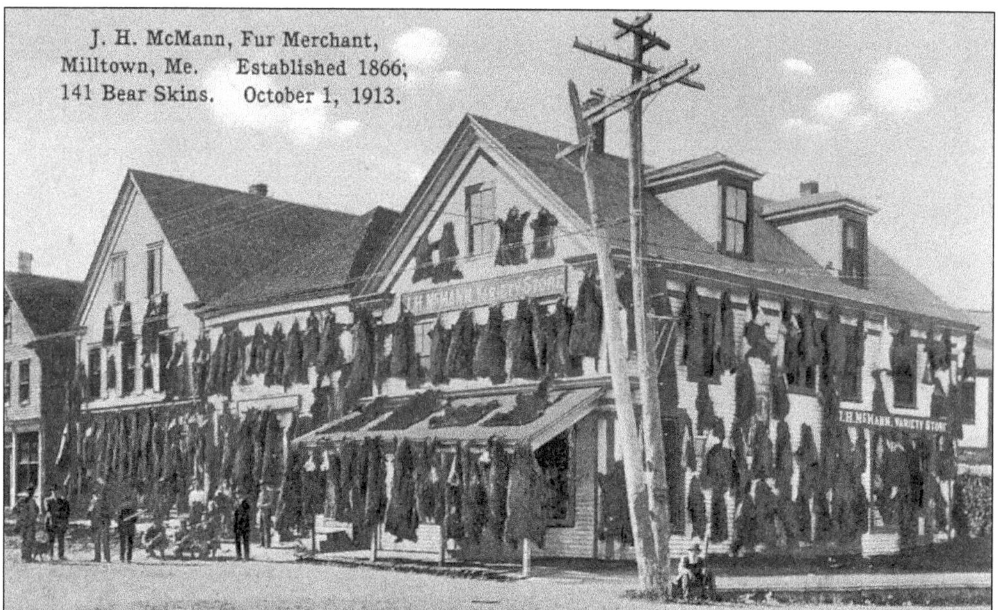

Another major fur dealer and trader was the McMann Company in Milltown. Located on the Canadian border, it was established in 1866, right after the Civil War. In this picture, the company displays 141 bear hides, demonstrating how abundant this animal was, at least in this area *c.* 1913.

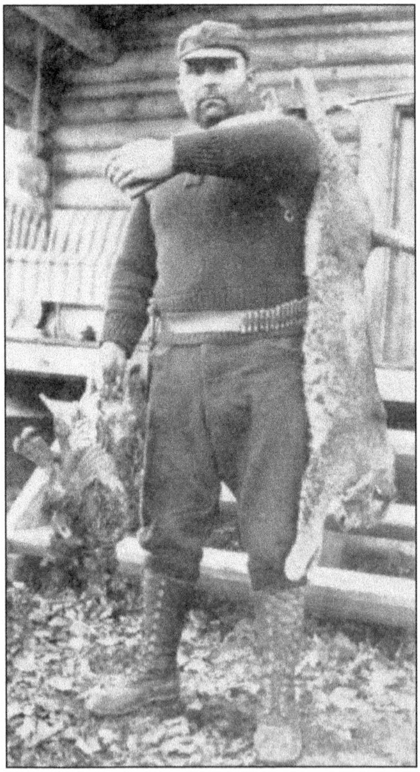

John Mechalick of Jonrac, New York, is shown here with a huge bobcat that he bagged while hunting grouse in Aroostook County. (From *In the Maine Woods*, 1933.)

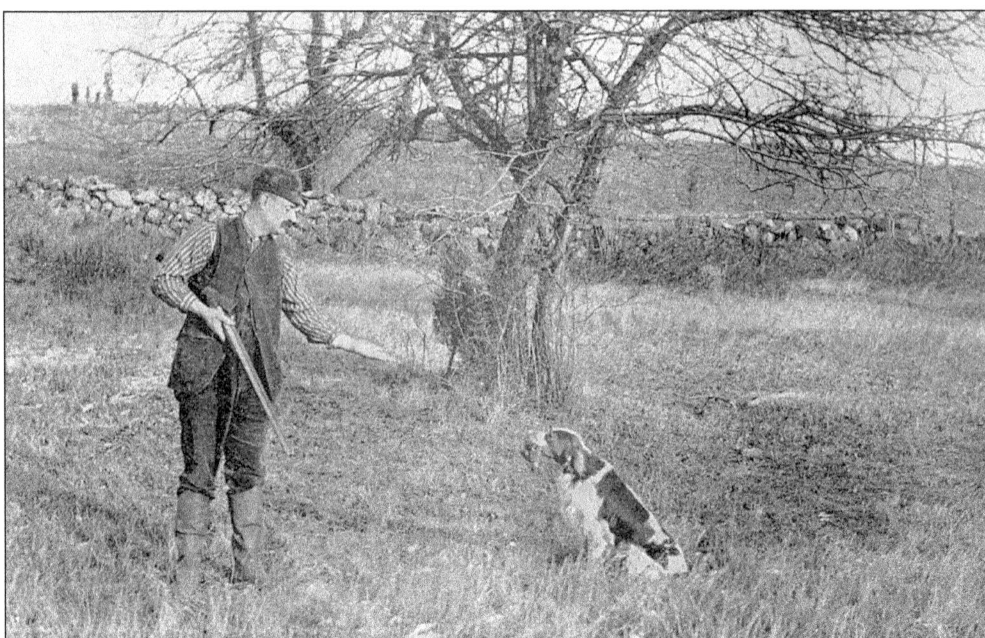

This spaniel has just retrieved a bird for the hunter. Upland bird hunting is a great sport and particularly enjoyable with a good bird dog. Not only do dogs help the hunter locate game, but they are also especially helpful in retrieving downed birds, minimizing the amount of lost game. (From *The Maine Central*, October 1896.)

Here a sportsman poses with his day's bag of ruffed grouse, while his partner checks his shotgun. In the great north woods, it was reported there were thousands of partridges, or ruffed grouse (also called birch partridge), and spruce partridge (also called Canadian ruffed grouse). It was said that "for the man with the shotgun these birds furnish unequalled sport, but hundreds of partridges are killed with the rifle." (From *In the Maine Woods*, 1932.)

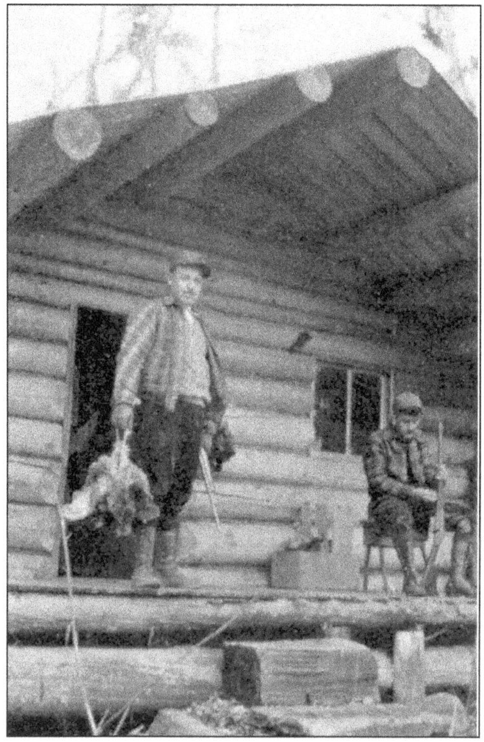

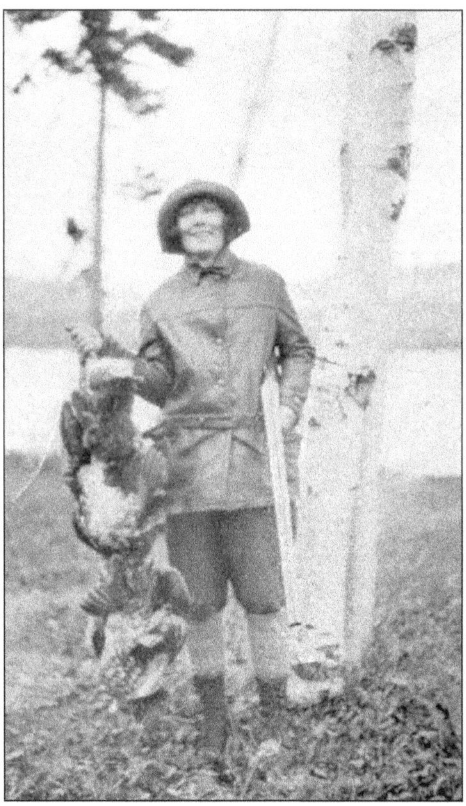

Mrs. P.S. Lewis of Laurel Springs, New Jersey, has just returned to camp with her bag of partridges. (From *In the Maine Woods*, 1930.)

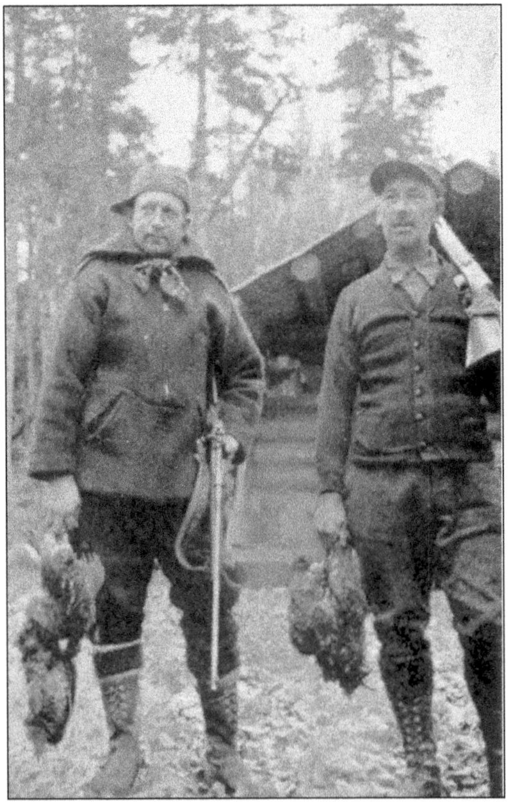

In this photograph, J. Baron and John Probaska of New York City are shown with their daily limit of grouse. Note the heads clipped from the body, as these birds were shot with high-powered rifles. V.E. Lynch wrote that "bird-shooting with a rifle makes good sport; seldom does a real hunter use a shot gun on them." He was referring to northern Maine. (From *In the Maine Woods*, 1935.)

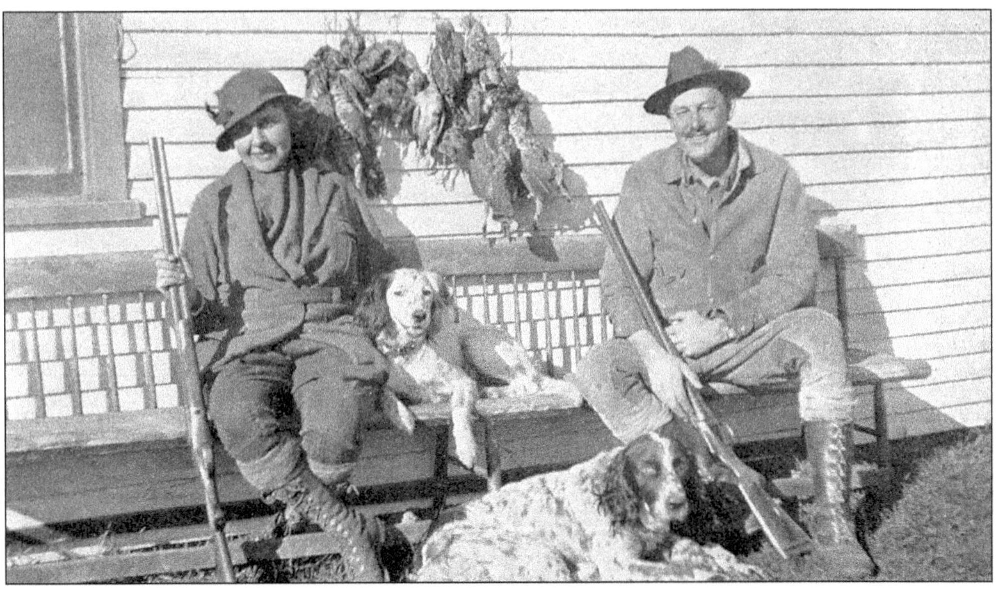

Mr. and Mrs. C. Blackburn Miller pose with their able assistants and an impressive bag of grouse and woodcock. It was advertised that partridge shooting and woodcock hunting was a premier form of sport in the Maine woods. (From *In the Maine Woods*, 1937.)

Two dogs anxiously await their hunter to join them in the field. A well-trained bird dog can add a great deal to the sport and make pursuit of game even more enjoyable.

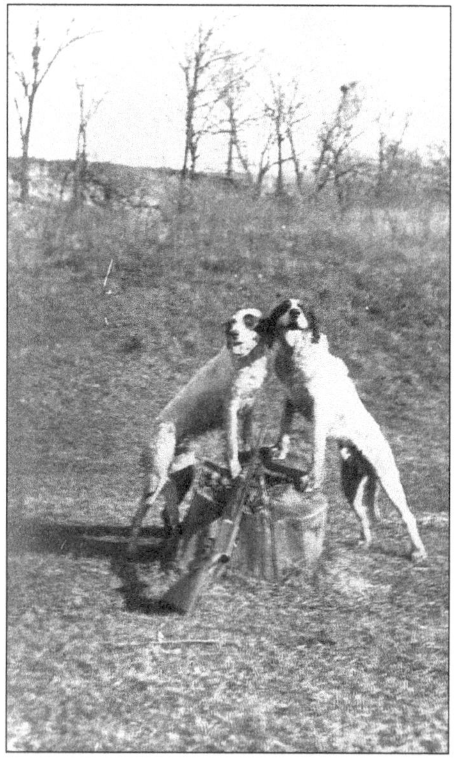

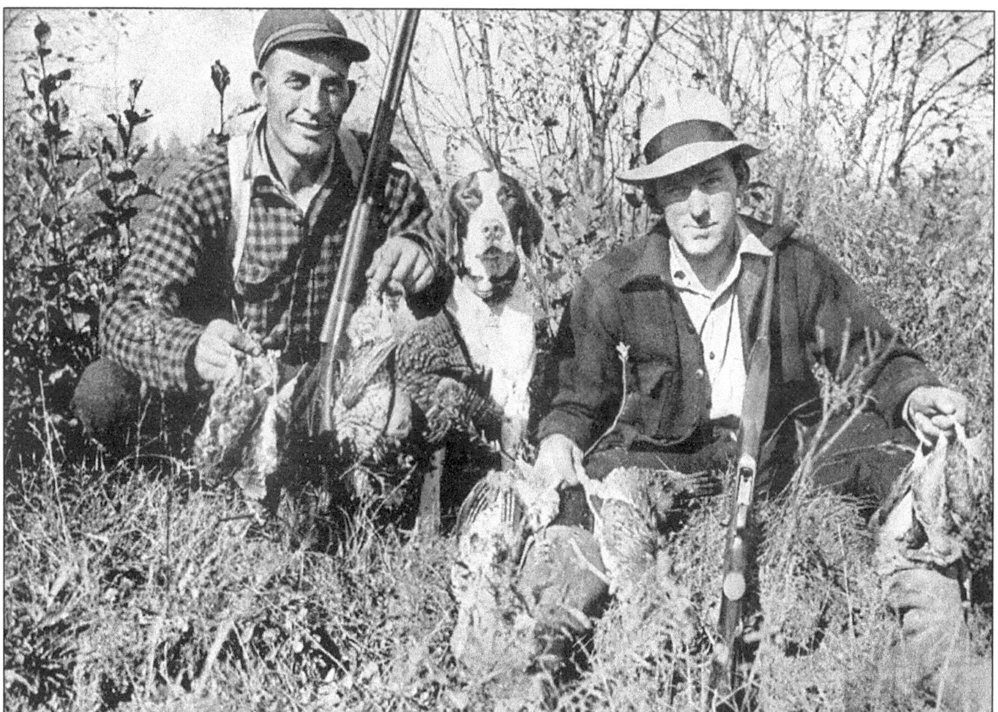

Two hunters with their dog show a huge bag of grouse and woodcock. This photograph was taken in the Mars Hill Region. (From *In the Maine Woods*, 1942.)

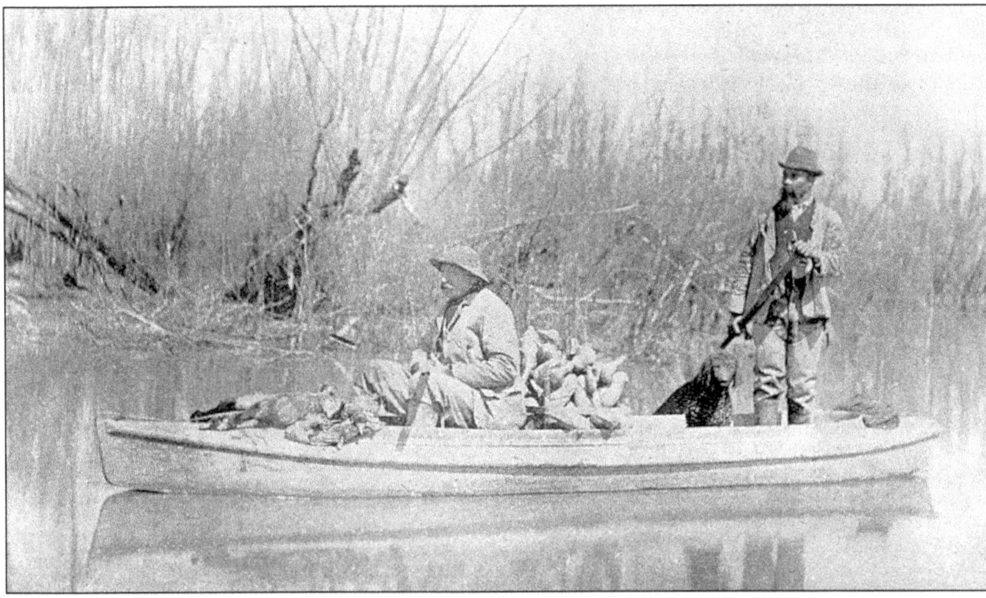

Here the guide paddles a sneak boat, while the hunter carefully watches for waterfowl. In front of the hunter is a pile of ducks, while in back of him are piled decoys, either set earlier or to be set later, to lure birds within shooting range. The dog sits patiently, awaiting the next retrieve. Close examination reveals that it has already been in the water. (From *The Maine Central*, October 1896.)

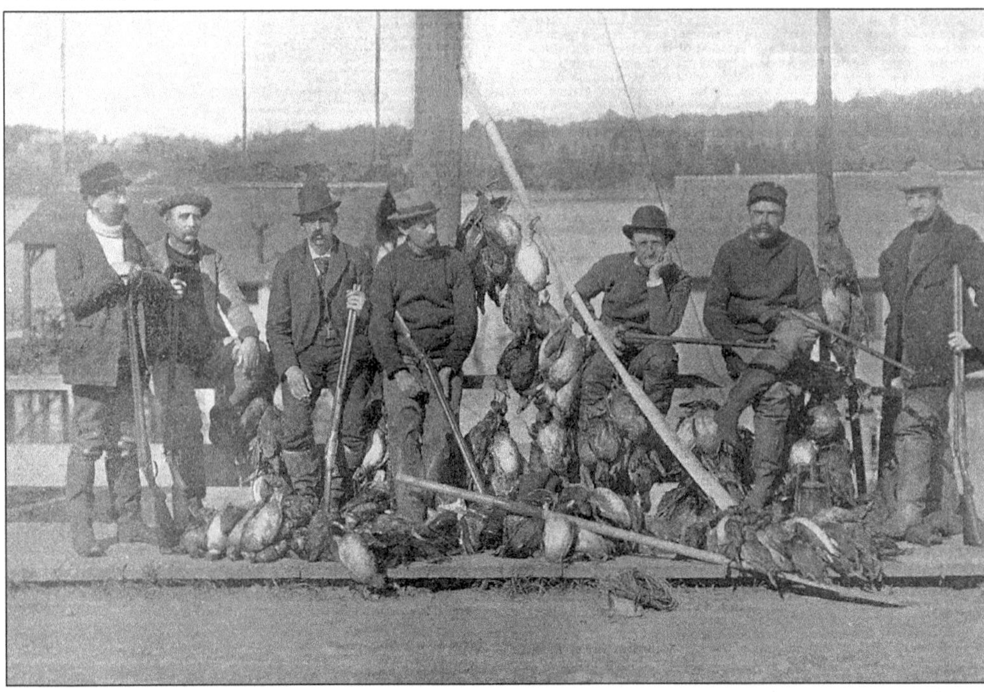

Hunting sea ducks off the coast is a different type of gunning. It provides great sport during the latter part of the season, when inland waters become frozen over and the birds move out. Larger bag limits are placed on sea ducks because of their abundance, even today. Here a group of hunters shows off the day's shoot. (From *The Maine Central*, October 1896.)

Four

Promotion and Advertisement

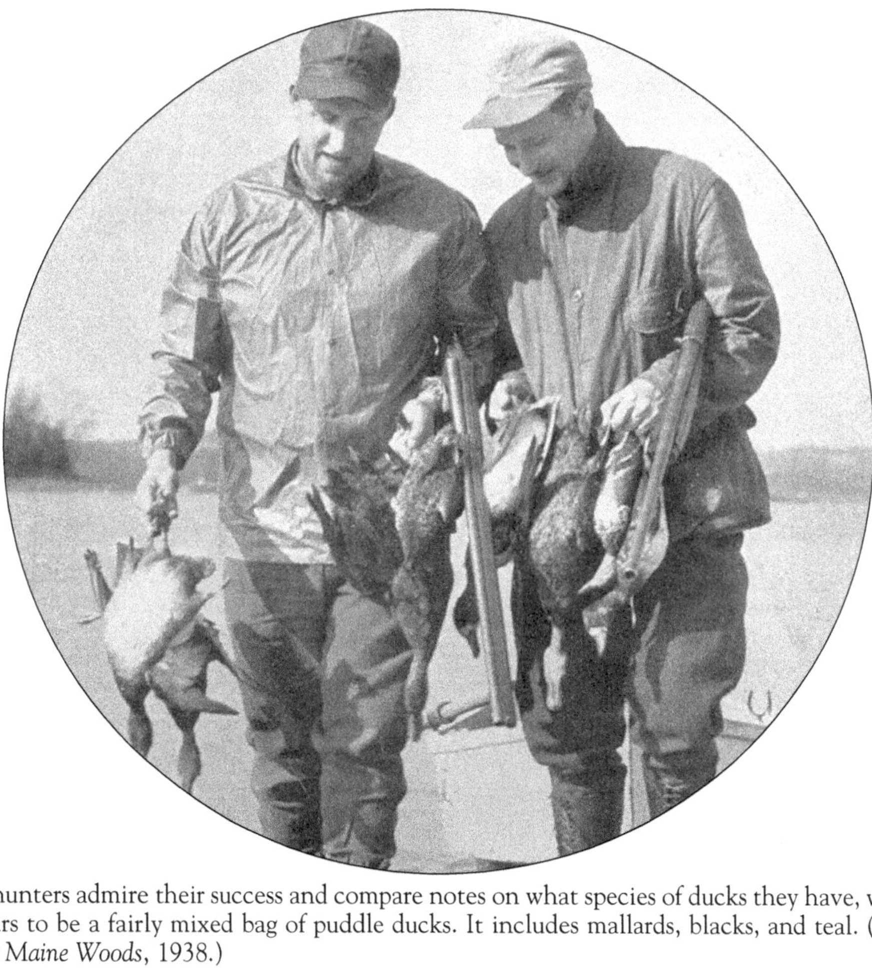

Two hunters admire their success and compare notes on what species of ducks they have, which appears to be a fairly mixed bag of puddle ducks. It includes mallards, blacks, and teal. (From *In the Maine Woods*, 1938.)

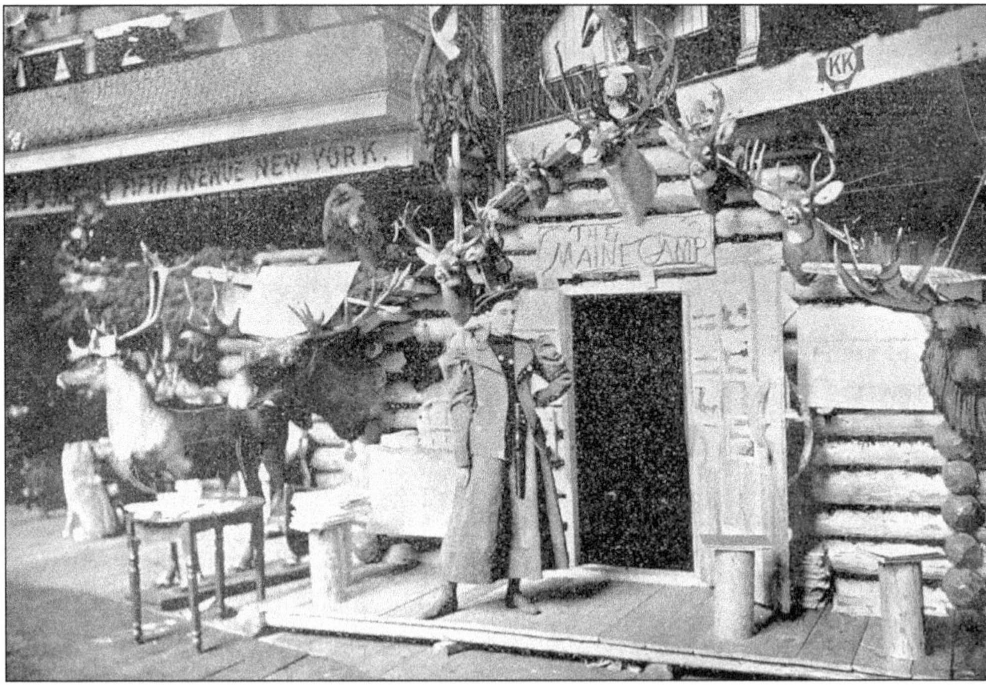

Cornelia Thurza Crosby, otherwise known as "Fly Rod" Crosby, was a great promoter of the state of Maine. In fact, she pushed for statewide guide registration and was awarded license No. 1 in 1897. Here, she represents the state in a special booth she designed for the Sportsmen's Show held in New York City in March 1896. They had far more visitors than they anticipated and, in later years, expanded upon their display. Well-known taxidermist and close friend Sumner L. Crosby provided the wildlife specimens. (From *The Maine Central*, May 1896.)

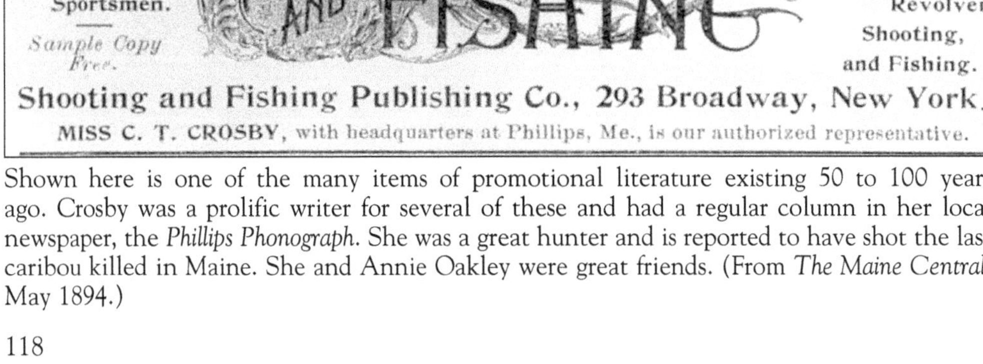

Shown here is one of the many items of promotional literature existing 50 to 100 years ago. Crosby was a prolific writer for several of these and had a regular column in her local newspaper, the *Phillips Phonograph*. She was a great hunter and is reported to have shot the last caribou killed in Maine. She and Annie Oakley were great friends. (From *The Maine Central*, May 1894.)

There were many regularly published magazines during the 20th century that promoted sporting pursuits, particularly hunting. Many of them centered on Maine or at least included Maine locations. Today, many of these are highly sought by collectors, while at least a few titles still remain in publication on a regular basis. V.E. Lynch of Ashland, well-known guide, trapper, and sporting camp owner, was editor of *National Sportsman*. (From *In the Maine Woods*, 1922.)

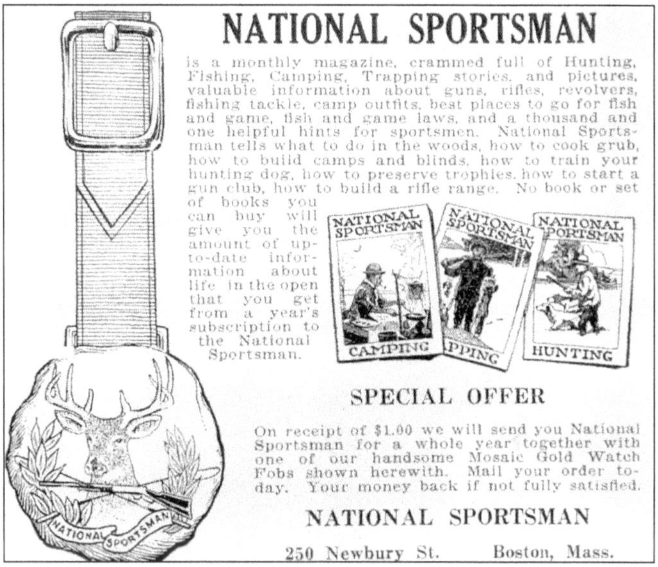

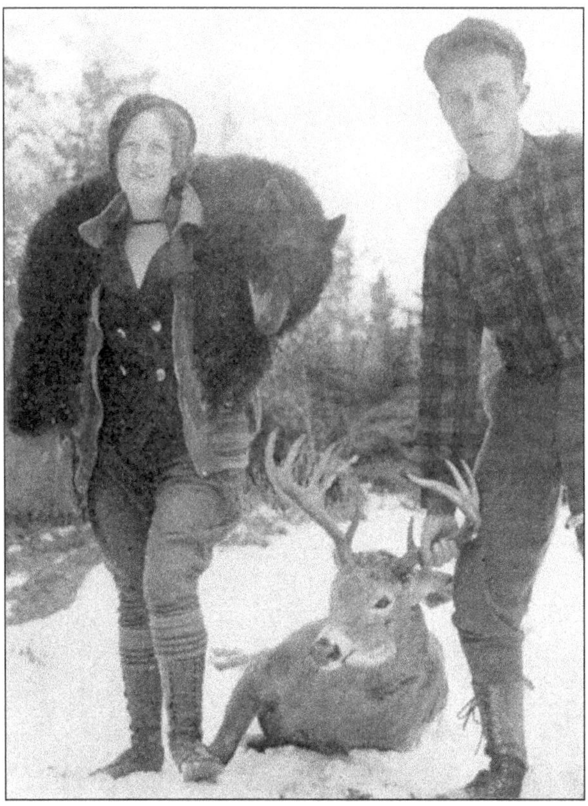

Fur, Fish & Game has long been a regular publication, covering many aspects of outdoor sports. Here, both Harding, the founder of the magazine, and his wife demonstrate that they know first-hand what they print. They were regular visitors to the northern Maine woods. (From *In the Maine Woods*, 1935.)

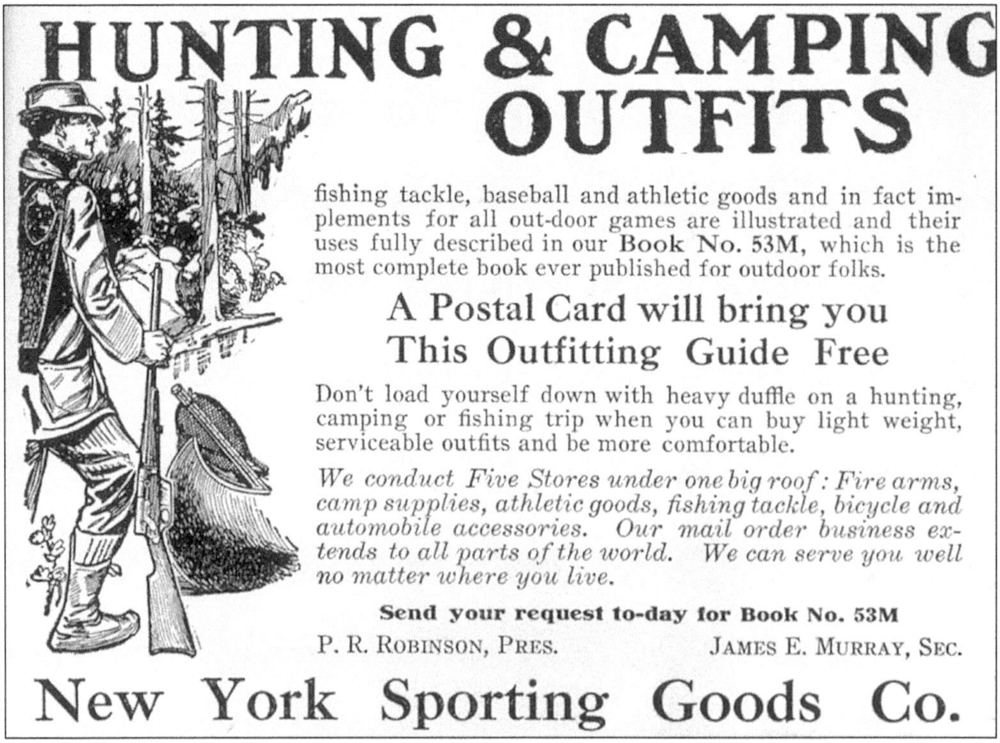

Outfitters were very important to sportsmen, particularly the hunter. Unlike the fisherman, game must be processed and the meat and hides must be taken care of. Hunting also requires a lot more gear, warm clothes, and supplies not necessary for the average angler. There were many shops located in popular hunting areas, but many people preferred to take advantage of mail order. (From *In the Maine Woods*, 1912.)

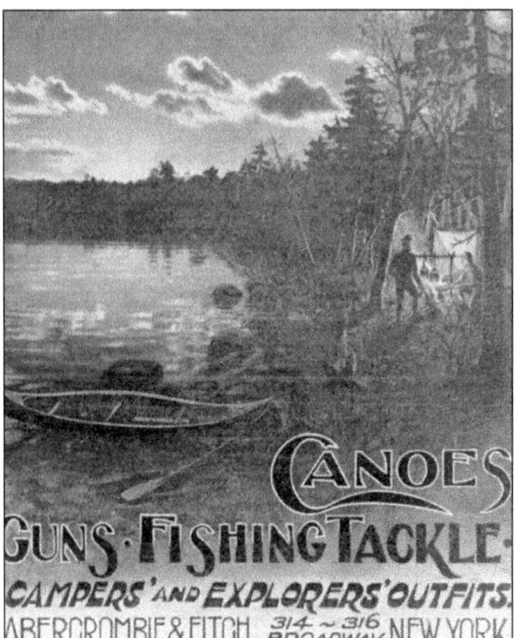

David Abercrombie, who was a trapper, prospector, and railroad surveyor, founded the famous outfitter Abercrombie & Fitch in 1892. One of his best customers, a lawyer named Ezra Fitch, who would rather hike the Adirondacks and flyfish mountain streams, joined him in a partnership that lasted just seven years. Abercrombie resigned and Fitch ran the business until his retirement in 1928. Today, Abercrombie & Fitch remains an active sporting-goods business in downtown New York City, having the reputation of supplying notables like Teddy Roosevelt, Ernest Hemingway, Amelia Earhart, and Presidents Taft, Harding, and Kennedy. (From *In the Maine Woods*, 1903.)

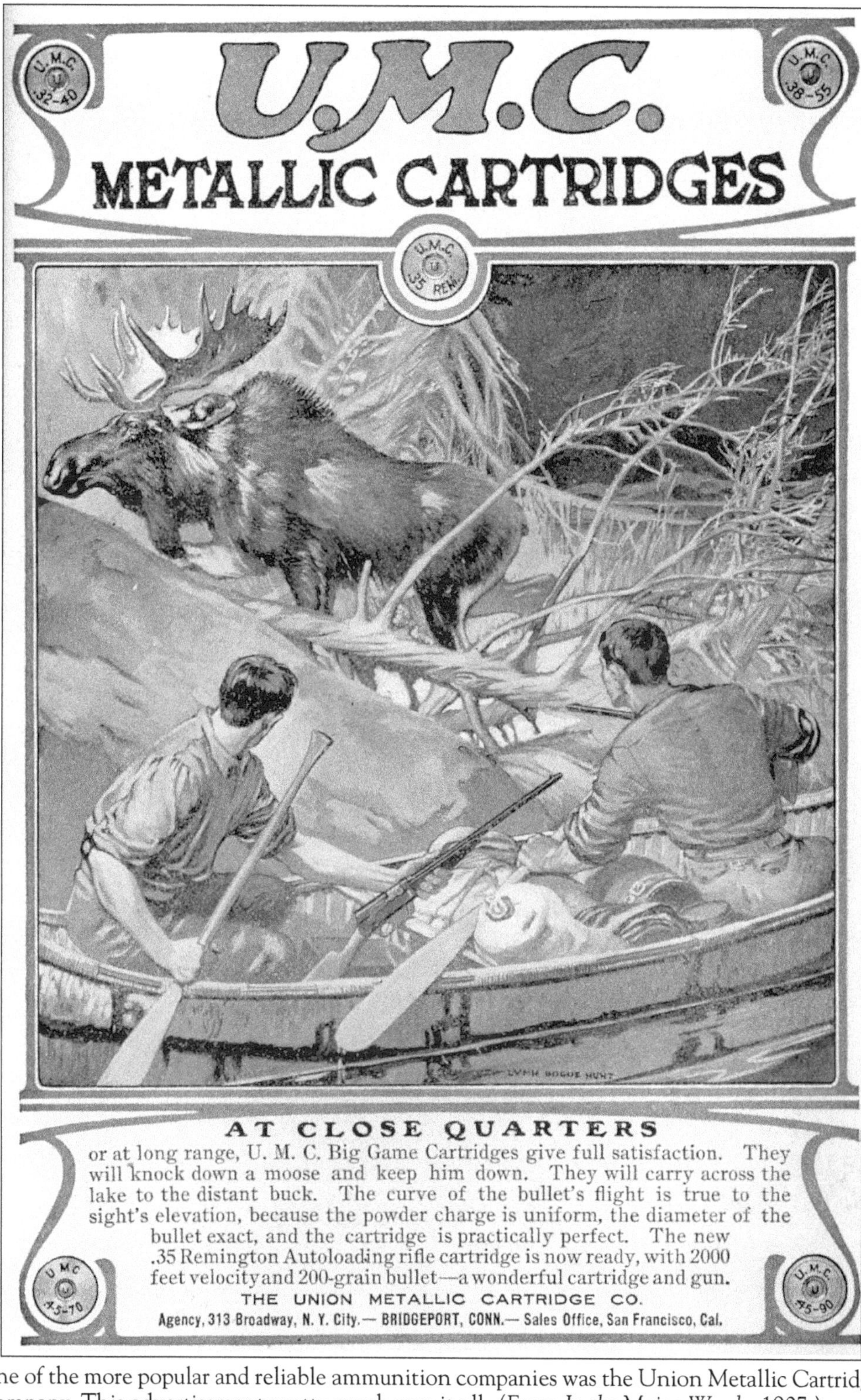

One of the more popular and reliable ammunition companies was the Union Metallic Cartridge Company. This advertisement pretty much says it all. (From *In the Maine Woods*, 1907.)

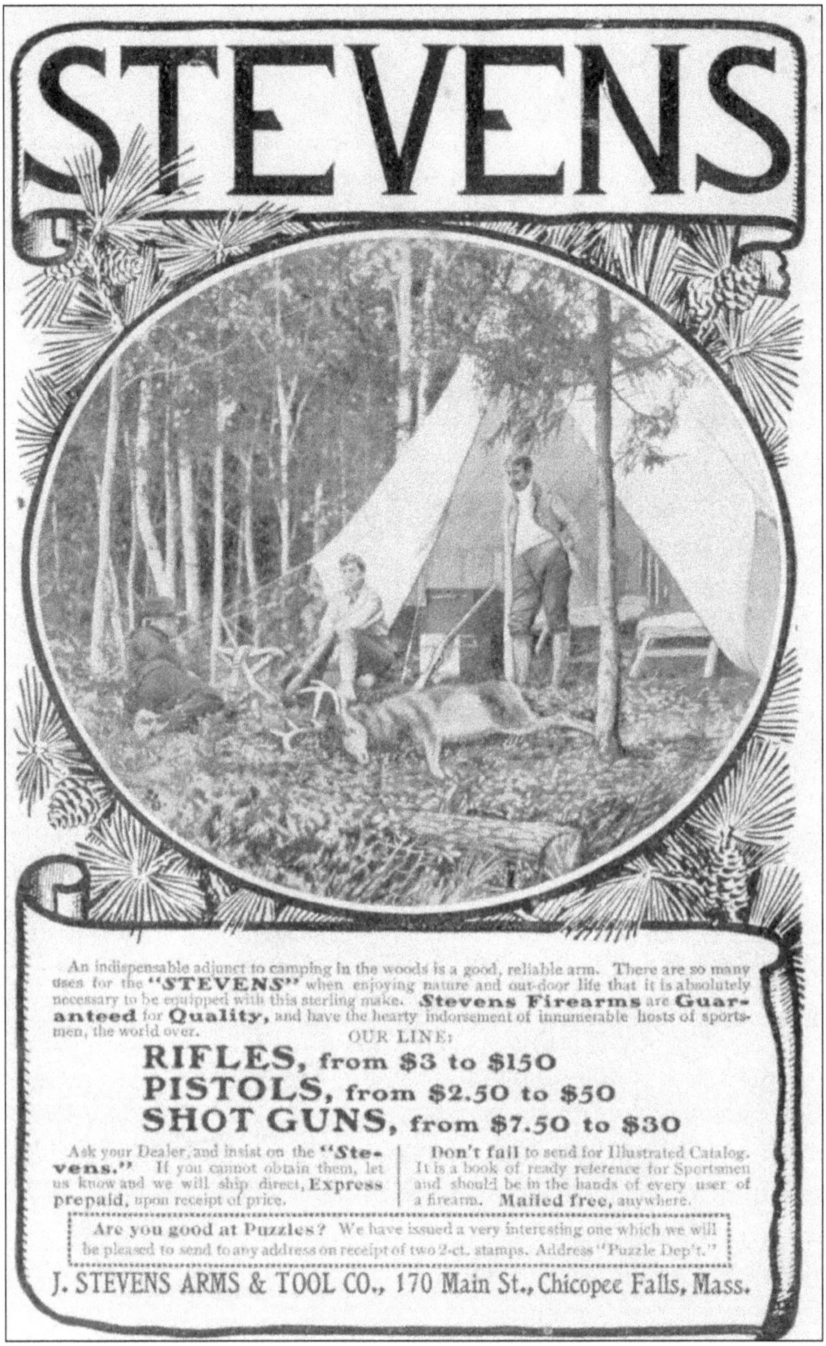

The Stevens Company produced a variety of firearms. It is a safe bet that most of the rifles shown in the foregoing photographs are either Winchester or Stevens rifles. For years, hunters debated about the best rifle for hunting in Maine, whether the .30-30 caliber or larger, even up to a popular caliber such as .45-70. As time went on, the lighter weapon seemed to have won out. They were light and easy to carry, yet large enough to do effective work at all times. Some people just preferred the heavier firepower, especially for animals like large moose and caribou. Shotguns were preferred for smaller game and birds. (From *In the Maine Woods*, 1904.)

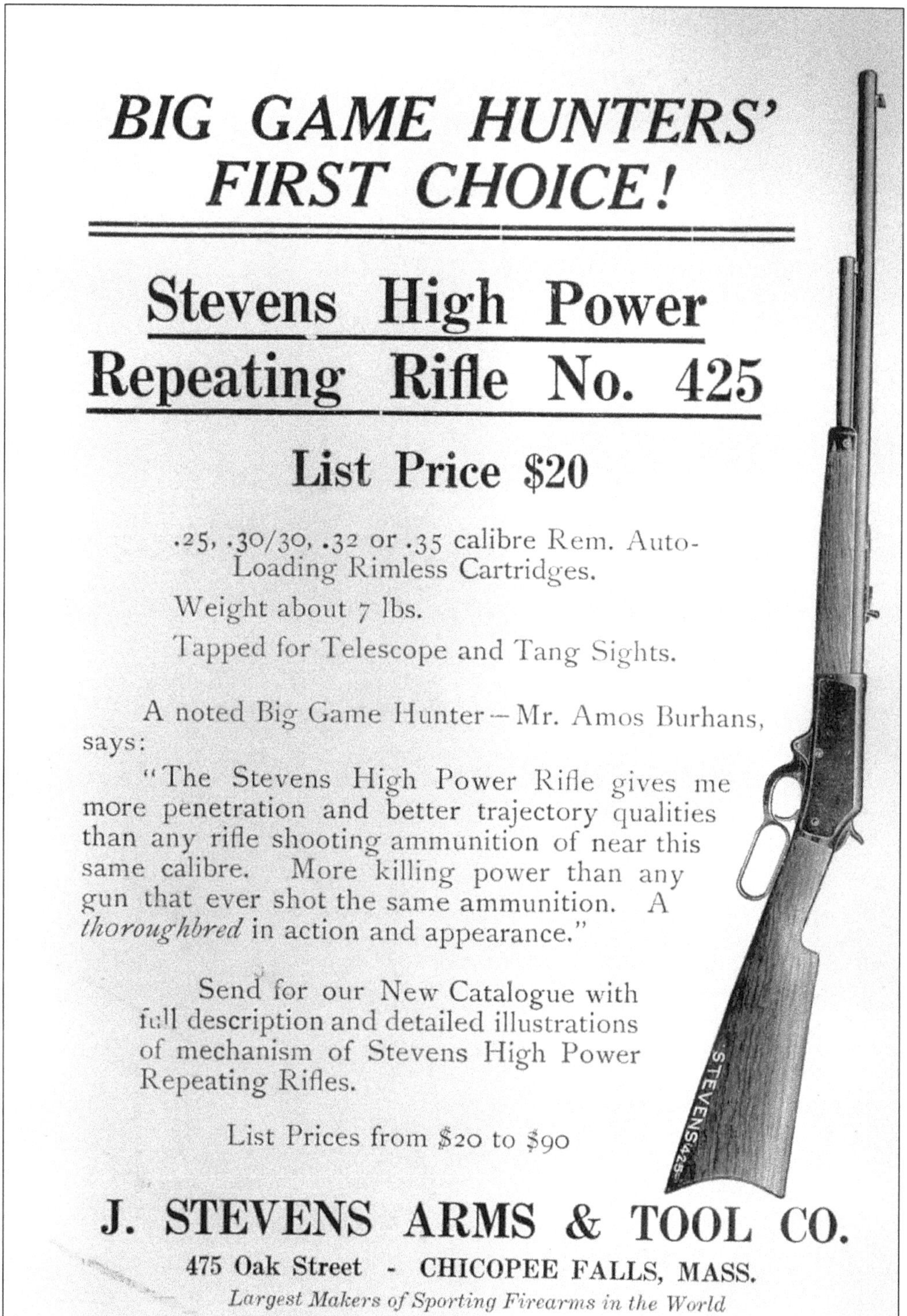

Here is a prime example of the Stevens lever-action rifle, perhaps chosen by more big game hunters than any other (with the possible exception of the Winchester). Even as early as 1912, this rifle was available in a range of calibers. (From *In the Maine Woods*, 1912.)

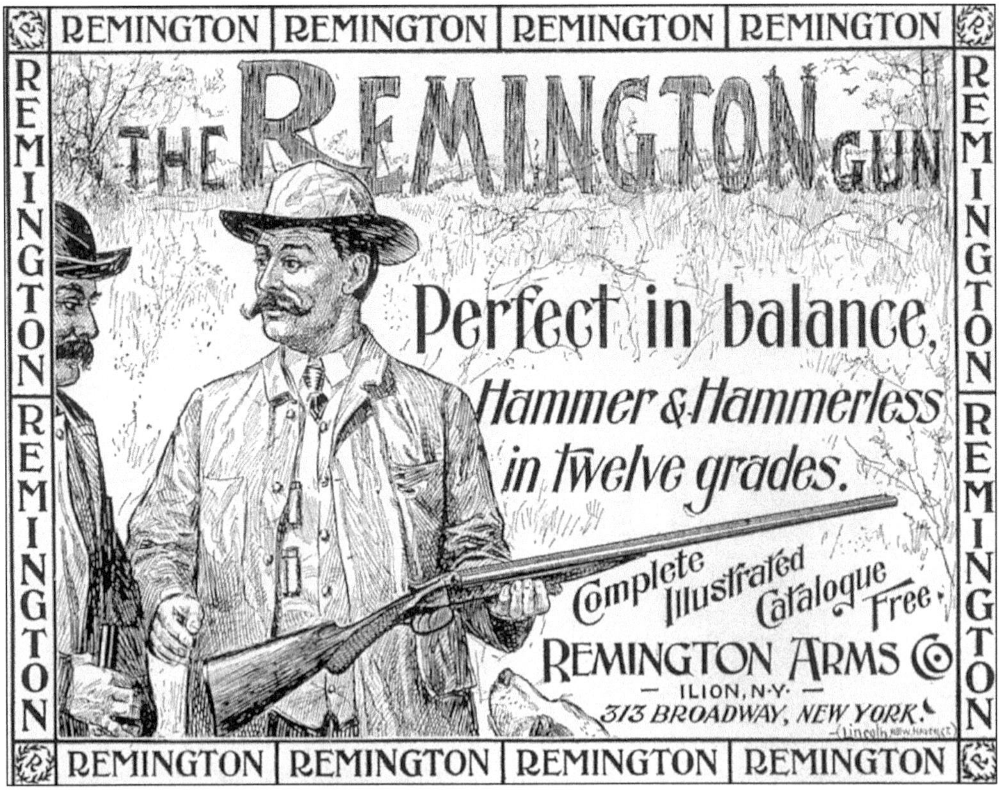

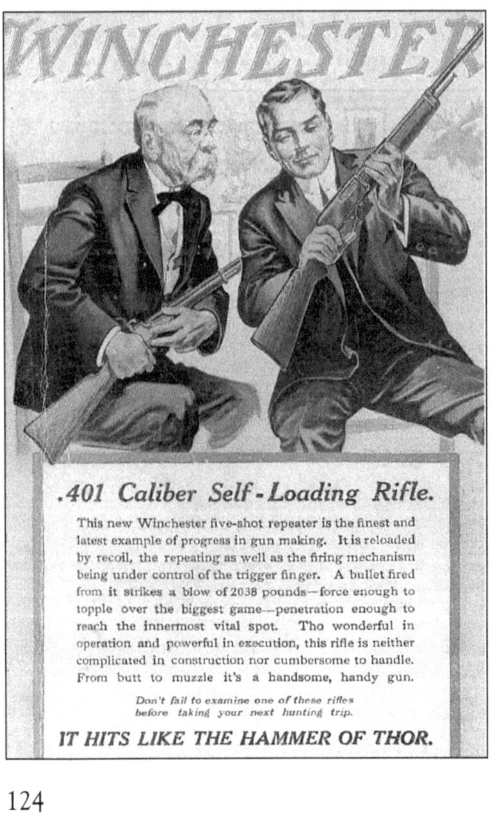

Another arms manufacturer, Remington Arms, was also very popular, particularly for bolt-action rifles and shotguns. There is no doubt among bird hunters that what they say here is true, Remington shotguns have great balance. (From *In the Maine Woods*, 1900.)

No treatment would be complete without a word about Winchester, probably the most famous of all the firearm manufacturers. Winchester rifles were common in the "Old West" and were standard issue for many of the U.S. Army companies. Winchester .45-caliber rifles and saddle carbines were among the most commonly found. Winchester rifles found their way into the Maine hunters' hands in popular calibers of .38-55, .44-40, and .45-70. (From *In the Maine Woods*, 1912.)

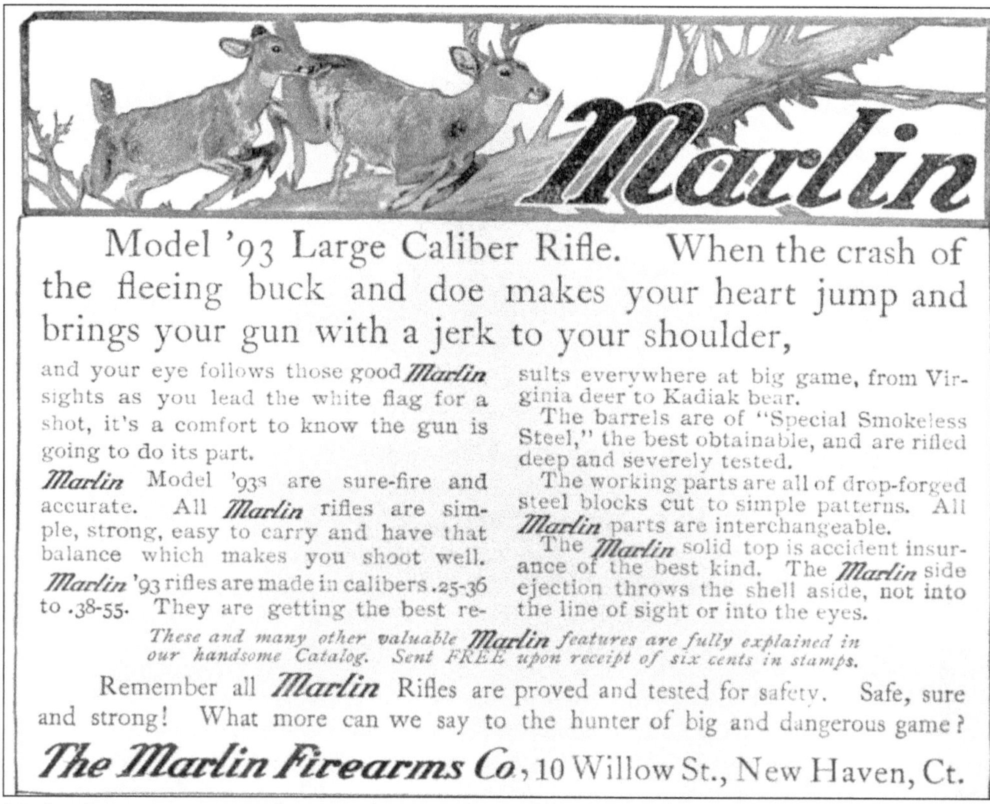

Marlin firearms were another popular item favored by many. The model '93 was highly sought and became as popular as some of the Winchester models, the '76 model included. (From *In the Maine Woods*, 1907.)

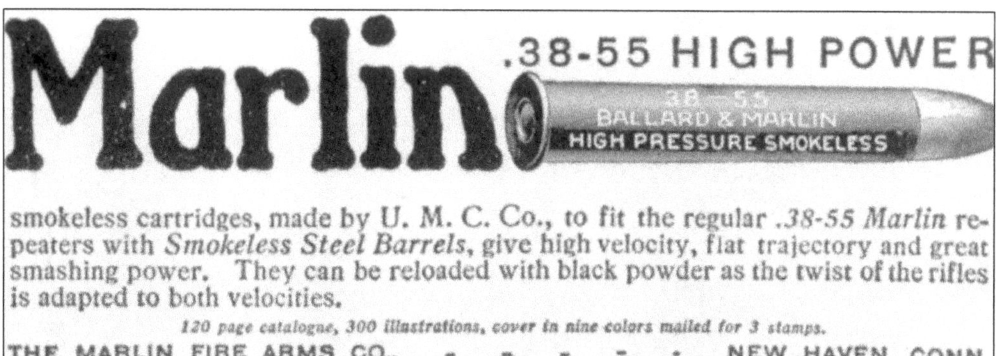

Marlin Firearms also produced ammunition for its rifles. At this time, smokeless cartridges became popular, and those producing them advertised them heavily. (From *In the Maine Woods*, 1903.)

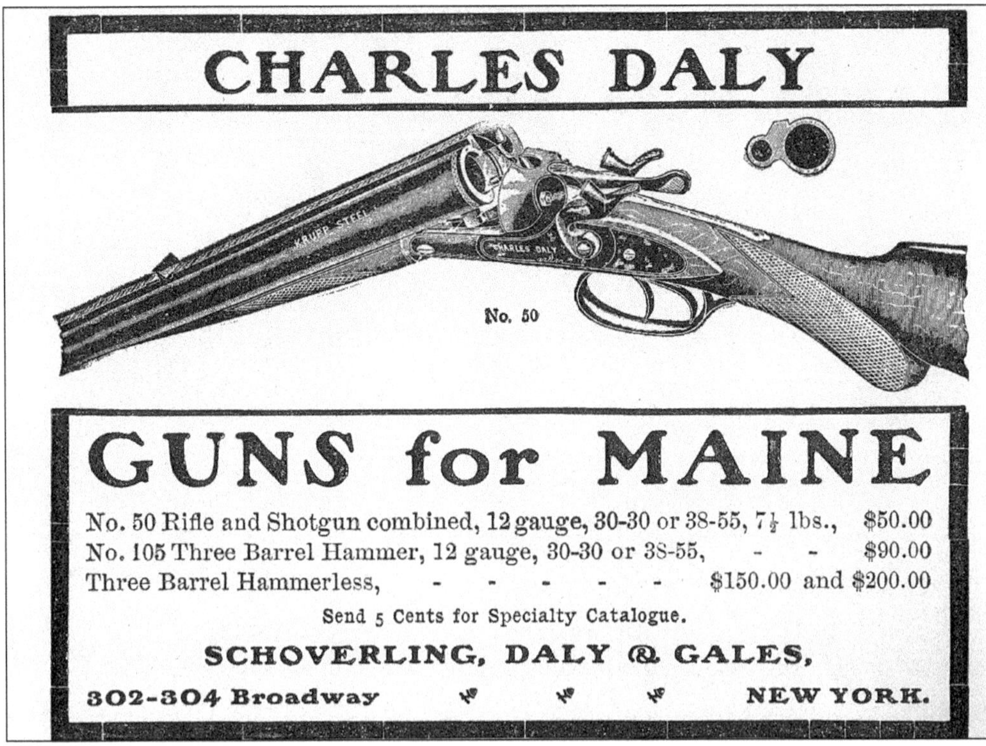

Even today, Daly shotguns are highly sought by hunters, but mostly by collectors because they have long been known to be the top of the line. In 1904, Charles Daly offered a variety of firearms, including combination rifle-shotgun in several caliber-gauge combinations. (From *In the Maine Woods*, 1904.)

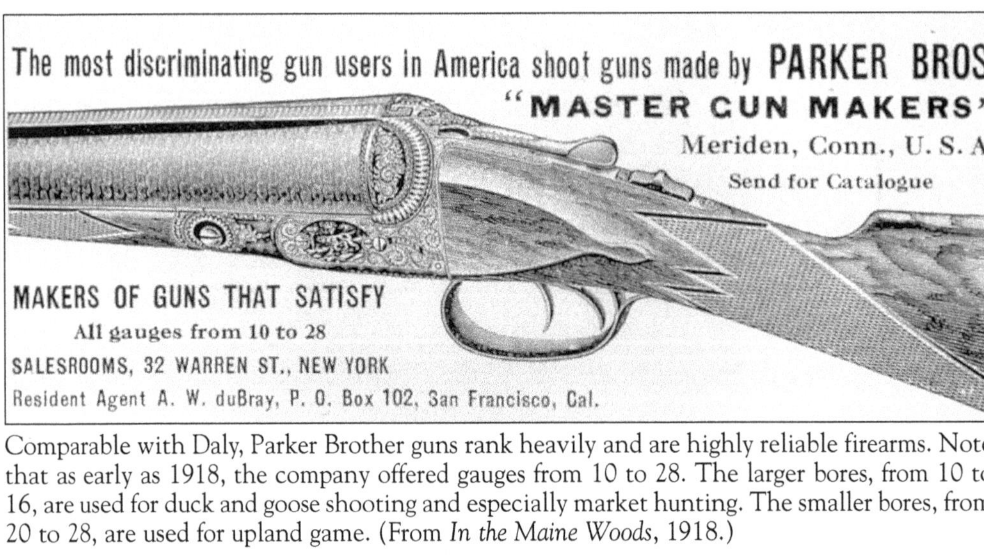

Comparable with Daly, Parker Brother guns rank heavily and are highly reliable firearms. Note that as early as 1918, the company offered gauges from 10 to 28. The larger bores, from 10 to 16, are used for duck and goose shooting and especially market hunting. The smaller bores, from 20 to 28, are used for upland game. (From *In the Maine Woods*, 1918.)

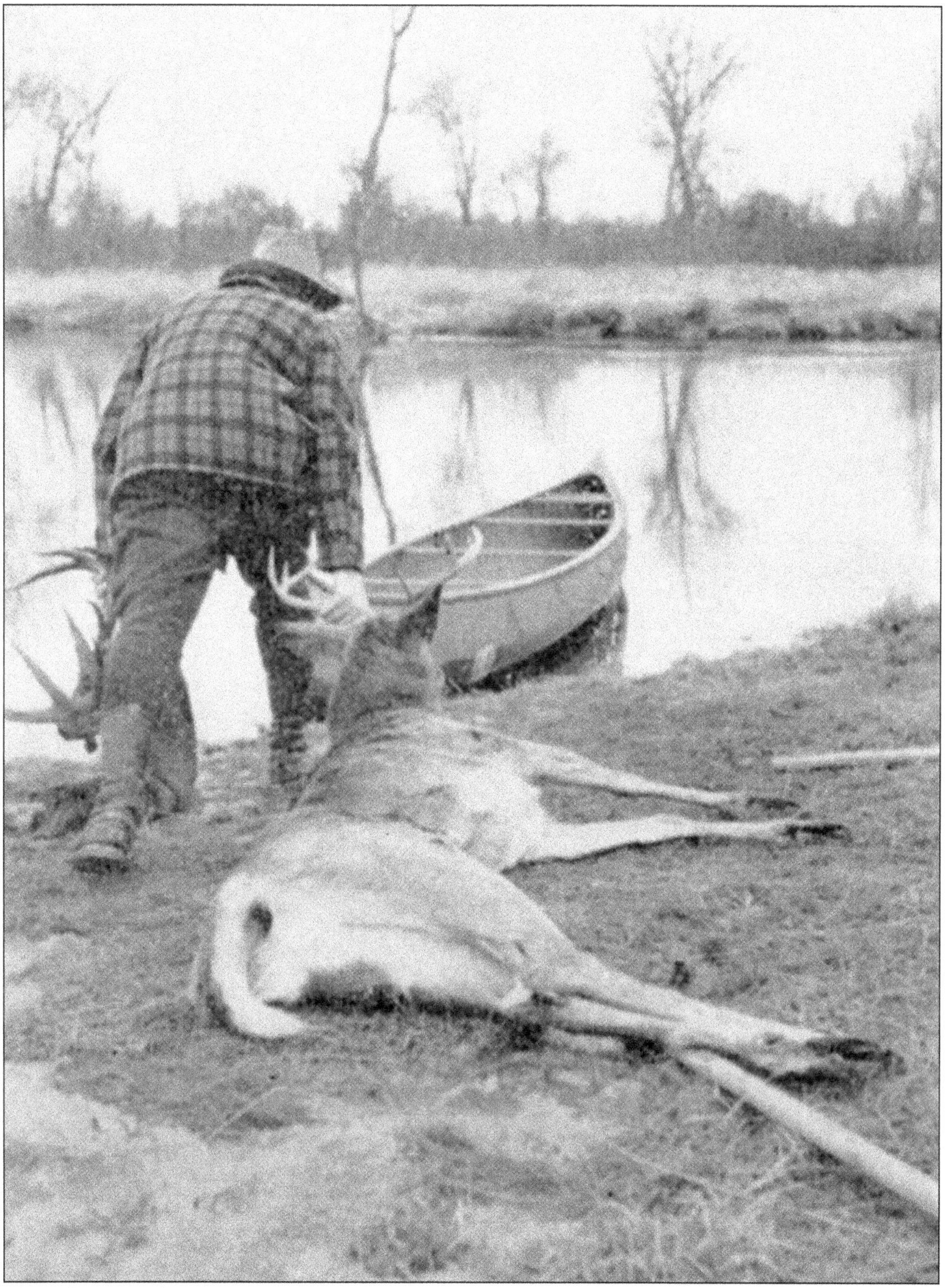

This photograph, taken by V.E. Lynch of Ashland, shows the end of the hunt. (From *In the Maine Woods*, 1933.)

BIBLIOGRAPHY

Bangor & Aroostook Railroad. *In the Maine Woods*. Various articles from various years.
Guide to the Rangeley Lakes. Portland: Loring, Short, & Harmon, 1879.
Hunter, Julia A. and Earle G. Shettleworth Jr. *Fly Rod Crosby. The Woman Who Marketed --Maine*. Gardiner: Tilbury House Publishers and Augusta: Friends of the Maine State Museum, 2000.
MacDougall, Walter M. *The Old Somerset Railroad.* Camden: Down East Books, 2000.
Maine Central Railroad. *The Maine Central.* May 1894, May 1896, October 1896.

www.ingramcontent.com/pod-product-compliance
Lightning Source LLC
LaVergne TN
LVHW071932040926
847296LV00039B/478